PENGUIN HANDBOOKS

SPROUSE'S HOW TO SURVIVE A TAX AUDIT

Mary L. Sprouse served with the Internal Revenue Service for seven years and was an audit group manager in Los Angeles, the country's largest IRS district. She has personally audited over one thousand income tax returns. Ms. Sprouse is now a practicing attorney specializing in tax law. She is the author of *Sprouse's Income Tax Handbook* and *Taxable You: Every Woman's Guide to Taxes,* both published by Penguin Books. Her office is in Los Angeles, California.

Sprouse's How to Survive a TAX AUDIT

What to Do Before and After You Hear from the IRS

MARY L. SPROUSE

PENGUIN BOOKS

PENGUIN BOOKS
Published by the Penguin Group
Viking Penguin Inc., 40 West 23rd Street,
New York, New York 10010, U.S.A.
Penguin Books Ltd, 27 Wrights Lane,
London W8 5TZ, England
Penguin Books Australia Ltd, Ringwood,
Victoria, Australia
Penguin Books Canada Ltd, 2801 John Street,
Markham, Ontario, Canada L3R 1B4
Penguin Books (N.Z.) Ltd, 182–190 Wairau Road,
Auckland 10, New Zealand

Penguin Books Ltd, Registered Offices:
Harmondsworth, Middlesex, England

First published in the United States of America by
Doubleday & Company, Inc., 1981
Reprinted by arrangement with Doubleday,
a division of Bantam Doubleday Dell Publishing Group Inc.
Published in Penguin Books 1982
Reprinted 1982, 1983
This revised edition published 1988
Published simultaneously in Canada

10 9 8 7 6 5 4 3 2 1

This book expresses the knowledge, experience,
and judgment of the author and does not necessarily reflect
the views of the Internal Revenue Service.

LIBRARY OF CONGRESS CATALOGING IN PUBLICATION DATA
Sprouse, Mary L.
Sprouse's how to survive a tax audit.
Includes index.
1. Tax auditing—United States. 2. Tax
returns—United States. I. Title.
KF6314.S65 1988 343.7305'2044 88-19702
ISBN 0 14 04.6850 1 347.30352044

Printed in the United States of America by
R. R. Donnelley & Sons Company, Harrisonburg, Virginia
Set in Times Roman

For William J. Sprouse and
Florence M. Sprouse

CONTENTS

I. UNCLE SAM WANTS YOU

"They're not going to put me in jail, are they?" the young, halting voice asked over the telephone. Usually the immigrants are the ones who ask, but not this time. Just your average scared-out-of-his-boots American. With a WANTED poster from Uncle Sam in his hand known as the audit letter.

"Of course not," I said lightly, wondering how he ever got such a notion and why he should believe me.

"I don't have to bring a toothbrush or anything, in case I have to stay?"

I looked around our drab but otherwise innocuous IRS office: The bright California sun was blazing through an expanse of windows without bars; the pleasant drone of midafternoon audits floated lazily on the air; a fellow auditor, dressed in Hollywood casual, drifted by and disappeared through a door propped wide open. You couldn't have kept a fly prisoner in that office, unless it petitioned to stay.

"Leave your toothbrush at home," I said, and he hung up with who knows what lingering fears.

I don't know what he would have done if I had said, "Yup. Kiss your wife and kids good-bye." Anyone who stands that much in awe of government would probably have come in dutifully anyway.

Almost one million individual taxpayers get the command from Uncle Sam each year to face front and center for an IRS audit. Few of them actually believe there is any threat of hearing that iron door clang shut behind them. Why, then, does almost everyone face the prospect of an audit with uneasiness, anxiety, and dread? Even auditors. I am an auditor and I know.

Come, now. Surely the IRS is not such an ogre that its own employees fear its fiery breath and gnashing teeth? No. It's not the words "Internal Revenue Service"; it's the word "audit." It's the nuisance value: rummaging through littered drawers and boxes, piecing together jigsaw scraps of paper, sorting, stacking, folding, stapling, bundling, adding. . . . It's the time lost from play, from work. It's the potential for harassment that any person in power wields and the insecurity and resentment of risking your future enjoyment on an auditor's whim. It's the guilt we all feel, from some real or imagined sin, that keeps us looking over our shoulders. But most of all, perhaps, it's wanting to keep some part of our lives hidden, not poked and prodded by curious, insensitive strangers. For an audit is without doubt an invasion of privacy, a limited one to be sure, but one that might accidentally stumble on a secret part of us.

It's hard to have a jolly time at an audit. Certainly no one at Internal Revenue expects you to come in dancing. If you understand the audit process, however, and know how to minimize its effects on your pocketbook and your life, it is possible to take an audit in stride and even emerge a winner, owing no tax at all. This presumes your intentions are honest. If they're not, you have bought the wrong book, although the cost is nonetheless tax-deductible.

This book is your guide, a *Through the Looking Glass* to lead you step by step through an audit Wonderland, from the selection of your tax return for audit to your first contact with IRS, then through the audit itself to the other side: the audit report and, if necessary, the appeal. Along the way, you will learn what records you need to keep, the best ways to avoid audit, how to court an auditor's favor, and how to survive victorious. You will also meet the Internal Revenue auditor and some of your fellow taxpayers in their best—and worst—lights. Welcome to Wonderland.

THE HOUSE RULES

A taxpayer told me heatedly the other day that the Internal Revenue Service is "illegal." He had as much chance of winning that argument as a horse thief protesting the hangman's noose, and I imagine he knew it as well as I did. He was more incensed than coherent, but because the word Constitution popped up in every other sentence, I believe he was trying to articulate the touching American faith that the Constitution possesses divine intervention and is invested with a sense of injustice that exactly parallels our own. One such band of diehards, whose sense of injustice runs to income taxes, clings to the proposition that income taxes are unconstitutional. In college, I had a teacher who would have described these individuals as "people who believe in Disneyland." This once-shining principle, which aborted the first peacetime income tax, in 1894, became as outdated, with the ratification of the Sixteenth Amendment, as the semaphore. In the tax-ripe years since 1913, the income tax has been granted the Supreme Court seal of approval and, as you may have noticed, is now as immovable and unassailable as the Rock of Gibraltar.

All this legitimacy has been inherited by the Internal Revenue Service, and, despite taxpayers' yelling "illegal," none of us working as auditors see ourselves as outlaws. The role of sheriff suits us better, enforcing the tax laws in a normally law-abiding town. For the Internal Revenue is an enforcement agency, an arm of the Department of the Treasury, charged with upholding the Internal Revenue Code of 1954 (as revised, amended, reformed, and confounded by Congress over the years). An important tool of enforcement is the audit of tax returns, and that is where you and I come in.

The Internal Revenue Service is a massive organization, divided into seven regions and fifty-eight districts, but as a taxpayer under audit, you will be dealing with the Service at its lowest level: an audit group in your local district office. Because the IRS is completely decentralized, taxpayers rarely have any direct contact with the headquarters, or National Office, in Washington, D.C. The auditor has complete authority to resolve your case without interference from above. More than one taxpayer has told me that he was going to "write the Commissioner," and none of them has ever believed that his letter will have no more impact than a tree falling in an empty forest. It's true. If you don't deal on the local level, you don't deal at all.

Each of the seven regions of IRS is headed by a commissioner, and each of these has five assistant regional commissioners under him, who are in charge of one division apiece. These divisions are Resources Management, Data Processing, Examination, Criminal Investigation, and Collection. There is also a regional director of appeals. From the moment you receive that letter asking you to appear for an audit, you will be dealing with the men and women of the Examination Division: the tax (or office) auditors and the revenue agents.

Over 55 percent of the 1.1 million individual taxpayers whose returns are examined each year come face to face with a "tax auditor." If you are a wage earner or own a small-to-medium-size business and file a Form 1040 or 1040A, the tax auditor is waiting to greet you. He does not make house calls, so you will be asked to bring your records in at a set appointment time. The only exceptions might occur if you own a high-volume business requiring a roomful of records or if you are severely handicapped or ill. A large percentage of tax auditors are women.

The "revenue agent," or field agent, audits primarily partnership and corporation returns. He has specialized training and an accounting background, and unless you are a partner, corporate officer, or tax representative, you will probably never meet a revenue agent.

The audit procedures and techniques described in this book are those used by office auditors. Many of them also apply to revenue agents. Because the Internal Revenue Service is decentralized, forms and procedures vary slightly from district to district, but in all important respects affecting you, the taxpayer, they are uniform.

The office auditor's bible is the Internal Revenue Code—the codification of our tax laws and the source of all audit authority. Interpreting the Code are three volumes of Regulations issued by the Commissioner of Internal Revenue. Although these Regulations do not have the force of law, the courts have consistently accorded them substantial weight, and they may form the basis for an audit adjustment. The auditor also relies on published Revenue Rulings, issued by the National Office and interpreting the Code with respect to particular sets of facts.

Other sources of Code interpretation are federal and Tax Court decisions, but an auditor is not bound by a particular decision unless the Commissioner "acquiesces" in it. If a case is acquiesced in, the Service will not litigate the same issue again, and auditors must rely on the decision as precedent. If the Commissioner does not acquiesce in a court ruling, every taxpayer who wants a similar ruling will have to take his case to court. Often the deduction is so small compared to the cost of litigating that most taxpayers simply pay up, muttering under their breaths. When the *Trujillo* decision declared, in 1977, that California state disability insurance was deductible as a tax, the

Commissioner nonacquiesced, with the result that no one in California was allowed the deduction except Mr. Trujillo himself. And because the deduction was then limited by California law to a mere $114 (usually but a few dollars in tax), only Mr. Trujillo took the issue to court. (The Commissioner has since reversed his position.)

The above is just one example of how difficult, time-consuming, or unprofitable it can be to play the audit game and beat the house. As I began planning this book, I realized anew how much the house rules (the Code, Regulations, and Internal Revenue manual) favor the IRS. I mention this because halfway through this book you're going to say, "The IRS must be paying her to write this. There's no way the taxpayer can win." When you reach that point, remember: the percentages are with the IRS. When there are two ways to survive the system and win, the Internal Revenue's and the taxpayer's, I will tell you both. In many cases, however, there is only one way, the IRS way, and the goal here is not to win, but, rather, not to lose. That's when you have to play by the house rules and count yourself lucky if it's a draw.

In 1987, office auditors and revenue agents assessed 5.9 *billion* dollars in additional tax and penalties as a result of all audits. Yes, billion. It doesn't sound as if too many of you out there are winning, does it? And yet 23 percent of those audited walked away without paying any more tax at all. (Stand up and take a bow, folks; you deserve it.) There are ways to win, but they're subtle, not spectacular. Don't set your sights too high. You're not going to bring the IRS to its collective knees. Monuments will not be raised to you. But if you don't lose a nickel on an audit, isn't that enough? You can win, and I will show you how.

II. AN AUDITOR IS . . .

If you enjoy a good insult, towering rages, hysterical weeping, or mail that ticks, have I got a job for you! Being an Internal Revenue Service auditor can be like riding an emotional roller coaster. Working with taxpayers is like working with nitroglycerin. Sometimes the simple act of saying, "Hello," can set off a pent-up explosion. One excitable woman even refused to go through with her audit because the auditor had called her by the name on her tax return.

"Tommy Winesap is your legal name, isn't it?" I asked tactfully, after she demanded to see the supervisor.

"Yes, but he had no right to call me that!" she yelled and promptly stomped out, leaving both of us somewhat dazed.

Taxpayers come in all shapes, all income brackets, and, often to an auditor's dismay, all temperaments. One favorite is the summer-storm taxpayer. Friendly, sometimes bantering, always polite, this taxpayer can lead an unwary auditor from sunshine to thunder at the drop of a receipt. Just when the auditor is beginning to believe that a job with public contact *can* be rewarding, the most random remark can loose a cloudburst of wrath.

"We were getting along so well," Laura said later, shaking her head in disbelief. "He was just the nicest man; then, all of a sudden, there he was standing over me, waving his arms and screaming."

Screaming was not the precise word. Bellowing was more like it. Loud enough, at any rate, to bring me running in case it was necessary to throw myself between her and the taxpayer. In the adjoining booths, other taxpayers were squirming uneasily in their seats, and one gallant gentleman had stood up ready for action. It is always a pleasant surprise to find out there are taxpayers still on our side, and if I didn't thank that gentleman then, I do now.

The audit had been going smoothly (sunshine) until Laura had asked about the theft of two fire extinguishers from the hallway of his rental unit. "I'll need to see the police report," she said routinely.

If you know the joke about the man who goes berserk whenever he hears the words "Niagara Falls," you'll understand what happened next. The words were "fire extinguishers," but the effect was the same. Nothing had ever outraged that taxpayer more than the theft of his fire extinguishers, and to be asked to actually prove it was just too much. It took myself and a physically more impressive male supervisor twenty minutes to get him back in his seat and sunny again.

Of course, there is always the taxpayer who lets you know exactly how he feels right from the start: suspicious, resentful, and raring to take it out on somebody. He is no hypocrite. He doesn't want to be there, he doesn't like you, and he's going to prove it. You can tell who he is by the snarl on his face when you greet him in the reception area. It's going to be a fun audit, but it's too late to do the only sensible thing: join the French Foreign Legion.

Auditing the outrightly hostile taxpayer is like riding a bucking bronco. He is going to flare and kick and fight you every step of the way. Nothing you can say will mollify him. No pleasantries, no compliments about his records. It might be all right if he would just maintain a strong silence, but this one is a nonstop talker, and every remark seems to be deliberately aimed at provoking the auditor. See if you can spot which comments in the conversation below are making the auditor grip the edge of his desk so tightly his fingernails are turning blue.

IRS: You're Mr. C. Red?

TP: Who'd you think I am? Santa Claus? I'm not here to give money away, I can tell you that.

IRS: Are you still living at 324 Mad Place?

TP: Why, are you afraid you won't be able to catch up with me?

IRS: No, sir. What is your telephone number during the day?

TP: Do I look like a sucker to you? Don't you ever call me at work. I don't want my boss to know I've got anything to do with you robbers.

IRS: Shall we start with your contributions, sir?

TP: You can start anyplace you like, because I'm not going to tell you anything. In fact, I don't want to talk to you at all. I want a hearing.

IRS: But we haven't even started the audit yet.

TP: I know my rights. I want to see your supervisor. It says right here in the letter—

IRS: Yes, sir. If you don't agree with my findings, you have the right to see someone else. But first I need to see your receipts for contributions.

TP: It's on my tax return. Isn't that good enough for you? Or do you think I'm a liar? I don't have to give you any receipts. You're interfering with my First Amendment rights. Freedom of religion. The government can't tell me who to give my money to. I'll take this to the Supreme Court. I'll sue you. . . .

And so it goes. When Mr. Red finally leaves, after one last, parting shot, the auditor will tear all the tape out of his adding machine and kick his desk.

Thank goodness there are a few taxpayers out there who do not approach us with the loathing reserved for lepers or the hatred afforded war criminals. We have a sign in our office that says: HUMAN BEINGS HERE. HANDLE WITH CARE. Someone disputes it every day, but a tip of the tax return to those of you who still give us the benefit of the doubt.

Sometimes, though, even the nicest taxpayers take us for that roller coaster ride. Not with anger, but with tears.

A middle-aged woman with a gray sweater that matched her hair sat across the desk from me. She was a plumber's wife, and we had gone through her itemized expenses quickly and pleasantly. She seemed shy, perhaps a little withdrawn, but amiable. I moved confidently on to the next issue.

"I see you have a rental," I said, flipping to the Schedule E.

Silence. I looked up to see the tears rolling down her cheeks.

"My son was murdered in one of the apartments," she sobbed at last.

I was a trainee, and she was my first taxpayer to burst into tears. I was horrified at being to blame for all this misery. Pretty soon we were both crying unashamedly, and I had to borrow a wad of tissue from a more experienced auditor.

Another heartbreaker was a frail, down-at-the-heels screen extra in his sixties. As we reached my office door, he said tonelessly, "I only have six months to live."

I went through the motions of a pointless audit, even to giving him a report for two hundred dollars tax, knowing he wouldn't live long enough for us to collect it. I wished him well clumsily, then watched him walk away with no hope, but a tax bill in his hand, and wondered how he felt toward his fellow man.

One problem is that we usually don't begin an audit until a year or two after the return is filed, during which time any number of calamitous events can and surprisingly often do happen to the taxpayer. From the taxpayer's occupation listed on the return, the auditor will expect a robust, husky person to walk through the door, only to see someone hobble across the threshold with a cane.

Taxpayers are laid off, disabled, have heart attacks, and even die between the filing of the tax return and the audit. One of my auditors lost five taxpayers in a six-month period, including a liquor-store owner shot in a holdup the week before he was scheduled to come in. Gallows humor being what it is, he has been ribbed quite a bit about this, and I always think twice about assigning him a taxpayer over sixty-five years old.

Another sad case of mine was a talented artist and film animator in his late twenties. He was tall, with dark curly hair and boyish good looks, and his Schedule C showed that his career was finally rocketing.

He was also blind. Shortly after filing his tax return, he had been stricken with spinal meningitis, which had cost him his sight. An artist who cannot see seems a senseless tragedy, but he was full of dreams and plans for an art museum for the blind, to be filled with new art forms of his own creation, designed solely for the sightless.

Although we are often moved by the misfortunes of our taxpayers, they cannot affect the outcome of the audit. Perhaps we are helped in this by being removed from the collection process. We live in a world of paper facts and we write paper reports. Someone else, the hapless revenue officer, has to deal with the cruel realities of collecting money that the unemployed, the crippled, or the bereaved relatives no longer can afford to pay.

Which does not mean that auditors escape unscathed. The auditor does have to face the taxpayer with the unpleasant truth and watch somewhat helplessly when she (usually) bursts into tears. Frequently this is the first the auditor finds out about the taxpayer's troubles. For many persons, an audit report is the last straw. "My husband's out of work, my son's on drugs, I need an operation, and now this. What am I going to do?" Frankly, I don't know what most of them do. They shuffle off, the auditor takes out a fresh sheet of paper, and the next soul shuffles in.

Actually, it is easy to become insensitive in a job like this, if only out of self-defense. Empathy is a strain five times a day, five days a week. There comes a time when the auditor has to tell himself it's just a job and he can't take the nation's troubles home with him every night. Another reason auditors develop fairly thick skins is that so many taxpayers abuse their emotional privileges. Like slapstick, too much tragedy can almost be funny. The lists of disasters recited by some taxpayers rival Rube Goldberg creations. True or not, they defy credibility, especially after the auditor has already listened to several hundred other sob stories. And, to be honest, too often these recitations are just that: ploys to win sympathy and a smaller tax bill. Not knowing whom to believe, the auditor tends to believe no one. Especially when the magnitude of the disaster rises in direct proportion to how much tax the sufferer owes.

Ultimately, the auditor must be equally compassionate to all his taxpayers. The fairness of an audit cannot be measured by who is best able to pay, but rather, who, under our system of tax laws, is required to pay.

III. WINNING THE IRS SWEEPSTAKES

It is April 16, and your worries are over. Your tax return has found its way home to IRS and is buried anonymously among the 103.5 million other returns that pour into the ten service centers every spring. You did not dip it in blood, edge it in black, or mail it in an obscene envelope, like some of your fellow citizens, who can't resist calling attention to themselves. There is no more reason for IRS to single out your return than for an ocean lover to pick up a particular grain of sand on the beach.

There are some persons who can't win anything. They have never been the millionth customer to crowd through the turnstiles of a department store. The local TV host of "Dialing for Dough" has never picked their names out of the telephone directory. They never find an empty parking space on a city street. But these same persons enter the IRS lottery and overnight they become winners.

"Congratulations! This is the Internal Revenue Service. You'll be happy to know that your name has been selected at random to come in for an audit." And just when you were beginning to think you never had any luck! I actually used this approach once and most persons took it good-naturedly. At least, they seemed to prefer it to a funeral announcement.

Each year, 1.1 percent of America's taxpayers receive from their government an offer they can't refuse. This percentage may seem too ludicrously small to worry about, but it represents over one million tax returns. And don't be fooled by the averages. As income rises, so does the percentage of audits. For example, 2.81 percent of taxpayers with incomes over $50,000 were audited. And 4.8 percent of those filing a Schedule C with gross receipts of $100,000 or more were examined. If you live in a metropolitan area, your chances of being audited are greater than if you live in a rural area. The Los Angeles and Laguna Niguel districts, for example, which cover California from Bakersfield to the Mexican border, audit .1 million, or 8 percent, of the total returns audited. The Manhattan and Brooklyn districts audit 5 percent, and Chicago, 4 percent. So roughly one fifth of all audits are conducted in just three major metropolitan areas.

Your audit risk is also high if you live in Nevada. In 1986, Nevada topped the list with an audit rate of 2.5 percent, compared to a .456 percent rate in Rhode Island, the nation's lowest. Other high percentage audit states included Alaska (2.2 percent), Wyoming (1.7 percent), Washington (1.5 percent), California (1.5 percent), and Texas (1.5 percent). Looking at urban centers, San Francisco led all other cities with a rate of 2.1 percent.

On a regional basis, the odds on winning audit roulette are greatest in the West and Southwest, least in the Central States.

Who fares best in audits? In 1986, it was the folks in Maine, with an average audit assessment of $1,947. The big losers? Oklahomans, who paid an average of $11,090, largely as a result of oil and gas shelters. Other hard-hit citizens were those in Alaska ($8,503), Florida ($8,005), California ($7,543), and Illinois ($7,412). The lowest assessments after Maine were in North Dakota ($2,043), Alabama ($2,220), New Hampshire ($2,506), and North Carolina ($2,675).

NOBODY'S PERFECT

Just what is the purpose of an audit, and how do you become one of the chosen many? The name of the audit game is "voluntary compliance." Although few taxpayers would admit that they pay taxes voluntarily and probably consider such a suggestion a real knee-slapper, the fact that they file tax returns without a loaded gun pointed at their heads is sufficient to make our tax system voluntary. This is in sharp contrast to other nations, where collecting taxes is a game of hide-and-seek. The IRS continually hosts foreign tax officials, who are openly envious of the integrity with which our tax system operates. No matter which side you're on in the debate over taxes, a government's need for revenue is hardly in issue, and the failure of our tax structure would cripple our government. Italy is a sterling example, although revenue is only one of that country's problems.

About ten years ago, the IRS could point to an almost perfect, 97 percent rate of voluntary compliance. That rate has plunged an alarming 15.5 percent, however, and voluntary compliance now stands at just 81.5 percent. This means that nearly one fifth of all taxpayers are actively plotting to get out of paying taxes, either by filing fraudulent returns or by not filing a return at all. Such unprecedented noncompliance endangers our tax system and can only lead to more pervasive and less restricted IRS intrusion into our lives.

The shadowy presence of the IRS is supposed to keep you filing, and an audit is supposed to keep you honest. Just because 81.5 percent of you file voluntarily does not mean that 81.5 percent of the tax returns are lily-pure. Voluntary compliance is not necessarily perfect compliance. A little exaggeration here, a little ignorance of the law there, gives the IRS sufficient room to audit.

I said that IRS audits 1.1 percent of all tax returns filed and that 18.5 percent of the population does not comply with our tax laws. Perhaps some of you are wondering, then, why the IRS is auditing voluntary compliers at all. This is simply because most noncompliers have not even filed a return, and if there's one thing an auditor needs, it's a return to audit. Failure to file is normally handled by the Collection Division, not by Examination.

The selection of your return for audit, therefore, does not mean that the IRS suspects that you have not complied with the tax laws or that your return is fraudulent. The IRS would continue to audit returns (although very few) if every audit produced no additional tax, not out of pure meanness but because laws are meaningless if they are not enforced. The IRS as an agency does not care whether an audit is win, lose, or draw if the audit has been fair and the law has been complied with. In practice, of course, the IRS expects most audits to be wins, but only because experience has proved that we, as taxpayers, are still somewhat shy of perfection.

As I like to counsel my taxpayers, "An audit is a learning experience." If an audit has been well conducted, the taxpayer will leave knowing exactly what the law is on the issues involved, how it can be complied with, and what documentation is needed to permit the deductions. The price of this education is sometimes high, but when a taxpayer leaves my office, I don't expect him, if he is sincere, to ever owe money in an audit again. The purpose of an audit is not to drill for noncompliance, but to dry the well up.

THE LUCK OF THE DRAW

The IRS will tell you that your tax return was chosen for audit at random. "At random" does not mean there is no system. It means that there is no discrimination against you personally in the selection of your return. Your return is not singled out because of your name, age, occupation, or marital status—unless one of those in some way affects your deductions. For example, filing a single return alone would not cause you to be audited, but there's a good chance it might if you also took a credit for child care. Bear in mind also that the IRS cannot possibly select your return for a reason that does not appear on the face of your tax return. One irate woman called to tell me, "I know why you're auditing me, honey. It's because I'm black." I couldn't convince her that there was no way we would know her race unless she had taken pains to scrawl it in large letters across the margins.

What about the preprinted label sent out with your tax package each year? Are you an unwitting accomplice in your own doom when you dutifully peel off the label and stick it smack dab on the front of your tax return? Is there a secret code hidden among all those numbers that tells the computer more than it has any right to know? Hardly. Conspiracy theories notwithstanding, the label is exactly what it purports to be. No microfilm dots, invisible ink, or cleverly concealed ciphers. If you want a career in espionage, don't join the IRS.

The meaning of three of the items on the label is obvious: they are your name, address, and social security number. The remaining three symbols require some explanation, but, alas, there is nothing sinister about them. The two letters in front of your social security number are computer shorthand for your name. Apart from the cultural shock of being reduced to two letters and a nine-digit number, you have nothing to fear here.

The other mystery letter and two digits to the right of your social security number simply stand for the IRS district where you filed your return. For example, D94 is the San Francisco district. The last remaining number, at the far right, represents the type of tax package mailed to you. A *1* means you received a Form 1040 and Schedules A and B. Package *3* goes to business people, and package *4* to farmers. Taxpayers filing a 1040A, or short form, have a *5* on their label.

Three quarters of all returns audited are preselected by computer at the service centers. Your return may arrive in the midst of several million other returns, but it does not escape the omniscient notice of the computer. When your return is fed into the "pipeline" at the service center serving your region, it begins a journey that ends at the Computer Branch.

On some days, your service center receives over a million returns. The envelopes are sorted mechanically according to the type of return, using the coded information printed in magnetic ink on the outside of the envelopes included in your tax package. Envelopes containing checks are identified without being opened using electronic impulses from the bank codes on checks. Extractors remove the returns from their envelopes, which are discarded unless the return was filed late. A document locator number (DLN) is stamped on each return and any accompanying checks or letters.

Returns with remittance enclosed are sent forward to record the payment before they join the other returns for examination. If the reason for payment is unclear, the IRS will telephone for an explanation. If there is no answer, the check is deposited anyway. A word of advice here: if you send cash instead of a check or money order with your return, the processing will be much slower.

Your return is now examined to make sure the purely mechanical items are complete (signature, social security number, W-2s, etc.). If schedules are missing, letters are sent requesting them. In some cases, but by no means all, employer and employee copies of W-2s are matched. A defect spotted here will be referred back to the taxpayer for correction. However, a failure to report all income as shown on the employer and bank copies of W-2s and 1099s can also generate a tax deficiency notice at a later date—or even an audit.

Your return is also checked for mathematical accuracy and the following errors: (1) medical expenses and casualty losses not reduced by the adjusted gross income limitation; (2) the dependent care credit claimed on a married filing separate return; (3) head of household claimed without naming the qualifying dependent; and (4) an incorrect mileage rate used for a business car.

Obvious errors are corrected and notices of additional tax due are sent. In some cases, a taxpayer may be asked to submit additional information to verify deductions or credits. This is not an audit, although you may request an interview if you disagree with the IRS assessment. If the correction is made before April 15, no interest is charged.

Now the moment you've been waiting for. Your tax-return information is ready to be fed, magnetic bit by magnetic bit, onto large magnetic disks for shipment to the National Computer Center, in Martinsburg, West Virginia. But first a double-check process makes sure the information on your return has been input without error. The service-center computer now processes this verified information for math or other errors evident from the face of the return—for instance, failure to compute the earned-income credit where all the qualifications appear to be met. Returns with errors must be perfected before they can be accepted by the National Computer Center's computer, which is quite a prima donna.

Refunds are approved by the supercomputer in West Virginia. Refund instructions are sent to the service center, which orders checks from regional payment offices.

Meanwhile, detection teams in the service centers look for false or fictitious returns. Holds can be placed on refunds claimed on suspicious returns, giving local offices a chance to investigate.

A math error never generates an audit. These corrections are made by "purple-pencil people" (conjure up your own image) at the service centers, and notices are sent to the taxpayers. Other errors involving the tax law may evolve into audits, but only if the taxpayer disagrees with the correction made by the service center. If he protests, the return will usually be sent to his district office, and he will be invited in to explain his position. Once the return has been sent to a local office, however, a full-scale audit may blossom if the auditor decides upon examining the return that a more in-depth audit is warranted.

LAYING ODDS—THE DIF FORMULA

Once the computer has digested your tax return, how does it determine you are good audit potential? The IRS has developed a computer program of mathematical formulas known as DIF (Discriminate Function System), which chooses returns with a high probability of "tax error," or additional tax due.

The DIF formulas are among the nation's most closely guarded secrets. The reason is obvious: if the details of these formulas became public, knowledgeable taxpayers and tax preparers would quickly use them to minimize their chances of audit, and the house the Sixteenth Amendment built would come tumbling down. I have probably come as close to the DIF formulas as any IRS employee—which is to say, not very. The formulas are housed in the Detroit Data Center, and as the Data Center's sometime public-information officer, I was allowed to view the well-locked file cabinets in which these precious national resources reside. The area, of course, was off limits to all but a handful of security personnel, and I was soon whisked away.

A team of systems analysts working at the Data Center extract the DIF formulas from extremely detailed data gathered during the Taxpayer Compliance Measurement Program (TCMP). Due to our continually changing economy and tax laws, the DIF formulas are updated every two or three years to reflect the corresponding changes in the income and deduction levels of the tax returns filed. TCMP projects are launched to collect data on these changes and involve auditors in every district in the country. A completely random sample of tax returns is selected from all income levels. Because of the randomness of the selection, many of these returns have no audit potential at all; that is, we do not expect there will be any additional tax due, because the returns represent taxpayers who are not itemizing deductions or taking any exemptions other than their own. It does not matter whether TCMP returns produce revenue. The purpose of the audit is strictly fact-finding. How much income does Mr. and Mrs. Average America make, how many exemptions do they support on that income, how many itemized expenses, capital gains and losses, or credits do they take? It is more like a census than an audit, and the only requirement of an auditor is that he be thorough.

Few taxpayers undergo a TCMP audit, so cross your fingers, because the audit is total. The tax return is combed line by line and personal questions are asked. Where, in a normal audit, a few dollars' discrepancy may be overlooked, even a dollar's difference must be recorded in a TCMP audit. Because the audit results evolve into the formulas upon which the coming years' audit success rises or falls, the amounts on each tax return after audit must be correct virtually to the penny. The audit will be long, arduous, and inflexible.

If this sounds grueling and merciless, it certainly can be, especially if your return involves more than the standard deduction. The IRS conducts no other audit as exhaustive as this. And if your auditor somehow overlooks a discrepancy, don't congratulate yourself yet. Your one audit will be reviewed *ad infinitum* all the way to Washington, D.C., and not one reviewer will hesitate to send it right back for correction.

Nor can you escape from a TCMP audit. Once the sample of TCMP returns has been chosen, there are, as in so many restaurants, no substitutions. You are "it," and this is a game of tag taxpayers rarely win. The *only* reasons that can be used to avoid a TCMP audit are that the taxpayer: (1) cannot be found, (2) is too ill, incompetent, or has died, and the guardian or executor cannot be located, or (3) is outside the United States and is unavailable for an interview.

However, there is a bright side to all this. Remember I told you an audit is a learning experience? A TCMP audit is practically a college education. When you get your diploma—the audit report—you are in select company indeed. And you have something to tell your grandchildren about.

THE WINNING TICKET

Once the DIF formulas are arrived at, they form the basis of a nationwide computer program that "scores" every tax return filed. From my observation, a score of 300 or better makes a return a semifinalist and eligible to enter the final drawing.

Why would your return score 300 and your next-door neighbor's be eliminated? The answer seems to depend in part upon the relationship of your deductions to income. Not too surprisingly, you are expected to have enough taxable income after deductions to live on. This is borne out by common sense. If you are married, with four children, you're going to need at least twenty-five hundred dollars left over after deductions just to feed the family. Not to mention clothing, toothpaste, utility bills, barbers, gasoline, and a movie or two. So if your taxable income takes a nose dive below zero, even a computer is going to ask, "So what are they living on?"

I know: What if your rent is overdue, the kids are barefoot, the car was repossessed, and you needed a root canal? What if every cent you have was borrowed from an unsympathetic brother-in-law or obtained through a grim clerk in the unemployment office? We realize there can be dozens of good reasons for a return that looks terminal (that's what an audit is for), but the DIF formulas play the averages. If your return is a nonconformist, you may be asked to explain why.

The IRS publishes a list of the average amounts of itemized deductions, such as medical expenses and charitable contributions, that taxpayers in various income brackets have taken in recent years. If this were all there were to the complex DIF formulas, however, you can bet you would never see it in print. Don't be misled. By keeping your itemized deductions within these ranges, you do not necessarily prevent an audit.

Your return is classified into one of eight "activity codes," ranging from a nonbusiness return with itemized deductions and a total positive income of under ten thousand dollars to a business return with gross receipts of over one hundred thousand dollars. Total positive income (TPI) is the sum of all positive numbers on your return. Losses are treated as zero. TPI has replaced adjusted gross income as the standard for selecting returns for audit. Under the old system, high-income taxpayers could avoid audit detection by claiming tax shelter losses that produced low adjusted gross incomes.

The computer is programmed to assign certain numerical weights, depending upon your income class, to significant line-by-line items on the tax return, as well as to selected relationships between these items and your total positive income.

The individual weights are then added into an index score for each return to arrive at the final DIF score, mentioned earlier. If your return is scored high—say over 400—you might as well start getting your receipts together. If the score is in the middle and lower ranges, whether you are selected for audit will probably depend on how many returns IRS plans to audit that year. The highest scores are chosen first, of course, then in descending order until the planned number of returns have been selected. In districts that audit a larger share of the audit plan, such as Los Angeles, there may be more demand for high-scoring returns than are available. This means that Examination will have to dip into the lower-scored returns to examine the planned number. In smaller districts—Boise, for example—with smaller plans and fewer auditors, only the highest scores might be audited. So there may conceivably be some geographically advantageous places to reside. Just don't tell Boise I sent you.

AND THE WINNER IS . . . AUDIT CLASSIFICATION

After your tax return is scored, it has two possible audit destinations: the service center's Examination Division or your local district-office Examination Division. The service center screens returns for potential "unallowable" items. These are usually adjustments that are evident just by looking at the tax return. Common examples are sales and utility taxes, deductions for personal living expenses, loss on the sale of a personal residence, personal legal expenses, and life insurance premiums. The service center also conducts audits by correspondence on simple itemized deductions, that is, expenses that can be verified by a small number of receipts and require little explanation by the taxpayer. Home mortgage interest, medical expenses, and church contributions are three examples. The taxpayer is asked to mail in his documentation, and an auditor totals the receipts provided and issues a report for any tax due. If the auditor decides the issue is more involved than it at first appeared or if the taxpayer requests an interview, the audit will be transferred to an office close to the taxpayer's home.

Returns with the highest audit potential (or DIF scores) now undergo the second phase of the screening process. At last, humans take over to prove that computers are not infallible. The computer may be a whiz with numbers, but it can't read or make judgments. The reason for a return's high score may be obvious upon inspection. For example, if you are over sixty-five years old, heavy medical payments, especially nursing care, do not seem unlikely and may not warrant audit. Or you may have attached copies of receipts or explanations for high or unusual expenses to your return when it was filed, and these may be sufficient (they are not always) to let your return go by. The human factor also makes allowances for the regional variations that the DIF formulas, which represent a nationwide average, do not take into account. The 1987 earthquake in Los Angeles must have knocked the Fresno computer on its memory banks when the casualty losses came pouring in. But visual inspection of these returns makes it possible to rule out the need to audit most of the taxpayers in the immediate quake area. Property taxes in Southern California also tend to be higher than the national average, according to local legend, and an auditor familiar with property values in a given area may discard a return on which real estate taxes might otherwise be considered a good issue.

Computer-selected returns are screened by experienced auditors who are usually on two-week assignments. Their function is to reject returns that are not really audit material. These returns are said to have been "surveyed." The auditors also "classify" the returns that are not rejected. Classifying a return means deciding which of the items on your tax return will be audited. Usually an auditor is limited to selecting a maximum of four items, or "issues," for audit. Auditing more than four issues is generally too time-consuming, and the IRS does not want to be accused of undue harassment. A favorite saying at IRS is, "Get the fast buck, not the last buck." A speedy audit of a few choice issues should achieve the IRS goal of voluntary compliance almost as well as squeezing a taxpayer dry, and it's a lot better for public relations. Of course, if your return has only one or two issues that look potentially profitable, only those issues will be classified. And, limit or no limit, if the entire return looks like the state of Denmark, every aromatic issue will be classified, although it may have to be given special treatment when an appointment is scheduled. And don't think that won't make it noticeable.

What is the classifier looking for? Every service center has its own guidelines, based on its own regional characteristics. And every classifier has his own set of inner guidelines, based on his own background, training, and experience. No two auditors will classify a return exactly alike. One auditor may know from past experience that a certain employer reimburses for all employee-incurred business expenses. That auditor will classify such business expense on every return on which it appears, where another auditor might pass it up. If a classifier does have specialized knowledge that most other auditors do not, he will usually write a note in the file to pass along to whichever auditor eventually gets the return.

The most obvious clue to a good audit issue is the amount of the deduction, and in many cases this is the sole basis of choosing one item over another. An expense that seems abnormally high may be exaggerated or require more proof than the taxpayer can muster. A deduction also has to be worth not allowing. There is no reason to audit an expense so small that even if it were completely "disallowed," the net tax would be close to zero. If a taxpayer is claiming $2,000 in medical expense, however, even if he can prove 75 percent of it, or $1,500, the auditor still has a nice, $500 adjustment, which usually yields enough tax to pay for the audit.

The potential for unreported income is not ignored, either. If the profession shown on the return is normally lucrative, a bad year may be viewed in an ominous light. Income is also considered a good issue for occupations where tipping or moonlighting is common. In addition, a classifier might question an investment showing an abnormally low yield or a business with high gross receipts and a pitiful net income. And if you are claiming a full house of exemptions, the classifier will check to see if your income seems sufficient to support them.

The classifier also looks for clearly nondeductible or suspicious deductions. Often, the taxpayer is kind enough to label these for us. One gentleman had drawn an extra line on his rental schedule to write in "Down payment $5,000." Because the law is black-and-white that a down payment is not deductible, this is known as an "automatic adjustment," and an auditor weeps with joy when he stumbles on a juicy one like this. An automatic adjustment is an easy day's pay: instant tax due with no arguments from the taxpayer—an open-and-shut case. Suspicious deductions are more subtle but include such items as contributions to a church school by taxpayers claiming exemptions for their children (tuition is not deductible) or entertainment expense claimed by a bank teller (no, I didn't make that up). While it is possible these expenses may prove to be allowable, there is a strong possibility an audit is needed.

WHEN THE ODDS ARE AGAINST YOU

There are also certain deductions an auditor learns to be wary of. These include items that are difficult to prove, such as *casualty losses* and *noncash contributions,* and areas that are somewhat technical and not commonly understood by most taxpayers, such as *depreciation.* Some deductions, such as *educational expenses* and *fellowship exclusions* are often abused (and audited) because the tax law must be interpreted to fit the facts of each case. In areas of the law where the lines between a deductible and a nondeductible expense blur, there are some taxpayers who find themselves near the border and quite a few who just think they are. Any taxpayer who ventures into one of these gray areas of the law stands an excellent chance of being audited.

An issue such as *bad debts* is another good audit choice, because most persons are unfamiliar with the legal requirements involved (an enforceable debt evidenced in writing and a realistic effort to collect) until after the fact, when it is too late. The Internal Revenue Code requirements of proof similarly make *automobile, entertainment,* and *gift* expenses a likely target for audit. And, of course, there are areas where quite a few taxpayers are out-and-out trying to get away with something, such as *hobby losses* and *vacation rentals.* Look, too, for deductions to be classified if there has been a recent change in the tax law. For instance, the *office in home* deduction was further restricted by the Tax Reform Act of 1986, and will probably be a popular audit issue for the next few years.

In addition to the above, there are other issues that are emphasized in each district, based on prior audit results. In Los Angeles, for instance, exemptions and casualty losses claimed by a single man are usually classified.

WHEN THE ODDS ARE IN YOUR FAVOR

Are there really any "safe" deductions, items you can claim on your return without worrying that they will be audited? Yes and no. That answer probably puts me right at the top of your list of all-time fence straddlers, but anyone who gives you an outright "yes" could be leading you straight down the garden path to audit trouble.

There is no deduction you can put down on your return that is guaranteed audit-proof. The best that can be said is that some deductions are *safer* than others; that is, you run less risk of their being audited, but even that may not be true, depending on the circumstances. There is only one exception to this rule, and that is for items that cannot truly be called deductions; for example, your personal exemption and the standard deduction. You are guaranteed these "deductions" by law. You do not have to meet any qualifications to take them, nor do you have to keep records to prove you are entitled to them.

Why is no one deduction entirely safe? The primary reason is that what kicks your return out of the computer in the first place is not necessarily the item that will be audited. Once your return has scored high enough to be selected by DIF, any item on the return is fair audit game. Although experience has given him a few reliable hunches, the classifier is not privy to the DIF formula, and he does not know exactly why your return was pulled. Besides, it's his baby now. He can classify or pick any deduction that appeals to his discerning eye or throw the return back like an undersized fish if there are no issues that seem promising to him. He is guided in his decision, you'll remember, by his own personal background, training, and experience, and every auditor has his own pet issues.

To give you an example, you might think that the interest on your automobile loan is a good candidate for safe deduction. Almost no one pays cash for a car, so claiming interest in itself is not suspicious, and the amount is usually no more than a couple of hundred dollars, not large enough, some would say, to entice anyone. But Joe, the classifier, has his own ideas on the subject. Just last week, he audited two taxpayers who deducted the entire amount of the finance charge in the year they bought the car, instead of spreading it out over the life of the loan. Now he has a nagging suspicion this might be a common error. The IRS hasn't given interest expense much emphasis lately, but he's thinking of starting a special project of his own. The fact that the adjustment will be only two to three hundred dollars doesn't bother him unduly. In the first place, an adjustment that size isn't all that small in office audit, especially when added to the other changes he expects the auditor to make. Besides, he's after compliance, isn't he? Several hundred dollars taken in error on, say, five million returns begin to add up. Perhaps, in his own way, he can make a dent in this pocket of noncompliance.

Automobile expense on a return coming into Joe's hands during his two-week stint classifying returns is no longer a safe deduction. Sure, the odds are your return will never be seen by Joe, but it does illustrate how circumstances can affect whether a normally safe item is audited, after all.

Similarly, an otherwise safe deduction can be audited in a sweep of an entire issue. As I mention below, union dues are seldom chosen for audit alone. But if, for some other reason, the classifier decides the miscellaneous expense as a whole should be audited, you will probably be asked to verify every item claimed in this category no matter how obvious it is that the expense must have been incurred or is too small to audit alone.

A deduction can also be safe or not depending on what kind of "shelter" you give it. The classifier is normally limited to selecting three or four issues. If there are *five* good issues on the return, the classifier may have to let one of them slide through. The one that got away, so to speak, is safe. (Note, however, that, where clearly warranted, a classifier can choose more than four issues.) Conversely, a deduction that would escape notice on a return with four better issues may be tapped for audit on another return where the choice is more limited. On the second return, the deduction is not safe.

Remember, too, that a deduction is safer only when the amount taken appears reasonable for that type of expense. You cannot claim any amount, no matter how extravagant, with impunity.

Now that you know why no deduction is audit-proof, let's get to the reason you're reading this section in the first place. What deductions are safer than others?

State income tax and *state disability insurance* are usually taken directly from the W-2 form and easily checked by the classifier for accuracy. The state-income-tax deduction may also include any balance due, which you paid with your prior year's state tax return. If the amount is in line with this year's withholding and if, based on your current deductions, it appears likely that you owed additional tax last year, I would not expect this issue to be classified.

Mortgage interest and *real-estate taxes* are seldom selected for audit unless the amounts claimed exceed the norms for your region or appear to seriously strain your resources. These items are unusually easy for the taxpayer to prove (one year-end statement from your loan company and a property-tax bill will do), so audit adjustments are rare. The exception is interest expense paid in a year when you bought or sold property. Escrow papers in hand, most taxpayers find themselves unsure which costs associated with buying and selling property are deductible, and the tax return for that year often turns out to include nondeductible "points" (those charged for specific services) and closing costs deducted as interest. If the classifier is alert to the fact that property has changed hands, an audit of the interest is likely.

Exemptions for your own children are almost never audited if you file a joint return. The IRS does not like to question the existence of family members, and when the children are living with both parents, there is no question of which is providing support. The only instances when this issue would be audited would be as the result of information received by an informant or during a special project. Children claimed by a single mother are more likely to be audited, especially if she is reporting a relatively low income. If you are a single father, you should be prepared for an audit at some time or other.

In certain areas, you are safe if you are not selected for audit when the deduction or loss is first claimed. One example is *capital loss carryovers.* IRS policy is to audit a capital loss in the year it occurred, and if it must be carried over, to let it be after that. The reason involves problems of proof. You are more likely to have the records you need to support your loss at the time it happened. Next year or five years from now, your records may be buried in the basement, lost in a fire, or unaccountably misplaced. So, unofficially, the IRS position is that if your loss is overlooked in the year it occurs, you are "safe" in all subsequent years.

This policy applies to *contributions carryovers* as well. For the same reason, the IRS tries to audit *rental depreciation* within the first five years after you acquire the property or convert it to rental use. Once that much time has elapsed, the depreciation is considered too old an issue.

Certain business expenses are seldom audited if the taxpayer is in an occupation in which these are typically incurred without reimbursement and the amounts seem ordinary and necessary. *Union* and *professional dues* come under this heading, as do *professional journals*. In the entertainment industry, an *agent's commission* equal to 10 percent of industry wages will not raise any eyebrows. If you are an employee in a narrow range of occupations (policeman, nurse) in which you are on call and would not otherwise incur the expense, *telephone* will usually not be questioned, but the amount claimed is expected to be small. With self-employed individuals, higher telephone expenses are tolerated.

The deduction for *drugs and medicines* is often too small to audit profitably. *Medical travel* is also frequently negligible and may escape audit even when medical expense as a whole is classified.

Two other small deductions that are not generally considered worth auditing are *tax-preparation fees* and the cost of maintaining a *safety-deposit box.*

Even if your deductions are not all "safe," you can still increase the odds in your favor if you:

- Attach documentation or other explanations of *unusual* deductions.
- Make sure all required supporting forms and schedules are correctly filled out and attached.
- Include income that wouldn't normally be uncovered if not reported to show your honesty and attention to detail (for example, $50 in lottery winnings or $75 for jury duty).
- Pay attention to neatness and legibility.

A TIE FOR FIRST—OTHER REASONS FOR BEING AUDITED

So far, we have been discussing only computer-selected returns, but 25 percent of all returns audited are selected manually, by other methods. You may be audited because you are a business associate of someone who is being audited. Or if you are an ex-spouse or a relative claiming related deductions. You may be audited if someone informs on you and the information seems reliable. (Be careful whom you antagonize.)

There are also some taxpayers who receive an "automatic audit." Regardless of DIF scores, their returns fall into certain categories the IRS has decided require mandatory audit. These categories currently include all returns with (1) positive income of $200,000 or more; (2) $100,000 to $200,000 of income, and taxable income less than $50,000; and/or (3) two or more Schedules C (business) or F (farm) and total losses of $25,000 or more. No suspense here. Just settle back and wait for our call.

Many persons are audited due to special IRS projects. Whenever a pocket of noncompliance is uncovered, hundreds or even thousands of returns may be audited to wipe it out. Current favorites are Schedule Cs with gross receipts of more than $50,000, because they have proved a rich source of unreported income. Other recent projects have involved matching alimony payments with the income reported by those who receive them, returns showing a sudden increase in exemptions, owners of S corporations with losses, and independent contractors the IRS believes are actually employees.

Sometimes a project encompasses an entire industry on a local level, for example waiters and waitresses, working at selected large hotels or restaurants, who as a class have not been reporting tips. And of course, tax shelters have long been on the IRS hit list, although the passive loss rules ushered in by the Tax Reform Act of 1986 may finally free agents and auditors to focus on other issues.

The underground economy is another target. Studies estimate that individuals fail to report between $285 billion to $800 billion in income. The result—an estimated revenue loss of $44 billion to $123 billion—means more audits in the future for persons who tend to "moonlight." Occupations included in that category are auto mechanics, plumbers, electricians, bartenders, security guards, carpenters, painters, tutors, and others.

Another large project, the Information Returns Program (IRP), involves returns reporting less taxable income than shown on the W-2s filed by employers, banks, dividend-paying corporations, real estate and stock brokers, and others. This computer matching program also includes IRAs (Form 5498), allocation of tips (Form 8027), mortgage interest deductions (Form 1098), and home sales (Form 1099-S), as well as income from royalties, awards of federal contracts, and income of Americans living abroad or resident aliens working in the United States. A notice of proposed changes to income (Form CP-2000) is sent to taxpayers whose income differs from the amount reported by payors. You may request a conference with an auditor if you disagree that additional tax is due.

You may also find yourself being audited because you are a poor judge of tax preparers. Selecting the right tax preparer is an art taught in Chapter VI, and it can be crucial indeed. If the preparer of your choice has found a niche on the IRS Questionable Practitioner

(QP) list, your return may be pulled along with every other client's for an intensive audit. I say "intensive" because every item on your return is fair game and you are asked to bring in proof for all issues. In no other type of audit, except TCMP, will you be asked to verify every deduction on your return, so if you are asked to, regard this as a good clue to your preparer's standing with the IRS. A questionable practitioner is one whose clients' returns have been negligently or even fraudulently prepared in the past. Even if you picked the shyster at random from the phone book, you may still have to prove that you are not negligent by association.

Some taxpayers who might otherwise have escaped notice court an audit by amending their returns to claim a refund. My guess would be that the IRS wonders why, if you knew you had this expense or supported this exemption, you didn't put it on your return in the first place. Claims are not automatically sent to Examination, however. If the taxpayer has a logical explanation for not claiming a deduction earlier or has attached supporting documents, not much fuss will be made over it. When a claim is selected for audit, any item on the return, not just the claim issue, may be examined.

Over one million returns have now been selected. You could be among the winners. First prize is an audit, and in the next chapter, you meet the IRS.

IV. DEAR TAXPAYER

It's time to notify the winners of the annual sweepstakes results. Actually this is a continuing process. Tax returns, or "cases," flow into the districts from the service centers as work is needed. With the exception of claims and special projects, these returns are always for the latest year available. Audit groups usually begin to receive the current year's returns five to six months after the due date (for example, 1987 returns will become available for audit in September or October 1988).

Taxpayers often complain, "I don't know why you waited so long to audit me." Believe me, we get to you as fast as we can. We just can't audit one million returns all at once. We hear your return ticking, though. By law, additional tax must be assessed on a tax return only during the three years after the date it was filed or the due date, whichever is later. Three years is the statute of limitations (unless fraud is involved), and if you have a return you are worried about, you can breathe a sigh of relief as soon as the three years are up. Actually you can breathe easier long before that. If your return isn't opened for audit within a year and a half after it is filed, odds are it never will be. The Examination Division is no more fond of "old" returns (filed more than twenty months ago) than it is of dead fish.

The fresh supply of plump young returns selected for audit are stored in the IRS larder after they have been classified, to await an order from an audit group. The audit market a return is destined for is generally determined by the taxpayer's ZIP code. Wherever possible, IRS audits taxpayers in the vicinity of their homes, and audit groups are located in areas of high "DIF fallout," that is, in the ZIP code areas where the largest percentage of taxpayers whose returns are computer-selected reside.

How many and what mixture of cases an audit group orders depends on its staffing. A group with trainees will ask for returns claiming exemptions and simple itemized deductions. A group of mostly senior, or business, auditors will want cases with Schedules C. If some of the staff will be on vacation or assigned to other offices, the order will of course be lighter. And following a personal preference of mine, if it is Christmas time, there will be no order at all.

A group can order cases in two ways: in bulk, to store if additional work is needed at a future date, or for immediate audit. If your return is in a bulk order, it may never be audited if the need for more work does not arise, and may eventually be shipped back to the service center once it becomes too old. Stockpiling bulk cases is done sparingly, however, and most bulk returns do get audited.

If your case is chosen to fill an order for returns to be immediately opened for audit, you have almost reached the point of no return. An audit letter is only a day or two away, and because I came to verbal blows with a taxpayer today over this point, let me acquaint you here with one of the facts of life. Once you receive that audit letter, you are going to be audited—rich, poor, sick, well, irate, insane, nine, ninety, dead. The audit, like the beat, goes on. (There is only one exception, which is covered below.)

There are a sizable number of persons who believe that at least dead you are safe from an audit. True, *you* are spared the irritation. That passes along with your estate to the heirs. But a return has been filed, and just because you are dead doesn't mean you were saintly. If a search of your earthly belongings fails to turn up receipts, there will be tax to pay, and the federal government gets first choice from among your estate's possessions.

Writing this, it does sound a little scandalous that the government should latch onto an audit like a terrier and refuse to be shaken loose for any reason, no matter how compelling. The irrevocability of an audit once it has been put in motion is really a form of failsafe, however. When a taxpayer learns he is being audited, no matter how influential he is, he cannot halt the audit and have his return sent back to the service center as if nothing had ever happened. An audit can only go forward; once it is begun, it must be completed. This axiom also prevents an IRS employee from giving preferential treatment to friends, relatives, himself, or strangers he feels sorry for. As mentioned before, we do not judge merit. Why should you be audited and another taxpayer be permitted to talk his way out of it because he is more unfortunate or just a better talker than you? When you come right down to it, do you want auditors as human as yourself to have the power to be as capricious, arbitrary, selfish, or illogical as humans sometimes are, or would you make sure they couldn't be?

THE AUDIT LETTER

Your return, you recall, is on the critical list to receive an audit letter. This letter will ask you to do one of three things: (1) mail in your receipts; (2) call for an appointment; or (3) come in for an appointment at a time shown on the letter. The type of letter you receive depends entirely on the particular needs of the audit group or the preferences of its manager, not on your return itself.

For our purposes, the letter you receive tells you to come in at a specified date and time. A sample appointment letter is reprinted here. Don't be put off by its length. When you get your appointment letter, read it. While it is not a treasure trove of information, it explains who may represent you at an audit, attempts to allay your fears, and briefly describes your appeal rights. In fact, some auditors believe the letter does too good a job of putting taxpayers at ease, especially when they come in waving the letter and immediately demanding appeal rights. Don't do this, folks. It's poor strategy, as you'll see in Chapter VII. The problem with the letter from the auditor's point of view is that it tells you that you don't have to agree with him. Now, of course, this is true, but the auditor would prefer to tell you in his own way and at his own time. Never forget that an audit is a form of power struggle, with both sides jockeying for advantage. The auditor benefits by your ignorance; he doesn't want you to know too much from the start. In addition, he doesn't want his authority undermined. His job is to convince you to agree to fair audit adjustments, and he doesn't expect the employer who gave him that job to turn around and tell his taxpayers they don't have to agree.

Your appointment letter also tells you which of the items on your return have been classified, or selected for audit. A separate page lists the most common deductions. Check marks are made in the

Internal Revenue Service
District Director

Department of the Treasury

Date:

Contact Telephone Number:

Appointment Clerk:

We selected your Federal income tax return for the year(s) shown below to examine the items checked at the end of this letter. We have scheduled an appointment for you at the time and place shown below. If you are unable to keep this appointment, please call the appointment clerk promptly to reschedule a more convenient time.

APPOINTMENT INFORMATION

TAX YEAR(S):

DAY AND DATE:

PLACE:

TIME:

ROOM NO:

To avoid any unnecessary repetitive examinations, let the appointment clerk know as soon as possible if your income tax return was examined in either of the 2 prior years for the same items and the examination resulted in no change to your tax liability.

If you filed a joint return, either you or your spouse may keep the appointment. You may also have someone else represent you; however, if you are not present, you must furnish your representative with a written authorization. You can get authorization forms from an IRS office by requesting Form 2848, or for limited authorization, Form 2848-D. Also, any individual may accompany you as a witness to assist in establishing the facts in your case.

We enclosed information guides to assist you in selecting the type of documents required to substantiate the items checked. It will save you time if you keep together the records related to each item. Without the requested documents, we will have to proceed on the basis of available information that may be incomplete. Therefore, we will need your cooperation.

The examiner will review your return and records. If we propose any changes to your tax liability we will explain them as well as your appeal rights. If you agree to the proposed changes, we will ask you to sign an agreement form. If you do not agree, the examiner will furnish you with a copy of Publication 5, Appeal Rights and Preparation of Protests for Unagreed Cases.

(over)

If you have any questions, please contact our office at the number shown in the heading of this letter. When you come in for your appointment, please bring this letter with you.

Thank you for your cooperation.

Sincerely yours,

District Director

Enclosures:
Information Guides
Notice 609

Please bring records to support the following items reported on your tax return.

- ☐ Alimony Payments
- ☐ Automobile Expenses
- ☐ Bad Debts
- ☐ Capital Gains and Losses
- ☐ Casualty Losses
- ☐ Child Care Credit
- ☐ Contributions
- ☐ Education Expenses
- ☐ Employee Business Expenses
- ☐ Energy Credit
- ☐ Exemptions (Child/Children, Other)
- ☐ Income—1099's & 1087's
- ☐ Interest Expense
- ☐ Medical and Dental Expenses
- ☐ Miscellaneous Deductions
- ☐ Moving Expenses
- ☐ Rental Income and Expenses
- ☐ Sale or Exchange of Residence
- ☐ Sick Pay or Disability Income Exclusion
- ☐ Taxes
- ☐ Uniforms, Equipment, and Tools
- ☐
- ☐
- ☐

Please bring all business and personal bank statements. Also, bring canceled checks, accounting ledgers and journals, notes, agreements, and invoices for the following items:

Schedule C

- ☐ All Business Expenses
- ☐ Bad Debts
- ☐ Cost of Goods Sold
- ☐ Depreciation
- ☐ Gross Receipts
- ☐ Insurance
- ☐ Interest
- ☐ Rents
- ☐ Repairs
- ☐ Salaries and Wages
- ☐ Taxes
- ☐ Travel and Entertainment
- ☐
- ☐
- ☐

Schedule F

- ☐ All Farm Expenses
- ☐ Depreciation
- ☐ Feed and Seed Purchased
- ☐ Fertilizers, Lime
- ☐ Gross Receipts
- ☐ Insurance
- ☐ Inventories
- ☐ Labor Hired
- ☐ Machine Hire
- ☐ Other Farm Income
- ☐ Repairs and Maintenance
- ☐ Supplies Purchased
- ☐ Taxes
- ☐
- ☐

Letter 889(DO) (Rev. 10–81)

boxes next to the issues classified on your return. Those are the only issues you must bring records to support. Do not be misled into thinking these are the only issues that may be audited, however. If the auditor suspects or discovers an error during the audit, he may extend the scope of the audit to include that new issue and ask you to produce additional documents. Similarly, if, because of a clerical error, the IRS fails to check one of the right boxes, you are still held accountable for the records once the error is discovered.

If your return is a nonbusiness one (no Schedule C), you will also find blue information notices attached to your letter. Some examples are included here. These notices tell you what records are needed to verify the deductions being audited. They represent the ideal, and if you follow them exactly, you should have no trouble in the audit. Unfortunately, most taxpayers don't find out what records they need for an audit until it's too late. That's why in the next chapter you'll learn all about record keeping—in advance of an audit—so that you can be smug instead of desperate when you read what these notices require. If exemptions are in issue, a questionnaire about the dependent will be sent for you to fill out and bring to the audit.

If you filed a business return, you will not receive these information notices. You may receive a variation of the appointment letter shown in this book, which lists the records you need to produce or includes a check sheet. Business owners have to bring in all the journals and ledgers for the business, even though not all business expenses are classified. They also must bring in bank statements for all savings and checking accounts, because income must be verified.

Also included with the appointment letter is Notice 609, which tells you the penalties and other undesirable consequences if you fail to provide the requested information.

If you want someone to represent you in the audit, the letter tells you to request a power-of-attorney form (discussed later) from your local IRS office.

PREAUDIT ASSISTANCE

Notice of your appointment date and time are written in the center of the appointment letter. The tax year(s) being audited and

OMB Clearance No. 1545-0526
Expires 11/30/84

Information
Guide

Contributions

To help us complete the examination of your return, please include the following with your records:

1. Canceled checks or receipts for church contributions.

2. Canceled checks or receipts for contributions to charitable organizations.

3. If the contribution was other than money show:

(a) Name and address of the recipient organization.
(b) What was contributed.
(c) The fair market value of each item on the date of contribution.

4. If you reported expenses for attending a church convention or similar activity, furnish evidence that you were an official representative.

For Privacy Act and Paperwork Reduction Act Notice, see enclosed Notice 609.

Department
of the
Treasury
**Internal
Revenue
Service**

**Notice 90
(Rev. 12-81)**

☆U.S. GPO: 1982—361-641/2218

OMB Clearance No. 1545-0526
Expires 11/30/84

Information
Guide

Employee Travel and Entertainment Expenses

To help us complete the examination of your return, please include the following with your records:

1. Statement from your employer showing:
(a) Employer's reimbursement policy.
(b) Amount and kind of expense reimbursed, charged, or provided.
(c) Specific expenses not covered by reimbursement policy.
(d) Territory assigned to you and a brief outline of your duties.

2. Explanatory statement from your employer if you are required to provide an office in your home or elsewhere or to use your home telephone in connection with your employment. Furnish receipts or canceled checks to verify these expenses.

3. Copies of expense vouchers submitted to your employer for reimbursement.

4. Receipts and records (diary) of expenses for business purposes:
(a) Lodging and meals while away from home.
(b) Gifts.
(c) Promotional items.
(d) Entertainment.

5. Verification of automobile expenses for business purposes:
(a) Invoice of purchase or lease of vehicles.
(b) Receipts for oil, gas, repairs, etc.
(c) Records of business mileage and total mileage.

For Privacy Act and Paperwork Reduction Act Notice, see enclosed Notice 609.

Department of the Treasury
Internal Revenue Service

Notice 93
(Rev. 12-81)

★U.S. GPO: 1982—361-541/2220

the address of the office where you are to appear are shown to the left of your appointment date. The phone number of the audit group and the appointment clerk's name are written in the upper right-hand corner of the letter.

Call the appointment clerk if you have any questions about what records to bring, if the appointment time is not convenient for you, if you need additional time to assemble your records, or if you want your case transferred to another office. When you call, tell the clerk that you have been scheduled to come in for an audit and tell her your name and the date of your appointment. Your name is the only identification you need, because all cases are filed alphabetically. If there is a problem locating your case, the clerk may ask for additional information or she may ask for your social security number to confirm your identity and make sure she has the right file (there are a lot of Smiths [and in my area, Garcias] out there). For starters, just tell her your name and the date.

Remember, the clerk is not an auditor. Your case, unless it has a Schedule C, is usually not assigned to an auditor until you walk in the door. This means that, although she can answer simple questions regarding record requirements, you cannot rely on her for tax-law advice. If your questions are technical, you will have to wait until you see the auditor, or seek outside advice. Even if the clerk were qualified to answer questions based on the facts of your case, she would not be able to give you an opinion as to whether your deductions will be allowed or not. As you have learned, the auditor is the sole judge of deductibility, and he cannot be committed to a position by anyone else, even a fellow auditor or his manager.

Although the clerk is unfamiliar with tax law, appointments are her business. Trust her. Don't muster up an excess of *hauteur* and insist on speaking to "someone in charge" just to switch your appointment to another day. The IRS is a business like any other business. If you are "someone in charge," I'm sure you do not handle routine clerical chores, and if you are not "someone in charge," you probably resent any implication that you cannot do your job. If the clerk cannot help you, she will say so and refer you to someone who can.

There is normally no problem in changing your appointment date. Just don't expect to change it to a Saturday or evenings when you are off work. The IRS keeps normal business hours, and unless you decide to mail in your receipts, you will have to take time off from work or school to attend the audit. You may also find that your audit group does not schedule audits on one day of the week, usually Fridays, to allow auditors to catch up on necessary paperwork. Audits do not begin later than midafternoon, to give you and the auditor time to do your return justice before the office closes.

If you need to reschedule your appointment, give the IRS as much notice as possible. This is a courtesy that allows the group to fit in other taxpayers who also want to reschedule. It is only a courtesy, because you can phone in up to the very day of your appointment to say you won't make it, without any harm to you. The appointment letter states, "We will consider the appointment confirmed if we do not hear from you at least 7 days before the scheduled date." This has no meaning in practice, because the IRS genuinely tries, within the limitations of the law, to be accommodating. IRS employees know that being audited is not your favorite activity, and I say it again: they are extremely sensitive to public opinion.

AUDIT BY MAIL

If you can't come to the office for personal reasons or because you can't afford the time, you may mail in your records. Again, as a courtesy you should call to tell the clerk you prefer to handle the audit by correspondence, although as long as your records reach the IRS before your appointment date, calling is not strictly necessary. Always mail a copy of your appointment letter along with your receipts. This will give the clerk all the information she needs to find your file and make sure your valuable documents don't wind up in a "Does anybody know where this should go?" drawer. I know this sounds like plain common sense, but we get envelopes all the time with papers stuffed inside, no cover letter, no identification. We take the liberty of assuming they came from someone under audit, who probably has an appointment at a future date, and look for a recurring name that would indicate the anonymous sender. Note that I advise sending a *copy* of your appointment letter, not the original, so that you have a record of the office auditing your return and a phone number to call if need be. If you mail in the original, at least make a note of this information. For the same reason, don't throw away and try not to misplace any correspondence you receive during the audit.

A word of advice about conducting your audit through the mail: It is never as advantageous as coming in for an interview, and it is downright unwise if the issues are more complex than itemized deductions. When you mail in documents, you limit the auditor to just those records. If the facts or receipts he needs to allow you the deduction aren't in the envelope, he cannot give you any credit for them. Often there are additional facts the auditor must have that he cannot infer from a receipt alone, and you have no way of anticipating all the questions he would ask if you were there in person. In many respects, you are asking the auditor to work in a vacuum, and if you think he will give you the benefit of the doubt, you are wrong. As you'll see later, an auditor can evaluate oral evidence and give you a reasonable allowance in certain areas, even though you do not have any records. If you do not come in for an interview, you miss the benefit of speaking to the auditor.

Because the allowability of exemptions usually turns on oral testimony, a correspondence audit is never recommended for this "easy" (in terms of the tax law) issue. Other issues better handled in person are: employee business expenses, bad debt deductions, casualty and theft losses, educational expense, income from tips, pensions, annuities, and rents, and gains from the sale of property.

If you still decide to chance it or simply have no choice, make sure you enclose an explanation of what each receipt is for and pertinent facts relating to the expense. Use the information guides to help you in giving all necessary facts. If you have no records at all for an expense, explain why and the circumstances that make it deductible. This is as close as you can get to oral testimony, but I cannot promise you that, without records to back up your statements, they will be given any weight. In evaluating oral testimony to determine its credibility, an auditor relies on the tone of voice, degree of nervousness, and other visible clues, as well as cross-examination, none of which is available when you write a letter.

Also include your telephone number. Your auditor may call to clarify the facts, but this is entirely dependent on how much time he has. The burden, or problem, of proof is yours, and an auditor is not expected to spend government time shifting the burden. Include your number anyway, in case you get lucky. Lastly, a correspondence audit is a slow audit. Be prepared for delays. The taxpayers who get immediate attention are the ones on the doorstep. The auditor has that one day a week reserved for working on correspondence cases along with quite a few other things. When you choose to present your case through the mail, you place yourself on a long waiting line.

POSTPONING THE INEVITABLE: EXTENSIONS OF TIME

If you do plan to present your receipts in person but need more time, you should ask for an "extension." How much you can get away with here is going to vary from group to group and manager to manager. It's also going to depend on the validity of your excuse. Some taxpayers seem to believe that if they put it off as long as possible, the audit will just go away. If the clerk believes you are simply stalling, you can rule out any grace period. Generally the clerk will be sympathetic the first time but increasingly unreceptive with each successive request. For this reason, you should be realistic in deciding how much extra time you need and make a genuine effort to keep the new appointment you agreed to. There is no hard-and-fast rule as to how many times you can reschedule your appointment, but three is close to tops. As for the amount of time IRS will wait to honor your presence, it may be as little as two weeks or as long as several months. The IRS will not sit out the filing season because your tax preparer is too busy, but if a taxpayer says he had an operation and will not be able to walk for three months, his file may be held pending. A letter from a relative stating the taxpayer is away from home for an indefinite stay will only generate an audit report. Either the taxpayer returns for the audit or asks that the audit be conducted where he currently is. I once had a taxpayer who flew all the way from Berlin for his audit, then flew back when it was over. He had his choice of Germany, but his records were all in Los Angeles. A more punctilious and precise man I never met, and it was a point of pride with him that in the end he owed no tax. He flew over six thousand miles to prove it.

This should give you some idea of the priority the IRS places on an audit. You are literally being asked to drop everything when you receive that ominous letter, and while you can secure reasonable extensions of time, when the time runs out the audit will go on, with or without you.

REQUESTING A TRANSFER

Your case is sent to the "post of duty," or office in the ZIP code area shown on your return. If you have moved since you filed the return, you may find yourself being audited from an office that is miles, states, or countries away from where you now live. If this is the case, you will have to call or write, asking to have your audit transferred to a closer office. If the transfer is to a different post of duty in the same district, a phone call is sufficient to put your case in motion. If the transfer is to another district, your request will have to be in writing. When your request is received, your case is forwarded to the appropriate office and a new appointment letter will be sent to you.

Suppose you have not moved but have appointed a representative to handle the audit for you whose business is not convenient to the IRS office that has your return. Can you have your case transferred to an office nearer your representative's? Policy and practice vary. The convenience of the government is the principal consideration in determining where the examination will be conducted, according to IRS Policy Statement 4-90. You may get the transfer anyway, but if it is denied, don't expect to win this one by fighting it.

Note: It is IRS policy to hold business audits at the place of business. Requests for a transfer closer to a representative's office are routinely denied. The one exception is if the place of business is too small to conveniently conduct an audit there.

A limited number of examinations conducted by office auditors take place in the field; that is, at the taxpayer's home or business. Normally they occur as part of an auditor's training and rarely after that. If you want to be the exception, you're going to have to come up with a reason airtight enough to support life in outer space, at least in my district. In the first place, field visits are reserved for business audits. The only nonbusiness field audits I know of involved taxpayers who for physical reasons could not even leave the house to reach a mailbox. Secondly, a business must possess such large quantities of records that you cannot possibly bring them all in. Whether your business has such a volume of sales and purchase invoices and other receipts will be judged by the auditor or group manager by looking at your return and considering the type of business. No one is going to come out and take a look—that would defeat the purpose. As a manager, I personally look for a high gross sales (several hundred thousand) of a low-cost item.

BEATING THE RAP—REPETITIVE AUDITS

Several pages back, I said that, with only one exception, once you receive that appointment letter you had better sit back and enjoy the ride, because the audit must go through. At this point, we're going to discuss the exception, which is the IRS equivalent of time off for good behavior. This is the "repetitive audit"; it is mentioned in the appointment letter. If you have been audited for the *same* classified *issues* in either of the *two preceding tax years* and owed no tax, you do not need to endure another audit this year. Whenever possible, classifiers try to spot prior no-change audits so that you will not receive a letter at all, but sometimes the audit is recent and the results are not recorded in time.

If you are in this enviable position and do receive a letter, call the office before your appointment date. Your appointment will then be postponed while the truth of your statement is confirmed and a decision is made whether to continue the audit. You may be asked to mail in copies of your prior-year appointment letter, no-change letter, and tax return. Or the group manager may request your audit file for the no-change year from the service center. This can take several months. Sit tight. When your file is received, the issues will be checked. If even one issue is different or if the deduction has significantly changed, you may be in for an audit anyway. The final decision is the group manager's. If everything appears the same, you are off the hook. Your return will be "surveyed" and returned to the service center. You will receive a letter stating your return is "accepted as filed." This letter must be distinguished from the no-change letter, which told you that you owed no tax in your prior audit. For repetitive audit purposes, the "accepted as filed" letter (L-359) is no good, because it is issued to tell you your return will not be audited. A no-change letter (DO 590) tells you your return *was* audited but with no tax result.

The repetitive audit procedures could also be invoked where an adjustment was made to only one of the classified issues in the prior year or where a new issue has been added to those previously no-changed. You could argue that the audit should be limited to the issue previously adjusted or never before audited. At least it is worth a try.

We have been talking about steps to take after you receive your appointment letter. What happens, though, when the letter is mailed to you but you never receive it? Should you lie awake at night in a cold sweat worrying about what the IRS is plotting to do to you because you never responded to a letter you never saw? Are you supposed to use ESP to make sure the IRS isn't trying to get in touch with you? Hardly.

The appointment letter is sent to the address on your return. If you have moved and left no forwarding address, the letter rebounds to the audit group. Your case has become a "return mail" case. Are we discouraged? No. At this point, a postal tracer may be sent out to track you down, we may write your last known employer, or we might get a more current address from a more recently filed return. In any event, an audit report is written and mailed certified to whatever address we may now have. If the letter doesn't come back, we yell, "Contact!" and expect to hear from you. If it is returned to us undeliverable, we move on to greener pastures. You cannot be assessed tax without notice, and your return will be surveyed and sent back to the service center. This is not another exception to the rule stated earlier that audits must go on, because even though the audit letter was mailed, you never received it, and the audit will be terminated. Note that we do look at the envelopes when mail is returned, and any undelivered mail that merely was unwanted does not qualify for this treatment.

You have your appointment, but do you have your records? In the next chapter, you'll learn the Internal Revenue Code's record-keeping requirements, how to live with them, and what to do if this information comes too late.

V. IT'S NEVER TOO LATE TO PANIC, OR DIGGING UP THE DEAD

There is only one surefire way to win when you play "audit" against the IRS. In Las Vegas, a man sitting next to me at keno got up for the fourth time to collect his winnings. My envy—I hadn't won a dime—must have shown, because he waved his way ticket at me and said, "You've got to have a system. All the big winners have a system." Oddly enough, that's true in an audit as well. You've got to have a system to beat IRS: a system of records. Without one, you're going to lose every time.

I know it's not easy. Unless you're an accountant or a bookkeeper, record keeping probably does not enthrall you. It's nit-picky, time-consuming, tedious, and hard to remember. It puts a crimp in your life-style, your self-image as a free spirit. You don't want to behave like Scrooge in public, in front of your friends and business associates—they're not going to think you're smart, just cheap. I agree. But, like a doctor telling you to take your medicine, I have to insist that you keep records, not haphazard, whenever-you-feel-like-it records, but daily, systematic ones. Unless you follow my record-keeping advice to the letter, I cannot guarantee you a no-change audit. It is the ounce of prevention that beats a dollar in tax.

You sit down across the desk from your auditor, real chummy, and you lean forward confidingly and say, "You know how it is. Nobody can get a receipt for every little thing. I don't have enough time as it is. You can't ask me to spend all my time getting receipts and keeping a diary of every place I go. When would I earn a living?" A plea with a ring of truth? Surely the auditor is nodding in agreement as she allows you the deduction anyway. Right? Let me tell you what the auditor really does as she writes, "No verification. Disallow in full." She says, "No one is forcing you to keep receipts.

You're the one who wants the deduction. Take your choice. Either keep receipts or don't put the expense on your tax return."

If you can't produce receipts, the auditor has a right to wonder how you arrived at the figures on your return. How do you know how much you spent if you didn't keep any record of it? As soon as you admit that the amount is only a best estimate, you are playing "my guess is as good as yours" with the auditor. Because the tax law places the burden of proof in an audit on you, this is a game you can't win.

What do I mean when I say the burden of proof is on the taxpayer? What ever happened to "innocent until proven guilty"? Nothing happened to it. It still applies, where it always did: in criminal trials. The IRS is not judging guilt or innocence. It is verifying whether you have receipts to match the expenses on your return. If an audit adjustment is made because you do not have receipts, the legal reason is not "The expense was not incurred" but, rather, "It has not been *verified* that the expense was incurred." No accusation is being made. Just a statement of fact it is hard to refute—you either have the receipts or you don't.

RECORD KEEPING MADE SIMPLE

Good record keeping doesn't have to be a career. For audit purposes, nothing more fancy than a shoe box is needed. And why not? The most difficult part of record keeping is not *how* to keep your records but *what* records to keep in the first place. I want to make sure you're saving the right documents. We'll worry about tidying them up later.

Every auditor appreciates a professional single- or double-entry set of books, but no auditor is going to send you packing if you don't have one. The overall quality of record keeping is so poor that most auditors are grateful if you just give it a good try. Because I want to make record keeping as easy as possible for you, the method I describe is the bare minimum you need to follow and still be a winner. Anyone who wants to add decorative touches of his own may do so with my blessing.

Those of you who chuckled when I mentioned a shoe box can have the last laugh, because this handy piece of cardboard makes an excellent, if unwitting, file box for storing records. Its length accommodates legal documents, and its depth permits you to organize it using dividers or gives you plenty of room to stack your documents up. I know it lacks sophistication, but it is practical, inexpensive, and the bare minimum.

The easiest way to keep receipts in a shoe box is to throw them in, one on top of the other. While no auditor will give you a standing ovation for this, it is acceptable. But you want to win, and to do that you must make sure you have every single deductible receipt. For this reason, we're going to use a refined shoe box method, which requires one-time preparation.

You're going to have one shoe box for each tax year. Write the year on top of the box with a felt marker or pen. Buy a package of legal-size envelopes. These envelopes will ensure no deductions are overlooked, because each one will be labeled with a tax-deductible expense or a taxable income item. You should have an envelope for each of the following:

Income (wages, interest/ dividends, prizes)
Exemptions
Medical
Taxes
Interest/loans
Contributions
Child care
Business expenses
Miscellaneous
- a) union and professional dues
- b) uniforms, equipment, and tools
- c) telephone
- d) education

Automobile
Major purchases (furniture, jewelry, appliances)

If your finances are more diversified, you may want to add such optional categories as:

Rental
Investments
Escrow papers, mortgages
Deeds
Insurance policies
Legal fees

Notice that I have not included any Schedule C expenses. This is because I cannot wholeheartedly recommend even a refined shoebox method for small businesses. I've seen it done, and it certainly beats nothing at all, but, leaving taxes aside, it is poor business practice. Find someone who can set up a simple set of books for your business and keep records diligently.

Those of you who are tax wise know that my list includes items such as major purchases and deeds, which are not deductible on your tax return. Why add them to the general clutter? Because none of us has a crystal ball. The price you paid for that nineteen-inch color portable will be of consuming interest to an auditor *if* some cad steals it. "How could I know somebody was going to steal it?" you argue justly, and the auditor shrugs and says, "Plan ahead." The time to start is now, with a thought to the unforeseeable and both eyes on the inevitable: taxes.

The categories I have listed are the most universal, and they should cover the spectrum of your income and expenses. Because the lives and livelihoods of all of us differ, however, there may be other deductions available to you, which you don't want to miss. You will need an envelope for these, too. I cannot list all the possibilities here, but I do have a suggestion. Call the local Taxpayer Service Division of IRS and ask them to send you a *Publication 17* (if you own a small business, ask for *Publication 334* and a businessman's kit, too). This is a comprehensive and comprehensible income-tax guide for the layman, and it is *free*. Familiarize yourself with the book, then skim the index for additional categories unique to your personal and business life. Prepare envelopes for each of these.

Now you've got a box full of empty envelopes. I can imagine your excitement. We've conquered the *how*. Now to tackle the *what*. What receipts or checks should you keep? Everything. Everything, that is, until you get home. Don't make snap judgments about tax deductibility on the run. Stuff every scrap of paper anybody hands you into your pocket or purse. It's not neat, but nobody's going to know unless you're searched.

If you can hang onto a receipt long enough to get it home, you have record keeping licked. Once you're settled in, transfer your collection of receipts to the shoe box. First write down the items purchased on the receipt if it is one of those cash-register tapes that show only a total. Then, however often the mood strikes you, sort these receipts into the categories labeled on your envelopes. If a receipt doesn't fit into one of these categories and you are unsure whether it is deductible, use your *Publication 17.* If an expense seems borderline, even after you research it, keep it, but make a note to call the IRS or ask your tax preparer about its deductibility before you claim it on your return. If a document fits into more than one category, for example a home loan statement showing both interest and taxes, put a note in one of the envelopes referring you to where the statement can be found. Follow a like procedure with monthly bills and canceled checks.

There is no need to keep a daily journal with nice, neat figures in nice, neat columns. The one exception is for business mileage, in which a log is a must. If you use your car for business, you might as well resign yourself to this right now. Keep a memo book in your car and write down the beginning and ending mileage and the purpose of your trip each time your business requires you to drive.

How long must each shoebox take up valuable space? The IRS, you recall, has only three years from the date a return was filed or the due date (or two years from the date the tax was paid), whichever is later. Therefore, the general rule is that receipts may be discarded after three years. This is tricky, though, so let me illustrate. Receipts for 1988 must be kept for three years, or until 1992. But that's *four* years. Yes, but only three years from the due date, April 15, 1989. Make a mental note to add four years to the date on the receipt.

Of course, some records should be kept much longer. If you own a business, it's a good idea to keep those records for seven years and any records on your employees for four years. Property records should be retained as long as they are needed to determine the basis of the original property or property that replaced it. Receipts for major purchases should also be saved until three years after you dispose of the property.

Finally, copies of past tax returns are often valuable in preparing subsequent returns, for example, if you are depreciating property. Records for the first six years you pay or receive alimony should be kept. If you sell business or investment property at a loss, you should keep the return for the year of sale for five years. You will also want to keep a return that generated a net operating loss or capital loss carryover for as long as it takes to completely use up the carryover.

A word of advice here. Never entrust your records to the safekeeping of your tax preparer unless he performs regular bookkeeping for you. Leave copies if you must, but always keep the original documents. You are responsible for verifying the amounts on your tax return—not your preparer. If your receipts are lost, don't expect your preparer to step forward, checkbook in hand. A distraught Filipino, obviously new to this country, called our office today, on the verge of tears, because he had given all his records to his preparer, who had "tricked" him and could no longer be found. There was nothing we could do for him except send him a report for additional tax due. I recall one questionable preparer whose entire clientele fell under audit several years back, and all of them had left their records with the preparer. Realizing the net was closing in, the preparer locked his office and went into hiding. His frantic clients were clawing at the doors, and with a misguided sense of jurisdiction were clamoring for us to help them. Several months later, the preparer had a heart attack, dying shortly thereafter, and I doubt if any of his clients ever saw their records again.

WHAT RECORDS TO KEEP

To give you some legal background, the Internal Revenue Code, section 6001, makes you responsible for keeping books and records that are adequate for audit purposes. As we have just seen, records are "adequate" if they exist, if they are in the proper form, and if you can readily lay your hands on them. Under section 7602, an auditor may compel you to produce whatever records he needs to conduct the examination of your return. That is the old one-two that makes record keeping a must and gives the auditor clout if he gets to you before I reform you.

Your return has been selected. You have received your appointment letter. This is the moment of truth. The auditor isn't going to take your word for anything. He doesn't *know* that everyone in your line of work has to spend X dollars to make as much as you did last year. You have to prove to him that you are worthy of belief. And you do that by backing up what you say with receipts.

What *type* of receipts should you bring to the audit? The Information Guides attached to your appointment letter list the documents you must marshal together to verify the items that are under audit.

If you have this information in advance, you will also know what type of records to house in that shoe box.

The most common items classified are listed below, followed by the documents you need in an audit to verify each one:

EXEMPTIONS: YOUR CHILDREN

Birth certificates; social security numbers if age five or older; if applicable, your divorce decree and the written agreement showing which parent will claim the exemption; copies of canceled checks and receipts for amounts you spent to support your children; a record of the amounts others spent toward the children's support; if applicable, a statement from the other parent that he or she did not claim the exemption; a record of amounts received from social security, child-support payments, welfare, and other outside sources. Note: It is rare for exemptions to be audited on a joint return. If you were divorced or legally separated before 1985 and you believe the other parent will claim the exemptions, keep receipts for *all* household expenses: food, clothing, education, even recreation.

EXEMPTIONS: OTHER THAN YOUR CHILDREN

A computation of the cost of the dependent's support; the amount of income or other funds received by or for the dependent; the amounts contributed to household expenses by each person living in the household; school records or other documents showing the dependent's address was the same as yours or a statement from the dependent that he lived with you so many months during the year; if the dependent did not live with you, canceled checks, money orders, or receipts for amounts you sent to him or spent for his support; a statement from others the dependent lived with that they did not claim him as an exemption. Note: You will be sent a Form 2038 to fill out about the dependent's support. This is to save time in the audit. You must still have checks or receipts to prove what you write on this form.

MEDICAL EXPENSES

Canceled checks, receipts, etc., for all medical and dental expenses; itemized receipts for prescription drugs and medicine (canceled checks are not acceptable, because they may include payment for nondeductible drugstore items); insurance policies for which you are deducting premiums; canceled checks or pay stubs for insurance premiums; a record of any expense reimbursed or paid directly by insurance.

TAXES

A. *Real-estate and personal-property taxes:* canceled checks or receipts for taxes paid; if you sold or bought real property, a copy of the escrow papers or settlement statement. B. *State and city income taxes:* a copy of your prior year's state or city tax return and canceled checks showing payment of income tax and estimated taxes.

INTEREST

Receipts or statements from creditors showing amounts of interest paid; payment books and purchase or loan contracts for installment purchases, plus canceled checks showing payment; year-end statement for mortgage interest. Note: Canceled checks alone will not verify interest paid, because the payment usually covers both principal and interest, with no breakdown of how much is interest.

You must also keep detailed records of how you spend borrowed funds.

CONTRIBUTIONS

Canceled checks, receipts, church statements, or letters from your church or other tax-exempt organization. If you contributed property instead of cash, a receipt or a record of the donee, what items were contributed, and the fair market value when contributed (you must estimate the fair market value). If the claimed value is over $5,000, you must have the property appraised.

UNIFORMS, EQUIPMENT, TOOLS, AND TELEPHONE

Receipts for purchases; a letter from your employer stating the telephone was required, and your telephone bills.

ALIMONY

A copy of the divorce or separate-maintenance decree; the current address of your divorced spouse, plus social security number if known; receipts or canceled checks showing payment.

CHILD CARE

Receipts or canceled checks; the name, address, and social security number of the person caring for your child, if available.

EDUCATION EXPENSES

A statement from your employer (if the education is required by him) stating the purpose of your study and that it is required, plus any reimbursement he provided; a transcript of courses taken and period of enrollment; canceled checks or receipts for tuition, travel and transportation, books, meals and lodging while away from home overnight, and others. Teachers must provide the type of teacher's certificate under which they taught, the date it was issued, and the subjects they taught.

CASUALTY LOSSES

Police, fire department, or damage reports; receipts or canceled checks showing the cost or other basis of the lost property and the date acquired; documentation of the fair market value of the property before and after the casualty, including appraisals or damage estimates if available; photographs showing the extent of the loss if available; repair bills or estimates to repair the property; copies of insurance reports showing the amount of reimbursement received or claimed; Small Business Administration loan application or amount received; records of other claims or suits filed.

BAD DEBTS

Promissory notes or other evidence of legal debt; full name and address of debtor; evidence of attempts made to collect the debt; evidence of the improbability of collecting the debt.

CAPITAL GAINS AND LOSSES

Stock sales: Brokerage statements indicating quantities of shares, selling and purchase prices, and dates of transactions; Forms 1099-B. For worthless stock, obtain a statement from your broker or a corporate officer to that effect and indicating the date.

Sales of real property (residential, rental, investment): Sales and purchase escrow papers; receipts for capital improvements to the property; Form 1099-S. For rental or commercial property, copies of your income-tax returns for the two years before the year of sale. For residential property, if the proceeds of the sale were reinvested, purchase escrow papers on new home.

EMPLOYEE BUSINESS EXPENSES

Automobile: Log or diary showing date of each business trip and business miles driven; odometer reading at beginning and end of year; receipts, credit card slips, or canceled checks for gasoline, oil, automobile insurance, lease payments, license fees, car washes, parking, tolls; automobile repair bills; purchase invoice for business automobile; letter from your employer stating the amount of reimbursement, if any.

Travel and entertainment: For entertainment, receipts (with diary preferred) showing the date, amount, place, person entertained, and business purpose or relationship; airline tickets, lodging and meal receipts, and log of taxi fares and tips for away-from-home expenses; letter from your employer stating you were required to incur these expenses and the amount of reimbursement, if any. Note: the Internal Revenue Code, section 274, requires strict record keeping for travel and entertainment. Auditors have been instructed to take a tough line in requiring the exact proof outlined in the Regulations. Watch your step here.

Home office: Letter from your employer stating that he does not provide an office and that you are required to work out of your home for his convenience. Receipts for interest and taxes or rent, home insurance, utilities, repairs to office, and office furniture and equipment. Total floor area in your home and the portion used as an office. A photograph of the office area, if available.

RENTAL INCOME AND EXPENSES

Income: Rent-receipt book for rents, deposits, and fees; a record of your tenants, the number of months they were in occupancy, and their monthly rent payments.

Rental expenses: Canceled checks, purchase invoices for materials and supplies, receipts for repairs, gardening, advertising, legal fees; receipts or canceled checks for labor, showing the name and address of the payee; year-end mortgage statement showing interest and taxes, or canceled checks for taxes paid.

Depreciation: Original purchase escrow papers showing cost, tax bill for the year of purchase, indicating assessed value in some states or appraisal of property where no assessed value is given; copy of prior-year rental schedule.

SCHEDULE-C INCOME AND EXPENSES

Income: Cash-receipts journal; bank statements or passbooks for all checking, savings, and trust accounts; duplicate deposit slips; sales invoices, cash-register tapes, or other records of income; records of all loans and canceled checks or receipts showing repayment; Forms 1099; information on any nontaxable income; brokerage statements; records for purchases or sales of real estate or other property.

Schedule-C expenses: Accounting ledgers and journals; work papers used in preparing your return; purchase invoices for cost of goods sold and purchase of capital items; copies of Forms 940 and 941 (payroll-tax returns) plus state payroll-tax returns; state sales-tax returns; canceled checks and receipts for all other expenses. For travel and entertainment, retain the records listed under EMPLOYEE BUSINESS EXPENSES, above.

Taxpayers with a Schedule C will be asked to bring in copies of the returns they filed immediately prior and subsequent to the tax year being audited. This does not mean those returns are also being audited. The auditor needs to get a feel for your business and to compare your income and expenses from year to year. If you have an inventory, the auditor will check to make sure it is being carried forward properly.

During the audit, you may be asked to estimate your family and living expenses on a Form 4822. The auditor knows the figures you put down will not be exact and will make allowances for that. Do the best you can to reconstruct your expenses for that year. Don't decide to be clever and overestimate your expenses so that the auditor will see just how bad off you are. That is totally to your disadvantage.

If you have saved all the documents mentioned above, the auditor will think you walk on water. March in fearlessly, lay your verification out in your neat envelopes, and lean back with a devil-may-care smile on your face. You will be invincible. Before long, you'll be celebrating a no-change audit.

Documentary evidence is usually all you need. On occasion, I have taxpayers who are intent on *showing* me their deductions. You've heard of Method acting? This could be called Method taxpaying. After a severe earthquake in 1971, victims were constantly appearing with shopping bags full of broken glass, knick-knacks, priceless antiques, even jars of food. One dramatic gentleman dropped a cracked roof tile weighing about twenty pounds on my desk with a thud that raised a cloud of dust and made my heart miss a beat. One eggshell of a man, who announced he was going to have a heart attack any minute, brought in a grocery bag brimming with empty pill bottles. The best that can be said for these flourishes is that they add credibility to your tale. They are worthless as proof, however, because they are not dated, nor do they tell the auditor the amount of your loss or expense. They do no harm, and they do give the auditor something to tell his readers about.

BLEEDING THE TURNIP, OR HOW TO MAKE DO WITH THE RECORDS YOU'VE GOT

I know you will have impeccable records from now on, but how does that help you when the audit is for last year's return? How do you make the best of a poor set of records?

If you don't have *any* records at all, I suggest losing gracefully. Call the appointment clerk and ask for an audit report. Don't waste time and money going down to the office to collect in person what you can get by mail. Take your licks and resolve to do better next year.

You can have rooms full of receipts, but if they are for nondeductible items, you are in the same sinking rowboat as the fellow who has nothing. Again, if you are unsure whether an expense is deductible, seek tax advice before including it on your return. If you know the expense is not allowable, don't show up with all the records anyway. Some persons clean out their closets just for an audit and wander in with everything from receipts for underwear to shoestrings. Often the paper is so yellowed, creased, and limp that the auditor is afraid it will fall apart at a touch. Coming in with nothing and admitting it is better than dumping a pack-rat assortment of unwanted miscellany on the auditor's desk. The person who does this is in effect admitting his ignorance to the auditor, who then begins to wonder about the accuracy of a return filed by someone with so little knowledge of even personal finance, let alone the tax law.

What if your records have been lost or destroyed through fire, theft, or a variety of other reasons (a neat maid, a dog who eats anything, the neighbor's two-year-old)? Then you have two misfortunes: the loss and the probable tax bill. You are responsible for safeguarding your records, and besides, it's too convenient an excuse. If all you had to do to escape audit was say, "I had them, I really did, but now they're gone," who would be left to audit? Thousands of people are already trying it out for size; for instance, the man who wrote in that he couldn't prove his burglary because his records were destroyed by fire. A neat double catastrophe, especially as he went on to admit that he had been convicted of the arson. But what if I can prove there was a fire, burglar, maid, dog, etc.? you say. So can the arsonist. What does that really prove, however? Only that an event occurred. Not that you ever had the records or that, if you did, they would have been the right ones to verify your deductions. Proof of the event may net you a little leeway and make the auditor more receptive to your oral testimony, but don't count on it.

To make the best of poor records, you may have to retrace your steps that year and try to obtain duplicate receipts. Ask your bank for copies of your canceled checks, write your credit-card and loan companies for statements, visit your doctor for another receipt, seek out your baby-sitter for a letter, whoever can verify how much you spent for what is claimed on your return. It is almost impossible to re-create your return 100 percent, so be realistic. Face the fact that you will owe tax, and concentrate on minimizing it as much as possible. Do weigh the time expended versus the tax consequence, however. You may not want to spend hours driving across town to pick up a duplicate receipt for a forty-dollar doctor bill when the tax on that item alone may be only eleven dollars. If you have a lot of small expenditures, they would, of course, add up and the effort may be worthwhile.

Some expenses, you will be unable to prove. The most common is cash contributions to your church. (Do give by check or keep a contemporaneous diary.) If you are a church member, obtain a statement from your priest or minister stating you attend regularly. This will give the auditor a reason to believe your oral testimony and will earn you some allowance, if not the whole amount. Casualty-loss deductions are also almost impossible to prove after the fact. If the items lost were recently purchased, visit the stores from which you bought them. Unless they were major purchases, however, your chances of success are slim. A statement from a third party that you owned the item, and a description of it, may help. If you failed to report a theft to the police, you are not going to be able to get a police report now. Again, the statement of a neighbor or friend that he knows you sustained the loss may give you credence and partial credit.

As I mentioned above, the record-keeping requirements for travel and entertainment are quite strict. Technically if you do not follow them to the letter, no amount of backtracking will get you a farthing. In practice, this is not yet always true. A statement from your employer that you traveled to certain cities on business and giving the dates will make it possible to pinpoint the air fare by calling the airline. You can write the hotels where you stayed, for a duplicate bill. The auditor knows you had to eat and will usually give you a reasonable per diem. Entertainment is tougher—a letter from your employer may state that it is necessary or you are expected to entertain, but unless he was present at the table, he doesn't know whether you ever entertained or not, or how much it cost. The persons you entertained may be induced to write, naming the dates, places, and business purpose, but you are still short the amounts (unless you showed them the tab). You can try it, if it isn't too embarrassing professionally, and see what it gets you. If you charged the meals, the credit-card company can send you copies of your charge slips.

Automobile expense doesn't fall under the same rigid Code provisions, but a log of the miles you drove must be kept at the time. Happily for taxpayers, if your employer will verify that you were required to drive for business, the auditor will go to great lengths to reconstruct how many miles you actually drove. Be prepared to tell her how far it is from your home to work, how often you drive to the office first, your route if you have one, or if not, the area you cover and the average number of stops and miles covered each day, and the number of miles you drove for personal business, e.g. vacation, shopping, recreation. See if you can dig up repair bills from your glove compartment or your garage, because these show your mileage readings. When the auditor reconstructs business mileage, your deduction is computed using the mileage rate instead of using operating expenses.

Use your imagination to find corroborating evidence. Sometimes evidence can be pieced together to come in the back door instead of the front. Ask your auditor for suggestions; he knows what it will take to convince him to give you the deduction. If you believe a piece of evidence will help your case, but obtaining it is going to be time-consuming or costly, find out first if the auditor is going to accept it once you produce it. Because waiting for banks, stores, credit-card companies, and others can take weeks or months, secure an extension of time on your appointment if necessary. Keep the auditor informed of what you are waiting for and how long you expect it to take, once she is involved in your case.

Do not expect the auditor to dig for you. The auditor will only contact third parties if it is expeditious for her. You cannot rely on help from this quarter. If a third party refuses to give you information, tell the auditor. She may make an independent inquiry, but, again, she may not. You were expected to keep the records at the time, and violins will not necessarily generate much sympathy. Although an auditor has the authority to summons information, this is only done when it is for the government's advantage. Of course, if witnesses are no longer available, there is nothing anyone can do for you.

A word about reconstructing records: Make sure the auditor knows the documents are duplicates. If they accurately reflect the money you spent, why is this necessary? Because the law requires that your records be timely kept. If the auditor suspects you are trying to give him the impression this is the original receipt and not a substitute, he may become suspicious of all your records. Passing off a reconstructed diary, for example, as one kept during the audit year, as required, may be fraud if done intentionally to deceive, because it is an attempt to claim a deduction with legally unacceptable evidence. If the auditor is told that the diary is the best estimate the taxpayer could make, the auditor is not misled into believing it is 100 percent accurate and will act accordingly. For this reason, if you ask a third party to state that you paid her four hundred dollars for child care last year, make sure it is dated this year, then states the year the payment was made. Backdating documents can also be fraudulent if done to intentionally deceive. You could run into trouble here, because an auditor usually won't tell you if she suspects there is something fraudulent about your documents, and you won't know about it until you receive the audit report. You can explain then that it was an innocent mistake, but it puts you on the spot and is generally bothersome. Remember to tell the auditor if the document is not an original.

If you are missing receipts, you must plead your case before the auditor. My advice is to be completely honest. You don't have anything to hide, you just don't have all your records. An auditor with any experience at all develops an ear for the truth, aided by a healthy skepticism. Be helpful and volunteer information. Ask the auditor to test your credibility by asking you questions. Without records you'll never get everything you claimed, but if the auditor can be convinced that you are an honest person, who through lack of knowledge or luck came to this sad pass, she will be more likely to give you credit for your oral testimony where she is allowed to by law.

THE FINISHING TOUCHES

After you have assembled your records, what is the best way to organize and present them? If you have the original of a document, bring it in instead of a copy. An original is easier to read, and an auditor is less wary of its having been tampered with. If you are mailing your receipts, you may want to send copies instead of originals, in case they are lost in the mail. This is acceptable if they are legible. Canceled checks should be photocopied on both sides. Even so, an auditor may request the originals. If they are mailed certified, you reduce the risk of loss. Along similar lines, sometimes an auditor will ask you to leave your records with him. This is usually done when an audit cannot be finished in one sitting. It allows him to work on your case between scheduled audits and eliminates the need for you to come in again. There is no reason why you should deny this request. Except for certain legal documents such as deeds, your receipts are not required for anything except tax audits. The IRS is the only organization you are saving them for. Have the auditor photocopy the legal documents, and leave the other originals. I have never known an auditor to lose a taxpayer's records. It is not common practice for the auditor to give you a receipt.

If you are following my advice, you already have your receipts separated by category. If not, you should do so. The auditor is going to cover each issue item by item before moving on to the next. He is not going to verify one medical expense, then one contribution, then one telephone bill, then go back to medical again. This is too disorganized and inefficient. Don't, under any circumstances, bring your receipts in organized by month. The auditor will have a nervous twitch by the time you leave, after watching you go through all your receipts month by month to take out medical, then go through all your receipts month by month to take out contributions, then. . . . There have been moments when I have wanted to tear the receipts right out of a taxpayer's hands and sort them into categories before I went mad waiting for the next receipt to be handed to me. Twelve envelopes of all the taxpayer's checks wrapped in their monthly bank statements are the worst.

If you have access to an adding machine and the time, add up the receipts in each category and staple the adding-machine tape to the outside of the envelope. The auditor will check the receipts against your tape and write down your total. If she finds your totals are trustworthy, she will begin to accept them without checking. This will expedite your audit considerably, and this is as much in your favor as the government's, because you will lose less time from work or more pleasurable activities. Speaking of trustworthiness, look out for duplicating an expense. Quite often, you will have a receipt and a canceled check for the same item. Associate these when you spot them. If you let it slide by, and add it twice, you risk losing your credibility with the auditor. Overlooking one or two of these is understandable, but any more than that and the auditor will think you are trying to slip something over, and every receipt of yours will be scrutinized and cross-checked. When duplicates pop up in different envelopes, the implications are even more serious, because it may seem intentional. One taxpayer tried this with receipts for his rental properties. The receipts were from hardware and paint stores and consisted of a yellow and a pink carbon copy. He had peeled these apart and filed the yellow under Repairs for one rental and the pink under Replacements for another. The properties were large, and there were hundreds of receipts in addition to the duplicates, but an auditor deals with numbers and receipts all day long. They take on individuality. The auditor handling this case remembered seeing those numbers before. This taxpayer was penalized.

What happens if your records are not organized? The auditor can tell you to come back when you finally get your act together. This does not happen often, but I have seen taxpayers sitting at an empty desk sorting their receipts while the auditor completes other work. It is a matter of degree and your attitude. The taxpayer who brings a bushel of papers and dumps them in a crumpled heap on the auditor's desk with a smirk will find this is his only satisfaction. The auditor will ignore both the heap and him until the documents are presented civilly. If there is any evidence at all that you are doing your best (and the records are not too voluminous), the auditor will work with you.

VI. H & R WHO?

Should you brave an audit by yourself? Pit your flimsy receipts against the assembled might of the United States Government? Do you have to be laughably arrogant or recklessly foolish to walk unarmed into the IRS camp? Or should you bring heavy artillery, a show of strength to prove you are a force to be reckoned with?

Overly dramatic? Perhaps, but not an uncommon reaction as taxpayers map out their strategy for "A" day. Some of them arrive so bristling with armor that we expect to see a tank parked outside. How much of those tax dollars you are trying to save do you need to spend on defense?

You are entitled to representation at an audit, and later, on appeal. The representative may come with you, or you may send him in your stead. You may also come alone, with just your receipts and an honest face to defend you. Whether you should hire a representative is not a decision I can make for you. Too much depends upon the facts of your particular case. I will give you my opinions, however, and facts that may help you decide.

Unless you are physically unable to be present, you probably do *not* need a representative at the examination level. I say probably because there are exceptions to everything: if the taxpayer is ill, out of town, senile, or insane, a representative is virtually a must. A taxpayer who speaks little or no English is also advised to bring someone who does, to act on his behalf or at least to translate. The IRS does not provide interpreters as a matter of course. In almost all other cases, the taxpayer can fend for himself quite nicely.

Why is a representative unnecessary at the office-audit level? The most obvious reason is that it is your return, your expenses, your life story. An audit is a fact-finding mission. The auditor spends the majority of her time developing the facts and only a small portion applying the law. You know the facts. You know the history of each receipt. Not F. Lee Bailey, or Ernst & Ernst, or anyone else, for that matter. There should be few questions you cannot answer by yourself.

A second reason you won't need a representative is that your meeting with the auditor is not your only chance to present your case, by a long shot. Why not wait and see whether you run into any problems before you run for help? If you have the correct documents (and you should from now on), the audit has an excellent chance of going your way. You may owe no tax without any hassle at all. If an unexpected problem does arise, tell the auditor you want to consult someone more knowledgeable. The auditor will wait. Often the auditor can explain the problem to you and tell you either how to resolve it or why it cannot be resolved as well as the outside expert you intend to hire. Don't hire someone needlessly, only to breeze through the audit with your representative ticking like a meter beside you while you answer all the questions and explain all the receipts yourself.

What if the audit isn't a breeze? What if you don't have perfect records? I've already told you that without the necessary receipts you can expect to pay more tax. A representative isn't going to change that. There is nothing magic about a C.P.A., an attorney, or a tax preparer. A representative is only as good as your receipts. The more razzle-dazzle, the more apparent it is that you don't have anything. A good set of records impresses an auditor, not rhetoric.

Besides, if you don't have receipts, you're going to have to rely on oral testimony. The auditor will need you personally to explain the nature of your expenses and how you arrived at the figures on your return. If you can convince the auditor of your sincerity and give her enough facts, you may be able to get some of your deductions even though you can't produce the right piece of paper. But *you* have to do it. The auditor can't tell how honest you are by how sincere your representative looks. As long as you have to be there anyway, you might as well come alone. No one is going to tie you down and force you to sign something you don't understand or agree with. If the outcome doesn't please you, seek outside help at that time.

I believe my advice holds true even if your tax return involves more complex or technical issues. You must decide, of course, and if you haven't the foggiest notion of how any of the amounts on your return were computed, you may want to bring a person who does. It may not be necessary, though. The auditor knows (or has ready access to) the law covering complex tax deductions on a Form 1040. He also knows how to interpret and extrapolate the necessary information from receipts and other supporting documents. He usually does not need an explanation. It is nice, but not necessary. In certain areas (tax shelters come to mind), the auditor may require additional facts, but this is normally information you must get from a third party, for example, the company promoting the tax shelter, and not from your representative. We frequently deal with representatives who know no more about a tax shelter, for instance, than we do; they have the documents the taxpayer provided them, but unless they are personally involved in the shelter, they have no facts about it. It is possible, therefore, to adopt a wait-and-see approach to the audit even when a return is complex. If the auditor cannot resolve the issues without information only your tax preparer can provide, he will allow you time to get it. Even then, you may be able to complete the audit alone by obtaining the information from your preparer without hiring him to represent you.

What taxpayers seldom realize or don't want to believe is that the auditor is a neutral party. The audit is not really you against the government. The auditor is expected to determine the correct tax, and it does not matter whether this is to your advantage or the government's. This quote is from Revenue Procedure 64-22, which your auditor is required to follow: "[I]t is the duty of the Service to carry out that policy for raising revenue by correctly applying the laws enacted by Congress; . . . and to perform this work in a fair and impartial manner, with neither a government nor a taxpayer point of view. . . . It is the responsibility of each person in the Service, charged with the duty of interpreting the law, to find the true meaning of the statutory provision and not to adopt a strained construction in the belief that he is protecting the revenue." In effect, then, the *auditor* is your representative. I understand your skepticism. Some auditors do identify too strongly with the government in the mistaken belief they are "protecting the revenue." Only two out of the many I have supervised or worked with, however, have assumed the role of self-appointed prosecutor. The majority of auditors try to be as reasonable and helpful as the law allows. Their function is to aid you in understanding the law and the audit process to the same extent as a paid representative.

REPRESENTATIVES—PRO AND CON

What are some of the benefits of having a representative? If you actively distrust the government or feel intimidated, a representative serves as an ally, a supporter, an extra measure of confidence. If some of the issues in question are borderline, involving gray areas of the law, a representative can research the law and argue your side of the case, presenting the facts in the most favorable legal light. He can give you a second opinion, one that may differ from the auditor's and that may affect your final decision. He may be able to explain an audit adjustment to you in a different way that is easier for you to understand. If he has an extensive tax practice, he may know some of the ins and outs of the audit process, which can be to your benefit. Depending on his expertise, he may save you tax if the auditor makes a computation error or overlooks a figure on your return. (The IRS does have case reviewers on the lookout for errors.) If you tend to the emotional, a representative can have a steadying influence and can keep you from losing your temper and any chance you might have of winning over the auditor. This will be a benefit for the auditor, too.

A representative *won't* get you any special consideration. All taxpayers are created equal. No one's going to lay down a red carpet if you come in with the most expensive legal talent available. In fact, sometimes it is advantageous to be unsophisticated. Just as an auditor tries to be more lenient if it is your first audit and presumably you didn't know all the rules, so an auditor may be more willing to give the benefit of the doubt to someone who through lack of education and outside help was unaware of the law's record-keeping requirements. You may be only one person, but so is your auditor. You are not really outnumbered.

A representative is also costly. If you are one of those persons whose "time is money," you may save by not having to appear personally for an audit, and this may outweigh the expense of hiring a second. Depending on the completeness of your records, however, you may still be required to spend time writing or talking to the auditor to clarify questions of fact. If you do hire a representative, remember: the auditor is not concerned about how high your bill is. He will conduct the audit as expeditiously as possible, but speed for speed's sake is not his goal. I have had representatives complain when I requested more information or refused to yield on a determination. "You're wasting the taxpayer's money," they say. "Every hour I spend on this case costs him that much more." The auditor is not costing you money—there is no charge for his services. The bill you receive is from your representative. One accountant carried on so about his client's endangered finances that I suggested he handle the case for free.

Does your auditor prefer to see you or a representative? I don't have an answer for that. I imagine opinion varies. I personally have no preference. It is easier to resolve the issues with you there to answer questions. On the other hand, I breathe a little easier when I face a representative alone, because he is more predictable and less prone to emotional outbursts than the taxpayer. Although he has some stake in the outcome, he does not take the audit personally, and becomes intractable only when he believes he is going to lose face with his client. Auditors have to work with individual tax representatives on a recurring basis and try to maintain a good working relationship. Sometimes this is done by allowing a representative to save face on one issue in exchange for cooperation in persuading the taxpayer to accept another adjustment. Rarely is there any spoken agreement; rather, it is an understanding springing from efforts of both to keep the audit machinery running efficiently. As an auditor, I often rely on the representative to act as a mediator, to convince the taxpayer I am right. This is because I know that the taxpayer trusts his representative more than he trusts me. The representative, if he is a professional and honest, will concede a correct adjustment and admit that some records are deficient. He also realizes that he will probably be working with me again and that over the years his track record with me will be considerably better if I believe he is ethical. If I can get the representative to back me up by appealing to him as a fellow professional, I know I can conclude the audit to everyone's (grudging) satisfaction.

While a representative is not necessary at the examination level, you may want one if your case is appealed. Again, though, you may represent yourself at all levels within the Internal Revenue Service. When you reach the formal appeals stage, you are running out of chances to persuade the IRS to your point of view (short of going to court), and you may want to give it your best shot. If the issue is one of fact, i.e., you have not presented adequate receipts or the auditor did not accept your oral testimony or your oral testimony revealed facts that deny deductibility, a representative will probably not be any more effective on appeal than you can be. If the issue is one of law, i.e., the auditor and you have applied the same facts and arrived at different legal conclusions, either due to conflicting case law or interpretation of the Code, a representative, who can advocate your point of view by presenting legal precedents in your favor and arguing why they should apply in your case, can probably get better results than you would on your own, unless you are an attorney or accountant yourself.

THERE ARE REPRESENTATIVES AND THERE ARE REPRESENTATIVES

Selecting the right representative is certainly as important as buying a stereo or a choice piece of steak. You wouldn't walk into a department store and point to the first turntable you see or march into a grocery store, put on a blindfold, and grab the first cellophane package that comes to hand. Yet many of you will pick a tax representative out of the Yellow Pages or ask your Uncle Fred or remember a neon sign you pass on the way to work. Into the hands of this stranger you will place confidential information about your family and finances that you might not tell your best friend. You may even grant this person a power of attorney and entrust him with the responsibility of absolving you of all liability to the IRS. You will then resolve to believe every word he tells you and to disbelieve everything the IRS says unless it agrees with your newfound guardian. Does that sound wise or even rational? Shouldn't you know more about someone than his name before you give him so much power to help or harm you?

I am sometimes appalled by the indifferent, perfunctory, negligent, and slovenly representation some taxpayers pay for. Often these taxpayers have given their representative complete discretion to act on their behalf and are oblivious to their peril. We will discuss how you can prevent the harmful effects of poor representation in Chapter IX. My point here is that you cannot afford to be so trusting. I do not intend to judge the merits of any one class of representative. You should know, however, what types of representative are on the market and which will be the most beneficial to you.

There are three categories of persons who are permitted to represent you in an audit. One class comprises certified public accountants, attorneys, and enrolled agents. The second class is unenrolled tax preparers, and the last consists of members of your immediate family and your employees. Anyone who does not fall into one of these three categories is not entitled to any recognition at any stage of an audit.

An attorney or a certified public accountant, of course, has specialized legal or accounting training and experience and in theory is more knowledgeable of the tax law than a person without these credentials. Not all attorneys, however, specialize in tax law, and it is best to inquire whether an attorney has a regular tax practice. In some states, qualifying attorneys may advertise as tax-law specialists. Both C.P.A.s and attorneys are bound to certain ethical standards of behavior.

An enrolled agent is a person who has passed a two-day Special Enrollment Examination, administered by the Internal Revenue Service and covering federal taxes and tax-accounting problems concerning individuals, partnerships, corporations, trusts, and estates. In addition, the enrolled agent must pass an extensive background investigation. He is then accorded the same status as attorneys and C.P.A.s. An enrolled agent is issued an enrollment card, and anyone professing to hold this status should be able to show you one.

A special category of enrolled agent is former Internal Revenue Service employees who have at least five years' experience interpreting and applying the provisions of the Internal Revenue Code and regulations. These former employees are not required to take the written examination but are subject to the background investigation. You may think you have made a real find if you stumble upon an ex-IRS agent or auditor to represent you, and there is no doubt that the information they possess can be valuable, especially in making the system work to your advantage. On the opposite side, although they do receive some deference, more is expected of them by their former fellow employees. They are expected to be honest and to realize when the auditor is right without putting up much of a fight, recalling the days when they were in the same boat themselves. Consequently, some of these employees turned representatives bend over backward to prove they're not pro-IRS, becoming unbearably arrogant and obnoxious in the process. If you do employ an ex-IRS employee, you should be prepared to go through the entire appeals process unless the case is a no-change.

Attorneys, C.P.A.s, and enrolled agents are the only persons authorized to practice before the IRS. This means they alone can represent you above the examination level—that is, at an appellate hearing. If you intend to appeal your case and you want a professional representative, it must be an attorney, a C.P.A., or an enrolled agent. You should consider this when you hire a representative, if you anticipate an appeal.

Persons who are authorized to practice before the IRS must adhere to ethical standards imposed by the Treasury Department and are subject to disciplinary action, including suspension or disbarment from practice before the Service. Among the duties imposed are diligence as to accuracy, furnishing information to the IRS upon lawful request, prompt disposition of matters pending before the IRS, avoidance of conflicts of interest, and not charging an "unconscionable" fee. Of course, the services of an attorney or a C.P.A. are probably going to be costly, and this is another consideration.

The unenrolled tax preparer may also represent you, but only at the examination level, i.e., the interview conducted by the auditor and an informal conference with a second auditor or the group manager. He cannot represent you at the appellate level. He may accompany you as a witness, but if he tries to advocate on your behalf, he will be asked to leave. Because probably fewer than 5 percent of all cases eventually go to the appellate level, an unenrolled tax preparer is usually quite capable of handling your case under normal circumstances.

The unenrolled tax preparer must be the person who prepared your return for compensation and who signed it. You may not go to a different unenrolled tax preparer and ask him to represent you. Neither may you be represented by a friend or neighbor who prepared your return as a favor and who did not sign the return or charge you for it. Such a person may accompany you and explain his computations or otherwise act as a witness, but he cannot advocate for you, that is, argue the tax law or the amount you should be allowed with the auditor.

You may also be represented by an employee or a member of your immediate family, generally limited to your father, mother, brothers, and sisters who are serving without compensation. These persons have unlimited representation; they may appear and advocate on your behalf at any level within the IRS.

GRANTING A POWER OF ATTORNEY

Once you select a representative, you must give him *written* authorization to represent you and to receive data and confidential information from the IRS. The law protects your privacy, and none of the information on your tax return may be discussed with a third party unless he has this written authorization. This is true for any representative, even a member of your family. Selecting a representative is a two-stage process. First, you must find a person who qualifies as a representative, and second, you must give him written authorization.

The most common written authorization is the power of attorney, and it is the only type we will discuss here. The Internal Revenue Service has its own power-of-attorney forms, the 2848 and the 2848-D. Although you are not required to use one of these IRS forms, it is best to do so. The commercial power-of-attorney forms you find in stores will probably not be accepted, nor will a plain, handwritten statement, even though they are valid under the law if they specify all the required information. This is because the Tax Reform Act of 1976 established severe civil and criminal penalties for unauthorized disclosure of tax-return information (see Chapter XVI). If an IRS employee accepts and acts in reliance on a commercial power-of-attorney form or a handwritten statement from the taxpayer and it is invalid, he is violating this law. What constitutes a valid power of attorney in this form has never been tested in court. The only forms your auditor can be sure are valid are IRS forms, because he has been given examples and guidelines, so these are the only ones he will accept.

Using the IRS forms is easier than devising your own, because you just fill in the blanks. The specific acts your representative may perform with your authorization are already listed, so you do not have to worry about spelling them out in the correct legal language. It is just as necessary to you that the power of attorney be properly executed as it is for the auditor. If it is invalid in the smallest detail, your representative will be powerless to act effectively for you.

You can obtain a power of attorney form from your local IRS office. Most representatives also have a large supply on hand. Your representative may present the completed form at the initial audit interview, or it may be mailed to the audit group in advance. The power of attorney must be in your file before the appointment clerk or auditor will discuss your case with the representative. A photocopy is acceptable.

It is important to distinguish between the two IRS forms. The 2848, Power of Attorney, is used when your representative is a C.P.A., attorney, or enrolled agent. All other representatives—unenrolled tax preparers, employees, and family members—should use the 2848-D, Authorization and Declaration.

Because the form must be correctly filled out in every respect, let's go through it item by item. A sample 2848 is provided. The 2848 and 2848-D are similar in all but three respects; these differences will be noted as we go along. The items on the sample form are numbered and correspond to the numbered items in the discussion below.

1. *Name, identifying number, address including ZIP code, and telephone number of taxpayer(s).*
Enter your name as it appears on the tax return, your social-security number (or employer identification number if employment tax is involved), your address, and your telephone number. If you filed a joint return, enter the name, social-security number, and address for both yourself and your spouse. If you filed jointly and are living apart, complete two separate powers of attorney.

2. *Name, address, and telephone number of representative(s).*
Enter the name of your representative, his address, and his telephone number. The name you enter must be a natural person. You cannot put down Expert Tax Service, for instance; instead, you must name an *individual* who works at the Expert Tax Service,

Form **2848** (Rev. February 1988)

Department of the Treasury Internal Revenue Service

Power of Attorney and Declaration of Representative

▶ See separate instructions.

OMB No. 1545-0150
Expires: 12-31-90

Part I **Power of Attorney**

For IRS Use Only: File So. / Level / Receipt / Powers / Blind T. / Action / Ret. Ind.

(Please type or print)

	Taxpayer(s) name(s)	Taxpayer identification number
1.	Lloyd Maple Connie Maple	123-45-6789 987-65-4321
	Address (number and street) 62 Birch Lane	Plan number (if applicable)
	City, state, and ZIP code Woodbridge, VT 05604	Telephone number 683-9442

hereby appoint(s) the following individual(s)*

	Name	CAF Number	Address	New Address	Telephone Number
2.	Lawrence H. Pall		936 Carlington Avenue Montpelier, VT 05602		732-8936

as attorney(s)-in-fact to represent the taxpayer(s) before any office of the Internal Revenue Service for the following tax matter(s) (specify the type(s) of tax and year(s) or period(s) (date of death if estate tax)):

	Type of tax (Individual, corporate, etc.)	Federal tax form number (1040, 1120, etc.)	Year(s) or period(s) (Date of death if estate tax)
3.	Individual Income	1040	1988

4. The attorney(s)-in-fact (or either of them) are authorized, subject to revocation, to receive confidential information and to perform any and all acts that the principal(s) can perform with respect to the above specified tax matters (excluding the power to receive refund checks and the power to sign the return, unless specifically granted below). See Regulations section 1.6012-1(a)(5) for information on returns made by agents. (List excludable powers below. Indicate if you are granting the power to sign the return.)

....

....

5. ☒ Send originals of all notices and all other written communications in proceedings involving the above tax matters to the appointee first named above, and a duplicate copy of all notices and all other written communications to the taxpayer named above, or

☐ Send copies of all notices and all other written communications addressed to the taxpayer(s) in proceedings involving the above tax matters to:

1 ☐ the appointee first named above, or

2 ☐ (names of not more than two of the appointees named above) ....

6. Initial here ▶ .... if you are granting the power to receive, but not to endorse or cash, refund checks for the above tax matters to:

3 ☐ the appointee first named above, or

4 ☐ (name of one of the above designated appointees) ▶ ....

7. This power of attorney revokes all earlier powers of attorney and tax information authorizations on file with the Internal Revenue Service for the same tax matters and years or periods covered by this power of attorney, except the following:

....

....

(Specify to whom granted, date, and address including ZIP code, or refer to attached copies of earlier powers and authorizations.)

8. **Signature of or for taxpayer(s)**

(If signed by a corporate officer, partner, or fiduciary on behalf of the taxpayer, I certify that I have the authority to execute this power of attorney on behalf of the taxpayer.)

.... (Signature) .... (Title, if applicable) .... (Date)

(Also type or print your name below if signing for a taxpayer who is not an individual.)

.... (Signature) .... (Title, if applicable) .... (Date)

* You may authorize an organization, firm, or partnership to receive confidential information, but your representative must be an individual who must complete Part II.

For Privacy Act and Paperwork Reduction Act Notices, see page 1 of the separate instructions. Form **2848** (Rev. 2-88)

9. If the power of attorney is granted to a person other than an attorney, certified public accountant, enrolled agent, or enrolled actuary, the taxpayer(s) signature must be witnessed or notarized below. (The representative must complete Part II. List representatives there only if they are recognized to practice before the Internal Revenue Service.)

The person(s) signing as or for the taxpayer(s): (Check and complete one.)

☐ is/are known to and signed in the presence of the two disinterested witnesses whose signatures appear here:

(Signature of Witness) (Date)

(Signature of Witness) (Date)

☐ appeared this day before a notary public and acknowledged this power of attorney as a voluntary act and deed.

Witness: (Signature of Notary) (Date) NOTARIAL SEAL (if required by state law)

Part II Declaration of Representative

I declare that I am not currently under suspension or disbarment from practice before the Internal Revenue Service; that I am aware of **Treasury Department Circular No. 230** (31 CFR, Part 10), as amended, regulations governing the practice of attorneys, certified public accountants, enrolled agents, enrolled actuaries, and others; and that I am one of the following:

- **a** a member in good standing of the bar of the highest court of the jurisdiction shown below;
- **b** duly qualified to practice as a certified public accountant in the jurisdiction shown below;
- **c** enrolled as an agent under the requirements of Treasury Department Circular No. 230;
- **d** a bona fide officer of the taxpayer organization;
- **e** a full-time employee of the taxpayer;
- **f** a member of the taxpayer's immediate family (spouse, parent, child, brother or sister);
- **g** a fiduciary for the taxpayer;
- **h** an enrolled actuary (the authority of an enrolled actuary to practice before the Service is limited by section 10.3(d)(1) of Treasury Department Circular No. 230);
- **i** Commissioner's special authorization (see instructions for Part II, item i) ;

and that I am authorized to represent the taxpayer identified in Part I for the tax matters specified there.

Designation (insert appropriate letter from above list)	Jurisdiction (state, etc.) or Enrollment Card Number	Signature	Date
10. b	Vermont		

Must be completed if the appointee is an attorney, certified public accountant, or an enrolled agent.

Only one of the above can represent you above the audit level.

e.g., Bart Convoy. You may name more than one representative on a 2848 if they are all C.P.A.s, attorneys, or enrolled agents. On the 2848-D, you may also name two or more representatives, but the individual tax preparer who signed your return is the only *unenrolled* preparer you may name. Any other named representative on the 2848-D must be a C.P.A., attorney, or enrolled agent. (Any number of family members or employees may be named.) It is not necessary to enter the representative's social-security number.

3. *Type(s) of tax and year(s) or period(s).*

If you filed a Form 1040, put down "Income Tax." If you own a Schedule-C business and filed 941s and a 940, write "Employment Tax." Powers of attorney are normally granted for the year(s) under audit. For employment-tax returns, enter the quarters for which returns were filed during the year(s) being audited, e.g., 8703, 8706, 8709, 8712 (if 1987 is the year in question). You must be specific in listing the years or periods or types of taxes: do not put down "all years," "1987 and subsequent years," "all periods," or "all taxes."

4. *Power to perform certain acts.*

This section is found on the 2848 but not on the 2848-D. This is because only attorneys, C.P.A.s, and enrolled agents may be given the power to act on your behalf. The only power an unenrolled tax preparer, family member, or employee is given is the power to receive confidential information. Of the acts that an attorney, C.P.A., or enrolled agent may perform for you, the power to sign an audit report (closing agreement) obligating you to pay additional tax is the most commonly used in an audit. A representative may also sign a consent to extend the statute of limitations, waive notice of disallowance of a claim, and delegate authority to or substitute another representative. If you want your representative to perform other acts, you must write them in on the lines provided.

You should avoid using the 2848-D if you have an attorney, C.P.A., or enrolled agent representing you, unless you do not want to give him the power to perform the acts listed above. A C.P.A., attorney, or enrolled agent may represent you at the appellate level with either a 2848 or 2848-D.

5. *Copies.*

If you want your representative to receive copies of the correspondence sent to you by the IRS during the course of the audit, fill out this section. Copies will be sent to not more than two representatives at differing addresses. Only one copy will be sent to representatives at the same address. Be sure to check the top box to receive copies yourself.

6. *Refund checks.*

Initial this section if you want your representative to receive (but not to endorse or cash) any refund check that might miraculously arise from the audit. Unless you will not be available to receive the check yourself, you should leave this section blank.

7. *Revocation.*

You must file a new power of attorney if you decide to change representatives or the powers you have granted your current representative. This new power of attorney automatically revokes the prior power of attorney unless you state otherwise in this section. If you want the prior power of attorney to remain valid, attach a copy of it to the new power of attorney and fill in the name, social-security number, and address of the person to whom you granted the prior power, and the date.

8. *Signature of taxpayer(s).*

Sign and date the power of attorney here. If a joint return was filed, both spouses must sign. Husband and wife may execute separate powers of attorney, however, if they desire. One spouse may not sign for the other unless a written authorization is attached. Spouses may each have his/her own representative, and either representative may see the joint return.

9. *Witnessing the power of attorney.*

This portion is completed only when a 2848 is being used for an unenrolled tax preparer, family member, or employee. The 2848-D is the proper form for these persons. Use the 2848-D if possible when your representative is an unenrolled tax preparer, etc., because it decreases the chance of error and because your signature does not have to be notarized and witnessed on the 2848-D. If the

2848 is the only form available, however, note that it requires two witnesses who are disinterested: you or your representative may not be a witness. Also note that when the 2848 is used for an unenrolled tax preparer, etc., you must strike through the authorization to act on your behalf in section 4.

10. *Declaration by attorney, C.P.A., or enrolled agent.* Your attorney, C.P.A., or enrolled agent must sign here and designate his status, the jurisdiction, and the date. Because this is completed by your representative, there is nothing for you to do here except to make sure he fills in all four columns. The 2848-D also includes this declaration.

If your power of attorney is incorrectly filled out and therefore invalid, you should be notified and given a chance to perfect it if your case is closed unagreed (Chapter XII) or goes to the appellate level. If you do not give your representative a power of attorney or an invalid one is in the file, your representative will only be able to present information, that is, the auditor will listen to him and look at your receipts; but she cannot tell him whether a receipt is acceptable, whether additional proof is needed, or what the probable outcome or additional tax will be. It will be a one-way conversation, and afterward the audit report will be mailed to you. If you come in with your representative, however, he does not need a power of attorney to sit in on the audit and receive confidential information. Both spouses who signed a joint return may receive confidential information about that return without a power of attorney from the other spouse. However, a spouse who was claimed as a dependent instead of filing jointly must have a power of attorney. If a husband and wife file "married filing separate," the husband must have a power of attorney to receive confidential information about the wife's return, and vice versa.

HEADING OFF AN AUDIT AT THE PASS—SELECTING THE RIGHT TAX PREPARER

Many taxpayers ask the person who prepared their tax return to represent them in an audit. This is a logical choice, and often a good one, because your tax preparer knows you and is familiar with your return and the documentation he used to prepare it. All right, he knows you, but what do you know about him? Selecting a competent tax preparer is even more vital than choosing a representative. If your preparer makes math or legal errors or is negligent, the most brilliant representative will be powerless to help you in an audit. Furthermore, as we learned in Chapter III, a poor choice of preparer can automatically entangle you in an audit along with all his other clients.

If you go to a tax preparer who is not an attorney, C.P.A., or enrolled agent, you need to be especially wary. Anyone can be a tax preparer. Some states require preparers to post a bond, but neither the federal nor the state governments require them to pass an examination to prove they are technically competent. The unenrolled tax preparer you pick out of the phone book may be less qualified to prepare tax returns than you are. For most of you, that should be a frightening thought.

Unfortunately for the unwary, there is no relief for even the most gross errors or outright dishonesty committed by your tax preparer. The IRS can take civil or criminal action against the preparer, but you alone are responsible for paying the taxes, interest, and penalties due through someone else's mistake. Read the fine print just above the signature line on the Form 1040 sometime. It says, "Under penalties of perjury, I declare that I have examined this return, . . . and to the best of my knowledge and belief, it is true, correct, and complete." When you sign your return, you are attesting that it is correct; if the return was prepared by a third party, you are ratifying his work as if it were your own. Crying on your auditor's shoulder is more than likely going to get you one reply: "You should have thought of that before you signed the return." Harsh? Maybe, but if the return had been filed correctly in the first place, you would have owed the tax anyway. Of course, that was before you spent the refund.

How can you be sure you haven't walked into the offices of Swindle, Cheat & Greed? You have to be your own policeman. The IRS is not permitted to publicly recommend or condemn a preparer (although heaven knows we'd sometimes like to). Your best bets are the favored three—C.P.A.s, attorneys, and enrolled agents—because they have proved their technical competence and have defined standards of conduct. The drawback here is the expense, and some of these practitioners are not interested in preparing 1040As and simple 1040s. There are nationwide firms that specialize in tax preparation, but most of them are franchises, and the quality of the returns can vary from office to office.

As your own policeman, what do you look for? In general, beware the tax preparer who suddenly pops up overnight like a mushroom in January, then closes his doors and silently steals away in April. These fly-by-season preparers are much less likely to know or care about tax law than the seasoned pros who make taxes their business all year long. Too many of them are after quick money, and they may cheat you as well as the government. Besides, where will they be when you're being audited?

Beware the preparer who guarantees you a refund or whose fee is a percentage of your refund. Given the unique combination of your income, number of exemptions, and deductible expenses in a given year, your total tax should come to a certain amount. Depending upon how much withholding or estimated tax you have paid, you will either owe additional tax or be entitled to a refund. No matter who prepares your return. The only break the preparer can give you is the full advantage of the law: he can guarantee that with his expert knowledge he will make sure you get every deduction, exclusion, credit, or exemption you are entitled to. But, even then, if you did not pay enough withholding or estimated tax, you can still owe tax with your return. A preparer who guarantees you a refund when you are not entitled to one is going to have to pull strings somewhere to make the figures come out as promised. If his take is a percentage of the refund, he's going to be even more freehanded, because the larger your refund the larger his fee.

Ask yourself also how much time the preparer takes to find out the facts. Does he ask a few superficial questions (or none at all) or does he ask for relevant information about each deduction before deciding whether to put an expense on your return? Does he tell you when an item is not deductible? Does he examine your receipts carefully, instead of giving them a hasty glance and tossing them aside? Does he explain the law to you or give you helpful hints to improve your record keeping? Does he tell you when a deduction may be questioned because the law is unsettled on that point?

Don't succumb to tax-shelter schemes or accept a deduction you've never heard of without asking the preparer to show you a legal citation or ruling to prove that what he claims is true. One preparer sold his clients shares in his "gold mine" for several thousand dollars (whatever they could afford to pay), promising them a ten thousand dollar depletion allowance for ten years. His clients forked over the money, and he duly wrote down ten thousand dollars on their returns as promised. They say you can't cheat an honest man, and most of them probably got what they deserved, because they all signed backdated papers to fit the deduction into the right tax year. Of course, the preparer took the money and ran, and the IRS recovered the tax, plus interest and penalties. The amazing fact was that none of these clients had ever thought to question this deduction from heaven, and swore to the end that it must be deductible because they had signed a contract that said it was. Another preparer claimed two thousand dollars in student exemptions on his clients' returns. If a deduction seems too good to be true, maybe it is. Ask to see it written down somewhere—besides on your tax return.

The professional appearance of the finished product is another clue to the preparer's pride in his work at least. Are the figures neat and legible? Did he spell your name and occupation correctly? Did he use a messy carbon that slipped for your copy? And although it's after the fact, was he mathematically accurate: Did he compute the correct tax or did you get an error message from your service center? I have seen returns that were thousands of dollars off—in the *government's* favor. That is something to consider before going to see him again next year.

Although this has nothing to do with the accuracy of your return, do not go to a preparer who bills you by the page. The Internal Revenue Service prints every form you need. If we don't print a form, you don't need it. We receive returns that could double as books, and every time I see one of these I say to myself, "Another person who paid for each page." A return recently crossed my desk prepared by a firm that is notorious for this sort of thing. I counted four IRS forms and *twelve* of their own forms, and this taxpayer was simply itemizing. Sixteen pages in all, probably at twenty dollars a page. At the outside, this return should have been no thicker than six pages. This firm had included a separate form for each itemized deduction, e.g., doctors, uniforms, education, plus the single Schedule A the IRS provides. Their forms were work sheets used to arrive at the figures, which went on the Schedule A. Tell your preparer to use scrap paper for calculations, and don't let him charge you a dime for it.

Whatever you do, never sign a blank return, always demand a copy of your return, and never put the preparer's address on your return so that your refund comes to him. Several years ago, the Los Angeles newspapers carried the sad story of a young tax preparer who had committed suicide when he realized the IRS had gotten wind of his refund scheme and was closing in for an arrest. He lasted barely one filing season, and as I recall, his scheme was this: He took his clients' documents, told them he would fill out their return when he found time, and asked them to sign two blank returns so that they wouldn't have to come in again. He then prepared two different returns, one claiming a small refund and one a large refund. He mailed the taxpayers the return with the small refund and the other to IRS. The returns were in the taxpayers' names, but in care of himself at his business address. When the refund checks arrived, he endorsed and cashed them, mailed the clients the smaller amount shown on their copies, and kept the balance. He amassed a small fortune before the bubble burst.

Finally, the best way to ensure an accurate return is to give it a thorough inspection before you sign it. You know whether you incurred an expense and approximately how much it should be. Don't be afraid to question items you don't understand. You're paying the preparer, not the other way around. And don't let temptation and a glib preparer cloud your judgment. Better still, try preparing your return yourself one year. You may find it's not that impossible after all, and you will know that it is an honest return.

STRICT ACCOUNTING—PREPARER PENALTIES

Until 1976, unenrolled tax preparers were accountable only to their consciences and God for their 1040 misdeeds. The taxpayer incurred all the penalties for negligence and fraud. A tax preparer who did not know the law or who willfully ignored it went scot-free. True, if they were actually stealing from the government for personal gain, like the preparer who committed suicide, they were guilty of a federal crime, but nothing they put down on your 1040 could be held against them.

Sound unjust? The IRS didn't like it either. Fortunately, Congress took heed, and the Tax Reform Act of 1976 added standards of conduct and record-keeping and disclosure requirements for preparers to the Internal Revenue Code. I'm going to highlight some of the rules your preparer now has to follow, so that you will know whether he is violating the law. This should help you in deciding if you have chosen a preparer you can trust. Even if the violation is unintentional and done in ignorance of the law, ask yourself, "If he doesn't know the law that directly relates to him, how can I be sure he knows the law that applies to me?"

These rules only apply to income-tax-return preparers who are paid to prepare a substantial portion of the return. They do not apply to your Aunt Harriet, who makes out your return as a favor and whom you reward with a bracelet to show your appreciation.

Your preparer is required to sign your return. If you go to a large tax-preparation firm, the individual who takes down the information and fills out the return must manually sign it himself. A rubber stamp or other copy of the person's signature is not acceptable. The preparer must also show his social-security number and his employer's identification number, if applicable. If the preparer is self-employed, he must check the "self-employed" box in front of his identification number. The preparer's business address must also be entered. The purpose of these requirements is obviously to pinpoint responsibility. If your preparer refuses to sign your return, you have reason to doubt its accuracy.

You must also be furnished with a completed copy of your return at the time it is given to you to sign. It is, after all, your return. You will need a copy for audit. You may need information from it to complete your next year's return. You may need it if you apply for a loan or become embroiled in a divorce. And how will you know whether any tax due or refund received is right if you don't have a copy of the return that was filed for reference?

Your preparer may not endorse or otherwise negotiate your refund check. However, under some circumstances, a bank may cash your refund check and give you the money or endorse it and deposit the full amount in your account. We have already seen the reason for keeping a preparer's hands off his clients' refund checks.

Standards of conduct are also imposed. Your preparer must not negligently or intentionally disregard the rules and regulations for preparing tax returns or willfully understate your tax liability. This requires him to ask questions of you if the information you give him seems to be incorrect or incomplete. If the Code requires specific documentation before a deduction may be claimed, e.g., travel and entertainment, the preparer must ask enough questions to satisfy himself that you have the required documentation. He must also keep up to date and knowledgeable on the tax law. The penalty for negligence resulting in an understatement of the tax liability is one hundred dollars per return. A five hundred dollar penalty can be imposed for willfull understatement of the tax liability; criminal prosecution is also possible.

Because the Internal Revenue Code provides penalties for a preparer's failure to comply with any of these new requirements, your auditor will ask you questions about how your return was prepared. Depending upon your answers and the facts she develops during your audit, the auditor may decide to penalize your preparer. If your return is unsigned, she will ask you the name and the address of your preparer. (An auditor can generally tell whether you prepared the return yourself.) She will also ask whether the return was completely prepared when you signed it, whether you received a copy at the time it was prepared, and who received the refund check. She will also want to know what receipts you showed your preparer and whether certain questions were asked.

It is surprising how many taxpayers try to cover for their preparers. Perhaps it is just an instinctive reaction to take someone's—anyone's—side against the IRS. Why so many of them want to take credit for their preparers' negligence or fraud, however, is intriguing. I can only surmise that they do not realize that if there is negligence or fraud involved, there are only two persons to blame for it. By hastily trying to get the preparer off the spot, you are putting yourself on one. Do you think he is going to be as gallant for you? This happens all the time, especially when the taxpayer brings his preparer with him to the audit. I have seen taxpayers completely change their stories at the not-too-subtle coaching of their alarmed preparers. Don't let someone *you* pay intimidate you. He needs your business, not the other way around. There are thousands of other preparers out there to choose from. If he has prepared the return properly, you cannot hurt him by answering the auditor's questions. If he has not, should you protect him? . . . He threw you to the audit sharks, didn't he?

AUDIT BY ASSOCIATION

If a person is known by the company he keeps, he is also known by the company he hires. Especially at the IRS. I have already alluded to the fact that each IRS office maintains a list of questionable, or problem, practitioners (QPs), whose track record in audits has put their honest intentions in doubt. Many of these preparers wound up on this list after special agents in the guise of fictitious taxpayers paid them a visit. The tax returns prepared for them were even more fictitious than the taxpayers, in some cases. Still other QPs found their way into the Hall of Infame as the result of audits in which the returns were so bad that the auditors, who hate additional paperwork, were motivated to write reports anyway.

When a preparer is on the QP list, all or almost all the returns he prepares will be audited. If the preparer is truly atrocious, and I have only known this to happen once, the audits will be pre-refund; that is, the taxpayer will not receive the refund claimed on the return until he has submitted to an audit. The IRS will not tell you that your preparer is the reason you are being audited. You can infer this if all issues on the return are being questioned or if everyone else in the waiting room went to the same preparer.

The QP program has been cut back since the penalty provisions of the 1976 Tax Reform Act were enacted, but it will probably continue to exist. Even if it were eliminated, however, each auditor has his own personal list, born of experience and nurtured by constant auditing. And he may prejudge you by the name written opposite yours at the bottom of your return.

What information or facts developed during an audit alert an auditor that a preparer is "questionable"? There are few written guidelines; the auditor frequently forms a judgment based on a "feeling" about the return that springs from subtle clues he may be unaware of but that he has learned to observe. One such clue is rounded numbers. Deductions for even amounts, like five hundred dollars or one thousand dollars, invite suspicion, because life is seldom so tidy. The use of commercial schedules available at office-supply houses, rather than IRS schedules, is a common practice among QPs (especially the twenty-dollar-per-page preparers). These are usually handwritten or typed, and the original or carbon is sent to the IRS. A data processed or photocopied return is rare from a QP. This tendency is not hard and fast, so don't be hasty in judging here.

The auditor will also make a judgment after seeing your receipts and asking you what information you gave the preparer. One or more of the following reflects poorly on the preparer: (1) the taxpayer incurred no expense and was not entitled to the deduction, (2) the preparer did not ask the taxpayer if any expense was incurred but put a deduction down, (3) the preparer did not ask how much expense was incurred and made up a figure, (4) the receipts the taxpayer gave the preparer totaled less than what the preparer put down, (5) the preparer gave the receipts a cursory examination, and (6) the taxpayer did not show the preparer any receipts for the deductions claimed.

A "key ratio" test is also used. If (1) the itemized deductions divided by the adjusted gross income on the return, or (2) the refund divided by the withholding on the return exceeds a certain percentage, the preparer might be questionable. I remember one preparer I was convinced was suspect because his name and address on his letterhead were in huge, bright red letters. A matter of personal taste, I guess.

Why should all this be a reflection on you? It needn't necessarily, and if you have the documentation to back up your return, it won't make any difference who prepared your return. It can give the auditor a "Show me" attitude, however. When you first walk in that door, all she has is that return to judge you by. If 75 percent or more of the returns with that preparer's imprint have not been crowd pleasers, the auditor is naturally going to be cautious. Besides, there may be the inevitable thought that you paid for what you wanted, that the very reason you went to this preparer was that you had heard or knew that he was unscrupulous. You will have to prove otherwise.

I hope I have given you some incentive to exercise care in selecting a tax preparer or representative. You can be a tremendous help in eliminating the abuses I have mentioned simply by being more aware of what these practitioners are doing with your return and your money. They cannot exist without ignorance and fear.

Now, on with the audit.

VII. WELCOME TO OUR PARLOR

Be truthful. What do you expect to find as you hesitantly approach that door ominously marked INTERNAL REVENUE? When you give the door a push, will it creak slowly open on rusty hinges like the entrance to the Inner Sanctum? Will you peer into an infernal gloom of flickering candlelight, only to be tapped on the shoulder by a bony finger and led through cobwebs to a cadaverous auditor sitting at a casket? You do expect it, don't you—just a little bit?

Ah, I wish it were so. Interiors by Hitchcock. But we didn't even dress it up like that in Hollywood, where it would have been appreciated. No sense of humor, I guess. When you come to an IRS office, you come to . . . an office. A touch of color here, a plant there. Appalling art. But nevertheless an office like any other.

Don't be in a dither to get to your appointment. It's important to arrive on time, but if you don't, you do not cease to exist in every financial institution across the country. Try to come at the stated hour as a courtesy to the IRS and yourself. If you come early or late, you are going to overlap with someone else's appointment, and unless you are lucky, this means a longer wait. On a busy day, audits are conducted like the assembly line in your favorite automotive plant. If you are scheduled for 9:30 A.M., that is when an auditor is available to see you, not at 9:00 A.M. or 10:00 A.M.

You will be greeted by a receptionist in a dense waiting room. Bring your appointment letter. It tells the receptionist your niche in the appointment schedule. She will relay the information that you are on the scene, and your case will be set in motion. If you are waiting for your representative, tell the receptionist, then let her know when he arrives. The auditor will wait.

Be prepared to stay at least an hour and a half if you filed a nonbusiness return and four hours if you have a Schedule-C business. In other words, don't put a dime in the meter, then sit on the edge of your chair watching the minutes tick by. An audit is miserable enough. If you put sufficient money in a meter, but the audit runs long, excuse yourself and fill it up again. An auditor would rather lose you for a few minutes than have you snarling about a parking ticket.

Above all, make yourself comfortable. Stop and get yourself a cup of coffee or a doughnut and bring them along. You only live once. I have audited while taxpayers drew, worked crossword puzzles, knitted, even danced the softshoe (the old vaudeville hoofer with twinkling eyes whose stoic wife whispered to me, "He's just like a little kid"; we should all be like that).

If you take a look around, you'll see that the office is humbly furnished with, for the most part, outmoded desks, chairs, and equipment. The reason for this "just folks" office design is, of course, public relations. It's tough enough to collect tax dollars without giving you an excuse to yell, "So this is how you waste the taxpayers' money!" I remember, a couple of years back, the IRS moved into the recently vacated corporate offices of a wealthy concern. The walls were wood-paneled, and chandeliers hung magnificently from the ceilings, and the corporation graciously moved out and left every luxurious bit of it, free of charge. I remember the employees watched longingly while the IRS tore the paneling and chandeliers all out.

BEHIND THE SCENES

While you are waiting, what is the auditor doing? If this is a normal day and you filed a nonbusiness return, you are one of four to six taxpayers to whom the auditor is going to say, "Do you have your receipts?" He has probably never seen your return until you walked in the door. Now, naturally enough, he wants to take a few quick minutes to become acquainted with it. This usually is no more than a brief scan to see what the issues are, whether your name is pronounceable, and what you do for a living. An experienced auditor will familiarize himself with your case as the audit progresses. If yours is a business return, the auditor has already thoroughly analyzed it long before you put in an appearance, when he decided what issues needed to be audited.

How much does the auditor know about you when the audit begins? Not much, actually. In the first place, she only has one of your tax returns, the one under audit. There is no "file" containing all your tax returns or the story of your life. Your credit-card company may be able to push a button and find out what shoe size you wear, but not the IRS. With patience, the auditor can get copies of your tax returns or a microfilm of the debits and credits to your tax account for a certain year, but that is the limit to her computer resources. Even that takes so much time that it's rarely worth it.

The auditor knows what anyone else would from looking at your tax return for a particular year. Are you married? Do you have children? Are you over sixty-five or blind? She knows whether you own a home or rent, whether you go to church, whether you drive for business. She knows what you do for a living, where you bank (if you use a Schedule B), and if you are a corporate shareholder. If she knows anything about analyzing handwriting, she may even have a clue to your personality.

If you have been audited for a prior year, she may have this information on a separate printout, plus the dollar amount you owed. She will probably be able to tell if your service center made any corrections to your return. From the outside of the case folder, she knows whether your case came directly to her group or was transferred from another office, how many times you've rescheduled your appointment, and whether you've seen or talked to another auditor and what action that person took, if any.

In exceptional cases, in which your audit is part of a special project or resulted from an informant's report, the auditor will have the information that led to the audit in the file along with your tax return. These facts may be conclusive, but you will be given the chance to explain why you should not be taxed or at least taxed on a lesser amount. For example, the audit of a restaurant's sales indicated the average tips per hour received by its waitresses. Based on the number of known hours a particular employee worked, a ballpark figure for total tips that employee probably received will be calculated. The auditor working a project case of this kind will have all the relevant facts before the waitress comes in, and will have computed the additional income. This predetermined audit adjustment will stand unless the waitress can conclusively prove that she did not receive the average amount and can show what the tips really should be. (Note: When a person fails to report income, such as tips, the IRS does not have to prove that the figure it has arrived at is right; the taxpayer must prove it is wrong.)

At some point you're going to wonder: What does the auditor get out of all of this? Why doesn't she hate paying taxes as much as I do? There's no quota system, right? Isn't that what the IRS always claims? Then, why doesn't she take my word about those three-martini lunches instead of hitting me with a bill for more tax?

It's true, the IRS has no quota system, and dollar amounts can never be used to evaluate an auditor's performance. But that doesn't mean the auditor is under no pressure to collect tax.

Where does this pressure come from? Forget Congress, the Commissioner, the neat layers of stratified managers who equate production with promotion. The auditor learns to weather management storms. For the auditor, the standards are set by DIF.

How does DIF exert its silent influence? By being right almost 80 percent of the time. When your case is handed to an auditor after running the gauntlet of screening, she knows there is better than a 75 percent chance you will come out of the audit owing tax. There is less than a 5 percent chance you will walk away with a refund. It's all down in black and white: computer printouts pointing out month after month that the DIF formulas work. (And heaven help the auditor rash enough to imply that they don't.)

To put it another way, only seventeen to twenty-five taxpayers out of every one hundred an auditor sees should leave her office without paying additional tax. She knows it, her manager knows it, and her fellow auditors know it. She can turn in thirty cases with no tax due one month or even two, but she had better not make a habit of it. It won't be long before she gets a reputation as a "no-change artist"—someone who can't do the job or, even worse, is giving away the revenue. That would be an integrity violation and could result in her being fired. With the computer looking over the auditor's shoulder, a quota system isn't really necessary.

After the auditor gives your return the once-over and readies her pencil and paper, she will come to the reception area, page you, and escort you to her desk. We try to keep your waiting time at a minimum, and as a manager, I believe you should not be kept waiting longer than ten minutes under normal circumstances if you arrive on time. I'm sure you noticed that I qualified that statement. There are times when the clock does strike thirteen, and I have restlessly prowled my office with a case in my hand unable to find a free auditor while the taxpayer twiddled his thumbs. Audits may run overlong, unexpected taxpayers may walk in, or half the staff may be out with the flu. We try to smooth these snags out, but it is not always possible. As a general guideline, be patient at least ten minutes. Usually the receptionist will keep a watchful eye on you and inquire if she believes you have been forgotten. If a delay is expected, you should be informed and told the reason. If you still believe you are being neglected, make a discreet inquiry. Don't leave in a huff. You'll have to come back eventually; why make two trips? This is one of those instances in which the IRS wins. If necessary, grin and endure it. You probably wait longer in your doctor's office, anyway.

ACT ONE

You'll want to size up your auditor. Fine. She's sizing you up too. After she introduces herself, the auditor will try to quickly put you at ease. This is partly out of empathy and partly to make you more responsive. The warm-up includes inquiring after your health, asking if the address on the return is correct, and soliciting your telephone number. She may also ask if you've been audited before. Not much chitchat, but simple questions that shouldn't make you feel pressured.

How you react now (or in the waiting room) can set the tone for the audit. Like most persons, auditors rely on first impressions. I can't dictate how you conduct yourself during an audit or toward the auditor. I do suggest that if you're not planning on being friendly and helpful, give it a lot of thought. It rarely pays to sail through an audit with the label "hostile" hanging around your neck like an albatross. You cannot intimidate your auditor. Believe me, it's true. You can only irritate her. And that means that you will be treated with less respect, not more, less patience, less sympathy. You may need all three. I hope this doesn't sound like a threat. I am merely trying to portray an accurate picture of human nature.

If you have opted for friendly and helpful (and this does not mean you have to agree with everything the auditor says), how friendly should you be? A smile and a pleasant manner will do. First and foremost, an audit is a business relationship. The auditor wants to conduct a professional and arm's-length audit. Do not call the auditor by his or her first name unless asked to. It's all right to make casual conversation, but don't ask personal questions. Please refrain from the sugar-daddy approach and drop the "honeys" and "dears."

The auditor is going to be writing during most of the audit. As she covers each issue and asks you questions, she will record the essence of your answers (we write as fast as we can, but we never get it all down), outlining the facts and any legal arguments you may make. She will also list the documentation you present: whether it is a bill or a canceled check, who the payee is, and the amount. She then computes the allowable deduction, summarizes her conclusion, and shows any adjustment. Nothing of a personal nature should go into the auditor's work papers, unless its directly related to a tax issue in question.

You may notice numbers on your case file or on correspondence sent to you that you do not recognize or understand. Frankly, I've run across a few that I cannot decipher. The tendency is to be suspicious of strange numbers somehow attached to our names. In fact, IRS policy is to remove all numbers except the social-security number from its computer-printed address labels to avoid alarming taxpayers. I examined a case file with the accompanying labels to see if there were any grounds for suspicion. None of us have anything to fear in this quarter. The numbers an auditor looks for are the tax year, the activity code, which indicates the total positive income on your return, and your social-security number. Numbers are for computers, not people, and in Examination, at least, we use them sparingly.

THE MOMENT OF TRUTH?

After the formalities are dispensed with, your audit begins in earnest. At this point you will be asked to present your documentation for each questioned deduction. The auditor will usually take each issue one by one and gather all the facts before moving on to the next. She will also be asking you questions about your expenses to make sure they fit the requirements of the law. And she may ask if you had additional income, either taxable or nontaxable.

There is no limit to how deeply an auditor may delve to verify the correctness of your return, but in practice she will rely almost entirely on the documentation you bring to the interview. If additional information is needed, you will be given time to produce it. This is true whether you simply left a receipt at home or statements must be obtained from third parties.

The auditor will rarely do any outside investigative work herself, unless fraud is suspected. Even then, she will make only a superficial investigation to confirm her suspicions. This may involve calling a third party to verify the authenticity of a receipt or, in the case of unreported income, obtaining a subpoena to examine bank records. If the auditor still believes that fraud exists, the case will be taken out of audit, and any further investigation will be done by the Criminal Investigation Division.

Because an audit is not a criminal investigation (unless a fraud case develops), there is no requirement that you be given a *Miranda* warning that anything you say may be used against you. Of course it can be used against you, and you do not have to answer a single question the auditor asks. This would be pointless, however, as you'll see below.

An auditor is under strict time limits. For this reason, almost all conversation will be directed to your tax return and your receipts. A great deal of your time will be spent watching the auditor totaling and recording your receipts. Every auditor has his or her individual style, of course, and some can keep a running conversation going while they work, while others only manage a smile now and then. Most of us feel an obligation to keep you mildly entertained, but, all in all, from the taxpayer's point of view, an audit is a bore.

An audit is not an excuse for prying into your private life. What constitutes prying can mean one thing to you and another to your auditor, however. A question you may consider highly personal may be routine to your auditor. But the question should have relevance to your tax return and the legitimacy of reported income and deductions or losses. If you don't feel a question is pertinent, ask the auditor why she needs that particular information. Probably the most personal questions involve exemptions, on account of which the auditor will delve into your marital status. This is embarrassing to some taxpayers who are divorced and living with someone else or have children out of wedlock. Another personal subject can be medical if you are under psychiatric care, have handicapped children, or recently underwent unpleasant surgery. The information you give the auditor is confidential, however, and should excite no comment. The auditor doesn't know you (she would have to disqualify herself if she did), and in many ways regards you as a doctor does a patient.

How an audit is conducted is within the auditor's discretion, so technically there are no questions he *may not* ask. If the question seems clearly outrageous and the auditor cannot explain its relevance to your satisfaction, do not answer it. Along similar lines, an auditor should never make personal comments about you, such as "I see you really like to live it up." You would have every right to protest such a remark. In one case, a taxpayer claiming a theft loss presented a police report that read, "Officer's investigation revealed victim met suspect in downtown L.A. and offered suspect a place to stay. Suspect has lived with victim for (3) weeks and has a key to apartment." My first thought when I read this was that this was an unusual living arrangement, but the taxpayer's life-style had no bearing on whether he suffered a loss, which he had. Any comment about picking up strangers on the street would have been totally out of line.

How much information should you volunteer? As an auditor I would say, "Gush your heart out." As your adviser, I would say, "Wait and see." You're out to win. The house already has the percentage points. Don't acccidentally expose your hand and ruin the odds altogether. What you don't know can hurt you. Quite innocently you may have claimed a nondeductible expense or failed to report a gain, because you did not know the tax law. If you begin to ramble on about this and that, you'll be like a person stumbling around in the dark. You may run smack into the tax law. The auditor will smile and write down every word you say and present you with a report for additional tax tied in your own ribbon. Information you reveal inadvertently can lead to your being audited for other years, friends and relatives being audited, and delinquent returns being filed for you. Answer the auditor's questions, but don't feel obliged to elaborate. Your answers to her questions may have the same unfortunate results, but at least make her ask the questions. You don't see the fox coming to greet the hounds.

Remember I said, "Wait and see." You have to provide enough information to convince your auditor that you are entitled to the deductions. If you have answered her questions and she is still unconvinced, you will have to go into more detail, until the auditor has all the facts she needs. Make sure you know exactly what information is still lacking, and stick to that subject.

I have been assuming you believe your return is correct. What if you have learned of an error since the return was filed? Should you admit your mistake? If the mistake involves an issue being audited, you might as well speak up, because the odds are excellent the auditor is going to find it. If she finds it with your help, you will have risen considerably on her credibility scale, which means that your oral testimony will be more acceptable, and if the auditor is wavering on what is a reasonable amount, you may receive the benefit of the doubt. If you say nothing, you simply lose out on winning her confidence. If the error is substantial, you may also end up with a negligence penalty, which is much less likely if you plead ignorance beforehand.

Suppose the error you discovered involves an issue not being audited or not even appearing on the face of the return. Some of you may think that honesty is stupidity in a case like that. That's a moral judgment I cannot make for you. Again, however, you stand a chance of being monetarily penalized if the error comes out without your help.

WHY YOU CAN'T BEAT THE SYSTEM—THE NO-SHOW REPORT

What if you refuse to give the auditor any information? Or never show up for your appointment? Or become angry and leave? What can the IRS do if you won't cooperate? At the beginning of this book, I told you the deck was stacked against you. Let me tell you how. The secret is called a no-show report, and it is your auditor's ace in the hole. Without the no-show report, your auditor would be powerless to make you do anything. Sure the Code requires you to present records upon demand, but who's going to make you? A summons backed up by a court order can do the job, but it's impractical. If all 1.1 million of you being audited suddenly decided not to cooperate, how could the courts possibly handle that many summonses? No, the power lies in the no-show report, and it works because the auditor controls your purse strings.

A no-show report is written any time a taxpayer fails to provide the information or documentation requested by the auditor, no matter what the reason. The theory behind it is simple. If you do not give the auditor the information needed to verify the issues being audited, you have not proved you are entitled to the deductions. Every classified expense on your return is reduced to zero and you receive a bill for all the tax due as a result of having your deductions thrown out. The burden of proof is on you. Either you pay up or you do what the auditor wants you to do, nicely. This is the enforcer.

You say you own a business and the issue is gross receipts. You say it's not going to bother you a bit if the auditor throws out all your income and sends you a refund. Sorry, friend, it doesn't work that way. The auditor doesn't toss out your gross receipts; she reduces your business expenses, thereby increasing your net income and your tax. Or she may jack your gross receipts up a notch or two if your expenses are outstripping your income on the return (see Chapter X).

Usually when we take this potshot with a no-show report, we hear a squawk and see the tail feathers fly. We get a response. Which is what we were after all along. Remember the no-show report when you're tempted to chuck the audit and walk out. It's all the same to the auditor. Either way, you receive an audit report—it's your choice how high you want it to be. Fact: You can't win this one even if your return is honest. A no-show report is like one of those weighted milk cans you throw baseballs at in carnivals.

THE GAME PLAN—TACTICAL DO'S AND DON'TS

The best audit strategy, of course, is to keep unimpeachable records. There are other tidbits of strategy, though, that can tip the scales in your favor. But first you should know what strategy the auditor is using.

In the auditor's game plan, control is the key. Your auditor wants to take control of the audit, and she wants to keep it. She wants to decide what issues to cover and in what order. She wants to ask the questions, in a certain order, and not be led astray. She wants you to be on the defensive, and she wants to make firm decisions and uphold them against attack. Control is the single most important strategy to the auditor. Let her have it. Why? Because you don't need to be in control, and because an auditor who believes she is running the audit is going to be less defensive and more willing to accept your suggestions as her own. Recognize your auditor's authority. You don't want to volunteer information unless the auditor asks; letting the auditor run the interview will just keep you from putting your foot in your mouth. Wait until your auditor has reached a final decision before you raise your objections and mount your arguments. If you have played your cards right from the start, there may be no adjustments to fight about.

Besides maintaining control, the auditor wants to keep you responsive. She begins by putting you at ease before the audit begins and by remaining receptive throughout the audit, encouraging conversation and listening sympathetically. Some auditors also try to keep you talking by not revealing their decisions until the audit is over. These auditors believe that if they tell you flat out an item is not deductible or you have a failure of proof, you will be on the defensive for the rest of the audit. They will write down all the information you give them, but you won't know what they are thinking until it is time to hand you the report. Many taxpayers mistake an auditor's silence as acceptance of their deductions and claim they've been misled when the harsh truth comes out. Don't be lulled by silence.

Some auditors do not tell taxpayers where they stand as the audit progresses because they like to make their decisions after they have an overall feel for the return and your credibility. They do not want to commit themselves to allowing you a reasonable deduction early in the interview, only to find glaring errors later that indicate they were foolish to believe you at the outset. Where the auditor has the discretion to allow a reasonable amount based on your oral testimony, she may prefer to wait until the rest of the audit confirms your honesty.

Try to get a feel for where the auditor stands as you go along by asking if you have provided enough proof for each issue or if additional information is needed. You can also come right out and ask if there will be an adjustment. It is to your advantage to know where the problem areas lie in time to prepare a cogent argument or a convincing explanation why you should be allowed a reasonable amount. Realize, however, that some auditors will hedge or refuse to make a commitment until they are good and ready.

The word "reasonable" keeps popping up. "Reasonableness" may be awkward English, but it is a key audit concept. Auditors are directed by the Internal Revenue manual to give weight to a taxpayer's oral testimony. Even if you don't have the verification required by law, in some areas, e.g. contributions and automobile expense, you may be able to talk yourself into a deduction (usually less than you claimed, however). If the auditor believes you, she is authorized to allow you a "reasonable" amount. It's easy to see that if you can win your auditor's confidence, this principle can be a tremendous asset. Getting the most "reasonable" allowance possible should be a vital part of your audit strategy.

It is essential that the auditor believe you. Priests and judges have a high credibility, but maybe you're neither of these. You're going to have to start from scratch. First, it is paramount that you have verification for most of your deductions. This is the cornerstone of faith. The auditor must know that a verifiable portion of your return is accurate. Second, your story must be plausible and not contradict other information you have given the auditor. Your return and your story must be consistent. One six-foot-two salesman said his firm did provide a company car, but they had switched to compacts, which were too small for him. He reasoned, therefore, that he should be allowed to deduct the expense of driving his own, private car for business. What kind of car did he drive? the auditor asked. A Toyota Corolla was his somewhat sheepish answer.

Your attitude and mannerisms may also affect the auditor's judgment. If you are too defensive, too touchy, she is apt to wonder if you have something to hide. Extreme nervousness is also a giveaway. One man I suspected of not reporting income smoked one cigarette after another; at the end of an hour, he had filled an empty ashtray to the brim. Another way to set off alarm bells is to be too anxious to deal. The first thing one wheeler-dealer said to me was, "I'll settle for 75 percent of everything." I all but dusted his receipts for fingerprints before accepting any one of them.

You can use the "reasonableness" doctrine to even greater advantage, because your auditor is under pressure to close your case in one interview. This means she would like to come to a mutually satisfactory agreement at your first meeting and send you on your way. The auditor's discretion to allow you reasonable amounts is a bargaining tool she uses to accomplish this aim. But it's a bargaining tool you can use too. If you're willing to give a little, both you and your auditor may come away from the audit each feeling he got the best of the deal.

If you don't agree with the auditor, don't use your appeal rights as a threat. Some rash taxpayers come in waving their appointment letters under the auditors' faces and demanding a hearing. If she knows you're not going to agree to her allowances, why should she give you anything? Why should she be reasonable? You've lost your bargaining power. Save the announcement that you want to appeal until the last possible moment.

Another proclamation it is best to save is that you forgot to put an expense on your return that should give you a refund. Let's face it, no auditor is ecstatic about giving away refunds. Sure, she'll give you credit for what you can prove, but she's going to make darn sure you deserve it, that is, you're not getting away with anything somewhere else on the return. A cry of "Refund" may result in the audit of most of your return instead of just what was originally classified. No one likes to have the wool pulled over his eyes, and your auditor doesn't want you bragging to all and sundry about how you got a refund for medical when you would have had to mortgage your house if the dumb auditor had looked into your business expenses. Remember, the auditor wants you to be on the defensive. Plop that receipt down as soon as you're seated and you've turned the tables. As much as that may satisfy your ego, a wary auditor is the last thing you need. She may spend the whole audit trying to find a way to offset your refund. She may be less reasonable. Wait until the audit is finished, then *ask* if that expense is deductible and produce the receipt. If the expense is for the tax year under audit and can be incorporated into the audit report without undue delay, you will receive credit for it during the audit. You do not need to file a claim.

For that matter, never take it upon yourself to correct your return during the audit by filing an amended return. Let the auditor make the corrections; that is what the audit is for. If you file an amended return, you will hold up your audit for months, accruing interest daily, while the auditor waits for the amended return to find its way into her hands. No one except your auditor can take action on an amended return while your case is open in audit.

How long your interview will last depends upon how many and complex the issues are, how many documents you have, and how well organized you are. Normally, a nonbusiness audit lasts a little more than an hour. A business audit is usually scheduled for half a day but will probably take longer than that to complete—we just don't like to keep you sitting more than four hours at a stretch.

Ideally, you will have brought all the records the auditor requires and the auditor can reach a decision and hand you a report in one sitting. Less bother for you and less for your auditor. If not, the auditor will give you two to three weeks to get whatever documents or information are still needed. Because an auditor's appointment schedule is usually filled with other taxpayers coming in for their first interview, you will normally be asked to mail this additional information in, rather than coming in a second time. There may be a delay if your auditor has a heavy interview schedule, is temporarily detailed to another office, or goes on vacation. Don't become alarmed if you hear nothing immediately.

If you are asked to submit additional information and don't meet the deadline, the auditor will send you a reminder; then, in ten days, he will write an audit report allowing you only what you verified in the interview. This is designed to get your attention and serves the same purpose as the no-show report, previously discussed. It is not intended to be final, although it will become final if you still fail to respond. Call the auditor if you are having trouble getting the information he asked for, and arrange for an extension of time. As long as you keep the auditor informed, you should be able to avoid any problems.

VIII. AUDIT ETIQUETTE

There ought to be a monument to the unsung taxpayer, that anti-hero who pays his fair share of his fellow citizens' taxes and submits to an audit with a smile on his face and a kind word for his auditor. It is a cruel trick of nature that these Galahad taxpayers quickly fade from memory and all the auditor remembers are the Al Capones. The notorious, it seems, make a lasting impression.

If you're bent on notoriety, jump ahead to the next chapter. The tips I have to give are for the pure of heart: the taxpayer who doesn't want his name mentioned through clenched teeth. The taxpayer who would rather be thought of charitably as he pockets his no-change and slips quietly out the door and into the auditor's subconscious.

There follow some "do's" (and even more "don'ts") from the *Book of Audit Etiquette,* written by the first auditor to ever hear those immortal words: "I'll write the President!" They were culled from every auditor's experience, and only a few of them are meant to be taken seriously.

Let's assume your auditor is in an exceptionally good mood. It's a sparkling, spring day, traffic was light, and her morning bagel was toasted just right. What luck! An auditor brimming with good will, who has no desire to quibble about how much a used bedpan is worth or whether that water pipe was a repair or an improvement. The last thing you want to do is curdle all this cream. So whatever you do, DON'T SAY:

1. *"You're the first breath of fresh air I've had in IRS."*
This is guaranteed to make your auditor suspicious. She knows you would rather be buried than talking to her, and she'll wonder why you're trying so hard to butter her up. One taxpayer did actually

gush this, and the auditor told me later, "I said to myself, 'Do I look that stupid?' " Your auditor doesn't expect to be complimented, and if you're not sincere about it, leave well enough alone.

2. *"The last auditor I had was: a) biased; b) sick; c) insane."*
How does that saying go? "You don't have to be crazy to work here, but it helps." One professional man even went so far as to claim *two* prior auditors were crazy. A statement like that not only defies the laws of probability; it usually means the taxpayer hasn't been getting his own way and is being immature about it. Some of the biggest bluffers say this with an air of confidentiality, which is supposed to dispel the suspicion the auditor is developing that their tax return is a fiction work of epic proportions. The real problem with this approach is that the auditor knows you'll tell the next person you see, "Boy, that last auditor I had was . . ."

3. *"How much of a cut do you get?"*
I won't say this is the "unkindest cut" because I am allergic to poor puns, but this one really grates on an auditor whose salary is probably lower than yours. Sometimes this is uttered with a perfectly straight face by hotheads whose holdings could support a Third World nation. In any event, this comment can be construed only as deliberately antagonistic, because few taxpayers actually believe it. Suffice it to say, the only cut your auditor gets is her proportionate share of government services.

4. *"I guess I'm not rich enough."*
There is a whole genre of grumbling in this vein, which implies that the IRS ignores millionaires and large corporations in its relentless persecution of the poor and middle-class. As a member of the middle class, your auditor may harbor the same feelings, but what do you expect her to do about it? As a government employee, she cannot engage in politics, and she is forbidden from taking any political stance on the job. The best she can do is to deny any discrimination (which is certainly true on her level) and to suggest you write your congressman. Quite naturally, she resents being blamed for national policies she had just as much to do with as you did.

5. *"I don't know why I bother to work. I might as well be on welfare."*
You'd be surprised how many taxpayers think this is original, but there's not an auditor alive who hasn't heard this cry of self-pity. The auditor is supposed to be overcome by remorse and alarm at the prospect of another public mouth to feed and decide the taxpayer doesn't owe a public cent. Don't hold your breath. Most auditors let this remark float right by. It's your life-style. Don't let us stop you.

6. *"I pay your salary."*
To begin with, depending on her tax bracket, your auditor pays between 15 and 33 percent of her *own* salary. In the second place, she doesn't work for you—or you or you. She works for the citizens of the United States, a collective union, and chances are, most of them want you to pay your fair share. Just because you pay taxes (not our salaries) doesn't mean you can have your way in an audit. Ironically, most of the taxpayers who play this game of one-upmanship are the ones who managed to pay no taxes at all. Those are starvation wages indeed, and if you see your auditor turning blue it is because she is trying to keep a deadpan Buster Keaton would admire.

7. *"I don't agree with you because I don't have the money."*
Come again? Nature hates a vacuum, and auditors are not wild about non sequiturs. Isn't there supposed to be an absolute truth? Either the audit adjustments are right or they're wrong. Sure, it's tough to be told you owe money when you can't remember what a nickel looks like, but collection is not our job. At least say, "I agree with you, but I don't have the money."

8. *"What's a nice girl like you doing in a place like this?"*
Oh, come now. You've spent too many Saturdays watching Gene Autry singing to his horse.

If you can avoid tossing out one of these original expressions (bite your tongue if you have to), half the battle is won. Keeping your temperament to yourself is by far the hardest part of audit etiquette. The rest of these rules should be a snap:

1. *Tell your auditor if you move during the audit.*
If the IRS cannot keep track of you, you're going to miss some important mail. A report stating you owe additional tax requires attention; if you get it late or don't get it at all, you may wake up one morning quite a bit poorer than you went to bed. By then, you will have to pay up before you can appeal, which is a distinct disadvantage and one that can be avoided if found out in time. Call your auditor or the group clerk and give her your new address. It helps us and it helps you. It's not a bad idea to make sure your post office is forwarding your mail also.

2. *Don't drop by without an appointment.*
Do the persons who do this also wander into their doctor's or dentist's office and expect to be seen? We'll take you if we can, but most audit groups have a full appointment schedule every day. To be fair to you, we like to give you our full attention. You cheat yourself if the auditor has to rush you in and out. Unless you just want to drop something off, call ahead and make an appointment. Along similar lines, don't walk in at noon or closing time—you will have wasted a trip. Auditors eat too. It may be your lunch hour and a good time to pop over, but it's also theirs. At the end of the day, you're likely to be turned around and pushed out the door. For security and labor-law reasons, IRS offices lock up promptly at closing time. Besides, do *you* feel kindly to a client or customer who collars you going out the door?

3. *Leave your video recorder at home.*
You will not be permitted to video record the audit. If you insist, you will be sent packing with that no-show report in your hand. You may be able to *tape* record the audit if you ask for approval in advance. Your recorder can sit right next to the IRS's. If you record their words, the IRS will record yours.

4. *Find out the names of employees you speak to.*
If you don't ask as if you intended to sue, IRS personnel will be happy to give you their names. Write them down. Knowing your auditor's name or anyone else's who serves as a source of information can prove invaluable. It will ensure that you receive consistent treatment and prevent delays in serving you.

5. *Don't ask for special treatment.*
By "special," I mean out of the ordinary. Procedures have been established for auditors to follow in all audits. What is procedurally required will be supplied to you. This does not include letters confirming appointments or extensions of time or receipts for payment you make. Don't hesitate to ask for something you want, but don't beat your head against a wall if you're told you can't have it.

6. *Stay home if you're sick.*
Why make yourself miserable? We can wait until you're on your feet again. We prefer to. If we wanted exposure to contagious diseases, we'd be in Africa as missionaries. One haggard woman collapsed into her chair, gasping, "I shouldn't be here. I've got hepatitis." The auditor agreed, sent her home, and bought a can of Lysol.

7. *Be brief and come to the point.*
Taxpayers are continually calling in, presumably because they have a problem and need information, and half an hour later we still have no idea why they called. We know that the cat is sick, the milkman delivered too much cream, the sink leaks, and Uncle Henry's boy never worked a day in his life. We have been saying, "Uh," "But," and "Ah" for twenty minutes without getting their attention, and from the tenor of the conversation they are just getting started. I have actually laid the phone down and gone on working while I listened for the squawking on the other end to stop. We love to help you folks—just tell us what the problem is and let us get a word in edgewise.

8. *Argue logically.*
I ask this for my own sanity. A wine salesman, whose accent betrayed he had immigrated to this country, pleaded with me for more automobile expense because he sent thousands of dollars to relatives in Europe every year. One shawled little old lady told me I couldn't be right about disallowing a medical expense; her preparer had said it was deductible and she believed her preparer. She had to take *three* buses to get to her preparer and only *two* buses to see me.

9. *Don't lie or try to bluff.*
Unless you know the organization, you'll only make a fool of yourself. Several months ago, a clerk in a law office (he let me know he

was working for an attorney in every other sentence) called to tell me he had just spoken with the Commissioner, Donald C. Alexander, about our handling of a client's case. I admit to deriving a devious pleasure from saying, "How wonderful! And where is our ex-Commissioner now?" This same clerk wrote the chief of the Examination Division about my lack of respect for attorneys. This drew a few laughs because I am an attorney, but of course he didn't know that. Other taxpayers, who confuse the state with the federal government, announce that they've written Sacramento and probably expect us to step back in awe. But what's in Sacramento? Then there was the machine operator who, after claiming he couldn't afford to pay, said he had five constitutional lawyers working on his case. We're sorry persons feel so defenseless that they believe bluffs will work. It's easier to deal with us one-on-one, and a lot more effective.

10. *Decide on one story and stick to it.*

There are some taxpayers who can turn on a dime. You can almost hear the brakes squealing and the tires screeching as they make a 180-degree swing to a better set of facts. As soon as it dawns on them that the first story isn't having the effect they intended, they switch gears and head off in another direction. Not knowing where they are going, they usually make matters even worse. The auditor's recorded history of your twists and turns will guarantee no one will believe you from that point on.

11. *Leave your children at home.*

Find a baby-sitter if you can. Audits are tiresome for adults, let alone small children. If you must bring them, don't let them run wild. Your auditor works better without a small person tugging on her hair, unplugging the adding machine, or running between her legs. Nor does she enjoy the sight of a baby chewing on your tax return. These distractions create errors and often interfere with other audits, especially if the young one is screaming at the top of his lungs.

12. *Restrain yourself.*

I know an audit is an emotional time in your life, but don't crack up under the pressure. Some taxpayers do things in our office that they would never dream of doing normally. A case in point: The issue was a large medical expense. My middle-aged, wifely auditor pleasantly asked what the expense was for. The taxpayer, a woman in her thirties, stood up with eyes flashing, "What's it for? I'll show you what it's for!" she yelled and tore open her blouse to reveal a mastectomy. Really, folks, we'll take your word. Very few of us are from Missouri.

13. *Don't kiss your auditor.*

I'm not really expecting you to, but, then, I didn't expect this gentleman to either. He was a handbag salesman, old-world, born in Corfu. After we had chatted several minutes, he pulled out his wallet.

"You remind me so much of my daughter. See?" Beaming, he showed me a picture of a strapping young woman. "She is a sergeant in the Israeli Army."

Without warning he grabbed me by my hair, pulled me across the desk, and planted a big kiss on my mouth.

"You are so much like her," he said, looking at the picture wistfully.

At that point, I knew I had lost all control of the audit.

IX. MINDING YOUR OWN BUSINESS

What has your representative been doing all this time? Do you know? Or are you one of those trusting souls who buy swampland in Florida? Do not be lulled into a false sense of security. It is essential to your financial health that you keep tabs on how the tax doctor you hired is progressing with your audit.

You must mind you own business, because your auditor cannot. She is not permitted to say so much as a discouraging word about the performance or conduct of your representative. No matter how incompetent, no matter how dishonest, he is your chosen representative, and we cannot interfere with that relationship or discredit him in any way. To do so would bring an entire profession down on our heads and expose us to suits for slander or libel. It cannot be our business; it must be yours. I hear auditors lamenting all the time, "If only the taxpayer knew what a mess his representative is making of this case." Our hands are tied. You have to get involved.

What type of behavior should you expect of your representative? The best word to describe a good representative is "professional" and all that it connotes: expertise, poise, considered judgment, high ethical standards. He does not enter the audit frothing at the mouth, deliberately throw a monkey wrench into the proceedings, and make reckless statements or decisions.

Certified public accountants work closely with the Internal Revenue Service to improve the quality, consistency, and efficiency of audits. Any IRS policy or practice that hinders these aims is rationally discussed and a mutual agreement is reached. Groups of C.P.A.s have even asked for more vigorous enforcement of the tax laws in certain areas to ensure fair treatment for those who comply. These professionals realize that cooperation with the IRS is beneficial to taxpayers in the long run. One mark of a good representative, then, is this willingness to cooperate and to work within the system to achieve the best for his client. He knows how to make the system work for him; he doesnt stand outside, ranting and railing against it.

Your representative must impress the auditor, not you. Don't let him dazzle you with rhetoric or play upon your dislike for the IRS. You may enjoy hearing his diatribes against the Service or watching him preen himself arrogantly in front of the auditor, but this is awing no one but you. Some representatives are so preoccupied with impressing their clients (or themselves) with their superiority that they will not listen to anything the auditor says even though it is vital. I once had to *write a letter* to a representative whose power of attorney was invalid, because he refused to listen to me when I called, on three separate occasions. He was a law student and knew far more than I, and because he had told his client not to talk to us and we couldn't talk to him (no power of attorney), his client got a no-show report and came into the audit with two strikes already against him.

Neither is your auditor impressed by insulting language or belligerence. A representative who exhibits hostility in an audit is using you as an excuse for expressing his own personal feelings. The professional representative has no ax to grind—he is not under audit. He is there to act as mediator, to maintain his composure, to be logical, rational, and unemotional. He can be objective and exercise better judgment than you can being emotionally and financially involved. Isn't that one reason you brought him along? If he uses the audit to vent his own emotions, how can he give you counsel? The letter printed here was written by a representative who is totally biased against the IRS and is exploiting his client to express his own hatred. You simply do not need this kind of "help."

A representative also prejudices your case by continually rescheduling appointments or by not appearing and neglecting to call. These representatives also stall for time, waiting until the last possible moment to show up or present requested information. Too many of these believe they are being clever and brag about knowing just how far they can push the system. This may flatter their egos, like walking a tightrope, but their acrobatics are not in your best interest. If there is a tax deficiency at the end of the audit, you will pay interest for each day of your representative's daring delays.

Re: Dishonesty and Ignorance of IRS auditor in an income tax audit

To: PRESIDENT JAMES CARTER
Commissioner of Internal Revenue
Secretary of the Treasury

I strenuously object to the dishonesty and display of total ignorance of the Internal Revenue code and the display of total disregard for what is right by the IRS auditor.

I request an appellate division hearing on the attempted thievery of my money. My reasons are:

Rental Loss: The auditor lies. (a) I proved the loss with receipts and checks for all legal and proper deductions; (b) I own the rental on which the loss was incurred; (c) all of the property was rented. Surely the IRS has a kindergarten type of training facility for the likes of this auditor.

Casualty Loss: The auditor lied again. (a) I presented my copy of the police report; (b) the invoice proving my ownership; (c) an estimate of repairs for the wrecked auto. Surely there are janitor or latrine orderly jobs open in the IRS for this auditor.

Business Expense: The IRS code says that all expenses incurred in the production of income are deductible. I regret that I did not take a copy with me. The auditor undoubtedly is incapable of understanding it anyway.

I read an article in the newspaper quoting the Commissioner of Internal Revenue: "The IRS audits all returns impartially and fairly by highly trained and qualified auditors. No auditor disallows proper deductions. In the absence of strict adherence to the regulations by the taxpayer, the auditors afford such leeway to the taxpayers in all fairness and consider whether or not the deduction claimed is reasonable."

There are a few million of us taxpayers who would like to see the Secretary of the Treasury and the Congress require, by legislation (legislation making dishonest auditors financially responsible to the taxpayer for all money lost as a result of the multitude of dishonest audits by IRS personnel) that the Commissioner stand behind his publicized lie. We know it to be a lie.

Letter written by a tax representative. The representative has tried to give the impression that his client is the one who is protesting.

Unless he has agreed to pay all interest, you have a right to be as unimpressed as we are.

Another bit of razzle-dazzle is to drag you through the entire appeals process when you don't have a strong case, again to convince you the representative knows all the ins and outs and you are getting your money's worth. But appeals take time and can be costly (and don't think he won't bill you at each successive stage). If the tax law is clearly against you or you have no proof, an appeal is wasted effort. Try to judge whether you actually stand a chance of winning. How? Listen to the reasons your auditor gives for not allowing an expense. Be objective—the auditor is not necessarily lying because she works for the IRS, and your preparer is not necessarily leveling with you because he doesn't. Ask to see the tax law on that point. Then listen to your representative's side of the story. Does he have a *legal* argument? Does the auditor indicate there are varying opinions in this area or does she state flatly that the expense is never deductible in a case like yours? Weigh both sides and make an independent decision. Don't be railroaded. Even if you stand to gain a few dollars, it may not be worth the other costs to you. Let me cite the extreme example of a representative who takes her clients through both levels of IRS appeals, then files a claim and generates a second audit through the same levels of appeal, then files a claim . . . until the statute of limitations or our patience runs out. This representative is fighting a war of attrition at the taxpayer's expense. Be wary.

I have seen representatives destroy a taxpayer's credibility in the audit interview as surely as if they had sat down and said, "You can't believe a word my client says." How does he accomplish this disastrous feat? He does it by jumping in hastily, when the auditor asks a question, with an answer of his own. ("Is this Mrs. Jackabee a relative?" Representative: "No, no she's not!") He interrupts his client's answer and contradicts it. ("She didn't mean that. What she means to say is . . .") He tells his client not to answer the question. He excuses himself and engages his client in a whispered conversation outside the auditor's office. He coughs, gives warning glances, or nudges his client. In no time at all, the auditor is convinced the taxpayer has something to hide that is roughly the size of the Goodyear blimp.

Then there is the representative who walks in with tax law he must have picked up from a tipster on the street. Some of the legal arguments these representatives use are so farfetched, even laughable, that the auditor is sure he knows better and is deliberately trying to confuse the issues because his client has a weak case. Or the representative who comes in with a citation to prove the deductibility of an expense and who, after the auditor discovers that it had nothing to do with the case, admits he never looked it up—he read it in the newspaper and thought it might apply. Someone was paying this man eighty dollars an hour not to research court cases and revenue rulings but to scan the financial advice column while he drank his morning coffee. Are we permitted to tell you this man is incompetent? No. In both of these cases, we have representatives who will not, under penalty of death, admit that the auditor is right when they know the auditor is right. Maybe they think their clients will interpret it as a sign of weakness. Who knows? But a representative who won't say die, even after rigor mortis has set in, is costing you money. Make it clear you want to know if your case is terminal.

You would think that a representative would at least look at the tax return he's representing, wouldn't you? But more than one has walked into my office without the least idea of what's on a return. I know, because *I* have looked at the return. I listen while these representatives make self-assured statements of fact about their clients which bear only a slight relationship to or completely contradict the tax return. They try to bluff their way through the audit when it becomes increasingly obvious that they don't place enough importance on their clients' interests to even take the time to familiarize themselves with the case. One representative didn't even try to hide his indifference. "I ordinarily wouldn't get up in the morning for a case like this," he said pompously. "He's my tailor, so I'm doing him a favor." If his tailor is reading this, I hope he sews this nabob into a suit and leaves him there.

On the lighter side, try to avoid the lunatic fringe. One evangelistic tax preparer, "Al, Everybody's Pal," told me there would be "no more audits in the ages. There ain't going to be no more audits because God asked me to do away with them." He was nice about it, however, offering to find me a job when the end finally came.

KEEP IN TOUCH WITH THE IRS

How can you tell if your representative is doing an adequate job for you? The only way you can mind your own business is to make sure you keep informed of what your representative is doing. Do not cut yourself off from communication with the IRS. Your auditor may not be able to tell you outright what your representative is doing wrong, but she *can* let you know what actions he has taken and let you draw your own conclusions. Without this feedback, decisions of vital importance to you financially can be made without your consent or knowledge.

The two things you do *not* want to do are these: (1) give your representative the authority to receive all correspondence from the IRS without copies being sent to you and (2) refuse to talk to anyone at IRS, because your representative so instructed you (unless you have committed fraud and your representative does not want you to incriminate yourself). Giving your representative carte blanche when he knows he has isolated you from all clues to his conduct is to be more trusting than wise. In one case where it appeared the taxpayer had nine thousand dollars more to spend than the tax return accounted for, the auditor called the taxpayer to ask if he had any non-taxable sources of income to explain the difference. The taxpayer, on the advice of his representative, would not say a word, even in his own defense. The auditor had no choice but to presume the nine thousand dollars was unreported taxable income and send the taxpayer a report for that amount plus a penalty. This case, which probably could have been resolved at the auditor's level, is now on appeal because of the taxpayer's refusal to communicate.

You will normally receive copies of all correspondence regarding your case, unless your representative tells us it should be sent to him alone. If you have not delegated this power and you do not hear anything from us within a reasonable time after the audit begins, call the auditor and find out whether any action has been taken or whether your representative has requested the IRS not to communicate with you.

Similarly, if you receive a request for additional information, a report, or other correspondence your representative had led you to believe you would not get (for instance, he assured you he had presented all the documents required), call and find out why there is a discrepancy in his story. I have known taxpayers to call after receiving a no-show report because the representative failed to appear, baffled because he had told them the matter was all taken care of.

PAYING FOR YOUR REPRESENTATIVE'S MISTAKE

What are some of the consequences of poor representation? You may be issued a no-show report or a report for more tax than you should owe. This can happen if your representative repeatedly fails to keep appointments, comes in without bringing your documents, or promises to obtain additional information from you but never does so. The word we use for this type of representative is "procrastinating," and someone with a reputation for such behavior gets short shrift (no extensions, no second appointments, and strict time limits). In short we won't bend over backward to give him (you) the little courtesies granted the better representatives.

Poor representation can also result in needless appointments, and as we have seen, needless or fruitless appeals, with the consequent delays and expense to you. On the opposite side, incompetence or ignorance can cost you your appeal rights. There are time limits within which you or your representative must act or, as we will see in Chapter XII, your case is closed and your only recourse (technically) is to the courts. You can no longer take advantage of the IRS's internal appeals process, which is far simpler and less expensive than court action. Anytime a procedure is closed to you because of your representative's action or inaction, you have been potentially harmed.

The audit is your business. Whether or not you want to be bothered, you stand to lose a lot. Keep your finger in the pie and a sharp eye on your representative.

X. AUDITING BY THE NUMBERS: The Pittances, a Case Study

Bags packed? Cameras ready? It's time for your tour to Fantasy Audit, where a mythical tax return meets a fictitious auditor for an hour of enlightenment. What sort of enlightenment? Think of this as an audit simulator, where you can learn about an audit without actually going through one. Following an auditor through an audit, even an imaginary one, step by step, will help you learn what problems of proof you may encounter in your audit and how you can prevent them beforehand. You'll also see what judgments the auditor makes about you and your receipts, how the scope and outcome of the audit is affected by your oral testimony, and what mixture of fact, experience, belief, and doubt come together as the bases of your auditor's decisions.

THE RETURN

We are going to audit the joint return of Noel and Annie Pittance, fictional residents of Lotus Land, where anything can happen. The Pittances' tax return, with its assorted schedules, is shown on the pages that follow.

Take a look at this return. How did it find its way to an auditor's desk? No matter how cautious the Pittances have been, they have unwittingly stepped on a DIF land mine. Let's see if we can figure out what might have set it off.

On the Pittances' return, three factors in particular stand out. Form 2106 shows us that Noel is claiming a substantial deduction for travel and entertainment expense. Because of rigid requirements of proof, these areas have been an audit gold mine for the IRS in the

1040 Department of the Treasury—Internal Revenue Service
U.S. Individual Income Tax Return 1987

For the year January 1–December 31, 1987, or other tax year beginning , 1987, ending , 19 | OMB No. 1545-0074

Use IRS label. Otherwise, please print or type	NOEL J AND ANNIE M PITTANCE 726 DATE PALM VISTA HOLLYWOOD, CA 90028	Your social security number: 978-26-1330 Spouse's social security no.: 872-64-3211 For Privacy Act and Paperwork Reduction Act Notice, See Instrs.

PRESIDENTIAL ELECTION CAMPAIGN
Do you want $1 to go to this fund? — Yes / No
If joint return, does your spouse want $1 to go to this fund? — Yes / No
NOTE: Checking "Yes" will not change your tax or reduce your refund

Filing Status (Check only one box.)

1 [ ] Single
2 [X] Married filing joint return (even if only one had income)
3 [ ] Married filing separate return. Enter spouse's name
4 [ ] Head of household (with qualifying person). If the qualifying person is your child but not your dependent, enter child's name here
5 [ ] Qualifying widow(er) with dependent child (Year spouse died ▶ 19).

Exemptions (See Instructions on page 7.)

Caution: If you can be claimed as a dependent on another person's tax return (such as your parent's return), do not check box 6a. But be sure to check the box on line 32b.

6a [X] Yourself 6b [X] Spouse

c Dependents

If more than 7 dependents attach statement

(1) Name (first, initial, and last name)	(2) Check if under age 5	(3) If age 5 or over, dependent's SSN	(4) Relationship	(5) No. of months lived in your home
NADINE		615-72-3772	CHILD	12
MARTIN	X		CHILD	12
MARTHA		443-68-2990	MOTHER	0

No. of boxes checked on 6a and 6b ▶ 2
No. of children on 6c who lived with you ▶ 2
No. of children on 6c who didn't live with you due to divorce or separation ▶
No. of parents listed on 6c ▶ 1
No. of other dependents listed on 6c ▶

d If your child didn't live with you but is claimed as a dependent under a pre-1985 agreement, check here ▶ [ ]
e Total number of exemptions claimed (also complete line 35) — Add numbers entered in boxes above ▶ 5

Income

Please attach Copy B of your Forms W-2, W-2G, & W-2P here.

If you do not have a W-2, see page 6 of Instructions.

Please attach check or money order here.

7	Wages, salaries, tips, etc.	7	59,735
8	Taxable interest income (also attach Schedule B if over $400)	8	68
9	Tax-exempt interest income. (DO NOT include on line 8.) 9		
10	Dividend income (also attach Schedule B if over $400)	10	
11	Taxable refunds of state and local income taxes	11	726
12	Alimony received	12	
13	Business income or (loss) (attach Schedule C)	13	
14	Capital gain or (loss) (attach Schedule D)	14	
15	Other gains or (losses) (attach Form 4797)	15	
16a	Pensions, IRA distributions, annuities and rollovers. 16a		
b	Taxable amount, if any (see page 11)	16b	
17	Rents, royalties, partnerships, estates, trusts, etc. (attach Schedule E)	17	-16,147
18	Farm income or (loss) (attach Schedule F)	18	
19	Unemployment compensation (insurance)(see page 11)	19	
20a	Social security benefits (see page 12) 20a		
b	Taxable amount, if any, from worksheet on page 12	20b	
21	Other income	21	
22	Add lines 7, 8, and 10 – 21. This is your TOTAL INCOME ▶	22	44,382

Adjustments to Income (See Instructions on page 12.)

23	Reimbursed employee business expenses from Form 2106	23	
24a	Your IRA deduction, from the worksheet on page 13	24a	
b	Spouse's IRA ded., from the worksheet on page 13	24b	
25	Self-employed health insurance ded., from worksheet page 14	25	
26	Keogh retirement and self-empl'd SEP deduction	26	
27	Penalty on early withdrawal of savings	27	
28	Alimony paid (social security no.)	28	
29	TOTAL ADJUSTMENTS ▶	29	

Adjusted Gross Income

30	Subtract line 29 from line 22. This is your ADJUSTED GROSS INCOME. If this line is less than $15,432 and a child lived with you, see "EARNED INCOME CREDIT" (line 56) on page 18 of instructions. ▶	30	44,382

Tax Computation	31	Amount from line 30 (adjusted gross income)	31	44,382
	32a	Check if: ☐ You were 65 or over ☐ Blind; ☐ Spouse was 65 or over ☐ Blind. Add the number of boxes checked and enter the total here ▶ 32a		
	b	If you can be claimed as a dependent on another person's return, check here ▶ 32b ☐		
	c	If you are married filing a separate return and your spouse itemizes deductions, or you are a dual-status alien, see page 15 and check here ▶ 32c ☐		
	33a	Itemized deductions. See page 15 to see if you should itemize. If you itemize, attach Schedule A, enter the amount from Schedule A, line 26, and skip line 33b	33a	27,233
Caution: If you checked any box on line 32a, b, or c AND you don't itemize, see page 16 for the amount to enter on line 33b.	b	Standard deduction. Enter amount shown below for your filing status unless Caution to left applies. Filing status from page 1: Single or Head of household, enter $2,540; Married filing jointly or Qualifying widow(er), enter $3,760; Married filing separately, enter $1,880	33b	0
	34	Subtract line 33a or 33b, whichever applies, from line 31. Enter the result here	34	17,149
	35	Multiply $1,900 by the total number of exemptions claimed on line 6e	35	9,500
	36	Taxable Income. Subtract line 35 from line 34. Enter the result (but not less than zero)	36	7,649
		Caution: If under age 14 and you have more than $1,000 of investment income check here ▶ ☐		
	37	Enter tax. Check if from ☒ Tax Table ☐ Tax Rate Schedules ☐ Schedule D or ☐ Form 8615	37	1,024
	38	Additional taxes (see page 16). Check if from ☐ Form 4970 ☐ Form 4972	38	
	39	Add lines 37 and 38. Enter the total	39	1,024
Credits (See Instructions on page 16)	40	Credit for child and dependent care expense (attach Form 2441) — 40: 400		
	41	Credit for the elderly or for the permanently and totally disabled (attach Schedule R) — 41		
	42	Add lines 40 and 41. Enter the total	42	400
	43	Subtract line 42 from line 39. Enter the result (but not less than zero)	43	624
	44	Foreign tax credit (attach Form 1116) — 44		
	45	General business credit. Check if from ☐ Form 3800 ☐ Form 3468 ☐ Form 5884 ☐ Form 6478 ☐ Form 6765, or ☐ Form 8586 — 45		
	46	Add lines 44 and 45. Enter the total	46	NONE
	47	Subtract line 46 from line 43. Enter the result (but not less than zero) ▶	47	624
Other Taxes (Including Advance EIC Payments)	48	Self-employment tax	48	
	49	Alternative minimum tax (attach Form 6251)	49	
	50	Tax from recapture of investment credit (attach Form 4255)	50	
	51	Social security tax on tip income not reported to employer (attach Form 4137)	51	
	52	Tax on IRA or qualified retirement plan (attach Form 5329)	52	
	53	Add lines 47 through 52. This is your total tax ▶	53	624
Payments Attach Forms W-2, W-2G, and W-2P to front.	54	Federal income tax withheld — 54: 9,790		
	55	1987 estimated tax payments and amount applied from 1986 return — 55		
	56	Earned income credit (see page 18) — 56		
	57	Amount paid with Form 4868 — 57		
	58	Excess Soc. Sec. & RRTA tax withheld (see page 19) — 58		
	59	Credit for Federal tax on special fuels and gasoline (attach Form 4136) — 59		
	60	Regulated Investment Company cr. (attach Form 2439) — 60		
	61	Add lines 54 through 60. These are your total payments ▶	61	9,790
Refund or Amount You Owe	62	If line 61 is larger than line 53, enter amount OVERPAID ▶	62	9,166
	63	Amount of line 62 to be REFUNDED TO YOU ▶	63	9,166
	64	Amount of line 62 to be applied to your 1988 estimated tax ▶ — 64		
	65	If line 53 is larger than line 61, enter AMOUNT YOU OWE. Attach check or money order for full amount payable to "Internal Revenue Service." Write your social security number, daytime phone number and "1987 Form 1040" on it. Check ▶ ☐ if Form 2210 (2210F) is attached. See page 20. Penalty: $	65	NONE

Please Sign Here

Under penalties of perjury, I declare that I have examined this return, and accompanying schedules and statements, and to the best of my knowledge and belief, they are true, correct, and complete. Declaration of preparer (other than taxpayer) is based on all information of which preparer has any knowledge.

Your Signature	Date	Your occupation
Noel J. Pittance		STOCKBROKER
Spouse's signature (if joint return, BOTH must sign)	**Date**	**Spouse occupation**
Annie M. Pittance	3/12/88	NURSE

Paid Preparer's Use Only

Preparer's signature ▶	Date	Check if self-employed ▶ ☐	Preparer's social security no.
Firm's name (or yours, if self-employed) and address ▶		E. I. No. ▶	ZIP code ▶

Schedules A&B (Form 1040)

Department of the Treasury Internal Revenue Service

Schedule A—Itemized Deductions

(Schedule B is on back)

▶ Attach to Form 1040. ▶ See Instructions for Schedules A and B (Form 1040).

OMB No. 1545-0074

1987

Attachment Sequence No. 07

Name(s) as shown on Form 1040: NOEL J AND ANNIE M PITTANCE

Your social security number: 978-26-1330

Medical and Dental Expenses (Do not include expenses reimbursed or paid by others.) (See Instructions on page 21.)	1a	Prescription medicines and drugs, insulin, doctors, dentists, nurses, hospitals, ins premiums you paid for medical and dental care, etc.				
		SEE STATEMENT ATTACHED	4,085			
		PRESCRIPTION DRUGS	310			
	1a			4,395		
	1b	b Transportation and lodging		23		
	1c	c Other LABORATORY	70	70		
	2	Add lines 1a through 1c, and enter the total here		4,488		
	3	Multiply amount on Form 1040, line 31, by 7.5% (.075)		3,329		
	4	Subtract line 3 from line 2. If zero or less enter 0. TOTAL medical and dental ▶			4	1,159
Taxes You Paid (See Instructions on page 22.)	5	State/local income taxes — 1987 w/holding: 2,123; 1987 estimated: ; Other years tax:		2,123		
	6	Real estate taxes		1,248		
	7	Other ▶ CALIFORNIA SDI	526			
		AUTO LICENSES	351			
	7			877		
	8	Add the amounts on lines 5 through 7. Enter the total here. TOTAL taxes ▶			8	4,248
Interest You Paid (See Instructions on page 22.)		NOTE: If you borrowed any new amounts against your home AFTER 8/16/86 and at any time in 1987 the total of ALL your mortgage debts was more than what you paid for your home plus improvements, attach Form 8598 and check here ▶ ☐				
	9a	a Deductible home mortgage interest paid to financial institutions (report deductible points on line 10)		10,676		
	9b	b Deductible home mortgage interest paid to individuals (Name & Addr)				
	10	Deductible points				
	11	Deductible investment interest				
	12a	Personal interest you paid				
		SEE STATEMENT ATTACHED	3,501			
		12a	3,501			
	12b	b Multiply the amount on line 12a by 65% (.65). Enter the result.		2,276		
	13	Add the amts on lines 9a through 11 and 12b. Enter the total.		Total interest ▶	13	12,952
Contributions You Made (See Instructions on page 23.)	14a	a Cash contributions. (Less than $3,000 ea.)		1,065		
	14b	b Cash contributions totaling $3,000 or more ea. ▶				
	15	Other than cash (Attach Form 8283 if over $500) ▶		1,500		
	16	Carryover from prior year				
	17	Add lines 14a through 16. Enter total here. TOTAL contributions ▶			17	2,565
Casualty and Theft Losses	18	Casualty or theft loss(es) (attach Form 4684) (see page 23 of the Instructions) ▶			18	2,122
Moving Expenses	19	Moving expenses (attach Form 3903 or 3903F). (See page 24 of the Instructions.)			19	
Miscellaneous Deductions Subject to 2% AGI Limit (See Instructions on page 24.)	20	Unreimbursed employee business expenses (attach Form 2106)		4,096		
	21	Other ▶ SEE STATEMENT ATT.	927	927		
	22	Add the amounts on lines 20 and 21. Enter the total		5,023		
	23	Multiply the amount on Form 1040, line 31, by 2% (.02). Enter here		888		
	24	Subtract line 23 from line 22. Enter the result (but not less than zero) ▶			24	4,135
Other Misc Deductions	25	Misc deductions not subj to 2% AGI limit. (List type & amount) GAMBLING LOSSES	52		25	52
Total Itemized Deductions	26	Add the amounts on lines 4, 8, 13, 17, 18, 19, 24, and 25. Enter the total here and on Form 1040, line 33a ▶			26	27,233

For Paperwork Reduction Act Notice, see Form 1040 Instructions.

Schedule A (Form 1040) 1987

SCHEDULE A, SCHEDULE B AND MISCELLANEOUS INCOME 1987

NOEL J AND ANNIE M PITTANCE SS # 978-26-1330

DOCTORS, DENTISTS, NURSES, HOSPITALS, ETC.		
HOSPITALIZATION INSURANCE	1,740	
DR THOMAS MD	300	
DR DARTOLI MD	1,000	
DR WILLIAMS DDS	645	
DR MARWAN DDS	150	
DR HILLMAN OP	250	
TOTAL TO SCHEDULE A LINE 1A...............		4,085
PERSONAL INTEREST YOU PAID		
CREDIT CARD & CHARGE ACCOUNTS	193	
AUTO LOAN	3,074	
FURNITURE LOAN	234	
TOTAL TO SCHEDULE A LINE 12A...............		3,501
CASH CONTRIBUTIONS		
HOUSE OF WORSHIP	520	
UNITED FUND	260	
DISABLED VETERANS	100	
PBS-KCET	75	
MUSCULAR DYSTROPHY	50	
LA CO ART MUSEUM	30	
HEART ASSOCIATION	20	
BOY SCOUTS	10	
TOTAL TO SCHEDULE A LINE 14A		1,065
NON-CASH CONTRIBUTIONS		
GOODWILL INDUSTRIES	1,500	
TOTAL TO SCHEDULE A LINE 15.................		1,500
OTHER MISCELLANEOUS DEDUCTIONS		
UNIFORMS/SHOES	252	
SACSB	240	
PROFESSIONAL BOOKS	200	
EQUIPMENT	175	
CONTINUING EDUCATION	60	
TOTAL TO SCHEDULE A LINE 21.................		927

past. This poor taxpayer track record has not been lost on the computer, and any taxpayer claiming travel, entertainment, or other unreimbursed business expenses can expect close scrutiny.

Remember the "key ratio" test from Chapter VI? It gives us two more clues to where possible land mines are buried. Adding up the Pittances' itemized deductions, we see they come to $27,233 (Schedule A, line 26), well over half (61 percent) of their adjusted gross income of $44,382. This may well be too far out of proportion with the "norm" reflected by DIF. If so, the itemized deductions taken as a whole may have triggered an audit.

The size of the refund can also determine audit selection. Not the dollar amount itself, of course, because that largely depends upon how much you are required to pay in. Rather, what matters is how high the refund is in relation to the total withholding. In the Pittances' case, the refund is a whopping 93 percent plus of the withholding on wages. There can be any number of reasons why this should be so, but the Pittances will have to make their explanations to an auditor.

Look at the return again. What does it tell the auditor about the Pittances? Both are wage earners. Noel is a stockbroker and Annie is a nurse. They have two children, one of them under school age, judging by Form 1040, line 6c(2). They are sending support to either Noel's or Annie's mother, who does not live with them. They have a small savings account and a duplex that they rent out, and they own their own home. Major purchases have been a car and furniture, which they financed through the furniture store. The Pittances took out no other personal loans, although they did make credit purchases with two credit cards. During the year, misfortune struck, and they suffered a major casualty or theft loss. Noel entertains and uses his car for business.

Aside from a few guesses about the Pittances' personal tastes and preferences, you can see that the auditor has little real knowledge about them. The return raises more questions than it answers. An auditor screening this return to select the best audit issues would ask: (1) If Noel is a stockbroker, why aren't any stock transactions shown on the return? (2) How old is the mother, and is she receiving social security (Form 1040, line 6c)? (3) Why is the medical expense so high when the Pittances have medical insurance (Schedule A)? (4) What is the employer's rate of reimbursement for the auto

SCHEDULE E (Form 1040)
Department of the Treasury
Internal Revenue Service (X)

Supplemental Income Schedule

(From rents, royalties, partnerships, estates, trusts, REMIC's, etc.)

▶ Attach to Form 1040, Form 1041, or Form 1041S.
▶ See Instructions for Schedule E (Form 1040).

OMB No. 1545-0074
1987
Attachment Sequence No. 13

Name(s) as shown on Form 1040: NOEL J AND ANNIE M PITTANCE
Your social security number: 978-26-1330

Part I Rent and Royalty Income or (Loss) CAUTION: Your rental loss may be limited. See instructions.

1 In the space provided below, show the kind and location of each rental property.

2 For each property listed, did you or a member of your family use for personal purposes any of the properties for more than the greater of 14 days or 10% of the total days rented at fair rental value during the tax year?

3 For each rental real estate prop listed, did you actively participate in the operation of the activity during the tax year?

		2 Yes	2 No		3 Yes	3 No
Property A	SEE STATEMENT ATTACHED ▶		X	▶	X	
Property B	▶			▶		
Property C	▶			▶		

	Line	Properties A	B	C	Line	TOTALS (Add columns A, B, and C)
Rental and Royalty Income						
4 Rents received		16,950			4	16,950
5 Royalties received					5	
Rental and Royalty Expenses						
6 Advertising	6	120				
7 Auto and travel	7	67				
8 Cleaning and maintenance	8	240				
9 Commissions	9					
10 Insurance	10					
11 Legal and other professional fees	11					
12 Mortgage interest paid to financial institutions (see instructions)	12	16,304			12	16,304
13 Other interest	13					
14 Repairs	14	2,495				
15 Supplies	15	75				
16 Taxes (do NOT include Windfall Profit Tax, see Part V, line 40)	16	1,836				
17 Utilities	17	560				
18 Wages and salaries	18					
19 Other (list) ▶						
OTHER RENTAL EXPENSES		600				
20 Total expenses other than depreciation and depletion. Add lines 6 thru 19	20	22,297			20	22,297
21 Depreciation expense (see instr) or Depletion (see Pub 535)	21	10,800			21	10,800
22 Total. Add lines 20 and 21	22	33,097				
23. Income or (loss) from rental or royalty properties. Subtr line 22 from line 4 (rents) or 5 (royalties)	23	-16,147				
24 Deductible rental loss.	24	-16,147				
25 Profits. Add rental and royalty profits from line 23, and enter the total profits here					25	
26 Losses. Add royalty losses from ln 23 & rental losses from ln 24, & enter the total (losses) here					26	(16,147)
27 Combine amounts on lines 25 & 26, & enter the net profit or (loss) here					27	-16,147
28 Net farm rental profit or (loss) from Form 4835. (Also complete Part VI, line 43.)					28	
29 Total rental or royalty income or (loss). Combine amounts on lines 27 and 28, and enter the total here If Parts II, III, IV, and V on page 2 do not apply to you, write the amount from line 29 on Form 1040, line 17. Otherwise, include the amount from line 29 in line 42 on page 2 of Schedule E					29	-16,147

For Paperwork Reduction Act Notice, see Form 1040 Instructions.

Schedule E (Form 1040) 1987

Form **2441** — **Credit for Child and Dependent Care Expenses** — OMB No. 1545-0068 — **1987**

Department of the Treasury Internal Revenue Service (X)

▶ Attach to Form 1040.
▶ See Instructions below.

Attachment Sequence No. 23

Name(s) as shown on Form 1040: NOEL J AND ANNIE M PITTANCE — Your social security number: 978-26-1330

Note: If you paid cash wages of $50 or more in a calendar quarter to an individual for services performed in your home, you must file an employment tax return. Get Form 942 for details.

		Line	Amount
1	Enter the number of qualifying persons who were cared for in 1987 (See instructions for definition of qualifying persons) ▶	1	1
2	Enter the amount of qualified expenses you incurred and actually paid in 1987 for the care of the qualifying person. (See What Are Qualified Expenses in the instructions.) Do not enter more than $2,400 ($4,800 if you paid for the care of two or more qualifying persons)	2	2,000
3a	You must enter your earned income on line 3a. See line 3 instructions for definition of earned income	3a	30,245
b	If you are married, filing a joint return for 1987, you must enter your spouse's earned income on line 3b (If spouse is a full time student or is disabled, see line 3 instructions for the amount to enter.)	3b	29,490
c	If you are married, filing a joint return, compare the amounts on lines 3a and 3b, and enter the smaller of the two amounts on line 3c	3c	29,490
4	• If you were unmarried at the end of 1987, compare the amounts on lines 2 and 3a, and enter the smaller of the two amounts on line 4. • If you are married filing a joint return, compare the amounts on lines 2 and 3c, and enter the smaller of the two amounts on line 4.	4	2,000
5	Enter percentage from table below that applies to the adjusted gross income on Form 1040, line 31.	5	x 20%

If line 31 is: Over– But not over–	Percentage is:	If line 31 is: Over– But not over–	Percentage is:
$0–$10,000	30% (.30)	$20,000–22,000	24% (.24)
10,000–12,000	29% (.29)	22,000–24,000	23% (.23)
12,000–14,000	28% (.28)	24,000–26,000	22% (.22)
14,000–16,000	27% (.27)	26,000–28,000	21% (.21)
16,000–18,000	26% (.26)	28,000	20% (.20)
18,000–20,000	25% (.25)		

		Line	Amount
6	Multiply the amount on line 4 by the percentage shown on line 5, and enter the result.	6	400
7	Multiply any child and dependent care expenses for 1986 that you paid in 1987 by the percentage that applies to the adjusted gross income on your 1986 Form 1040, line 33, or Form 1040A, line 15. Enter the result. (See line 7 instructions for the required statement.)	7	
8	Add amounts on lines 6 and 7. See the worksheet in the instructions for line 8 for the amount of credit you can claim	8	400

Form 2441 (1987)

(Form 2106)? (5) Were the repairs to the rental really improvements (Schedule E)? There are two other things that bother me about this return: There are too many round, even numbers, e.g., 1,000, 300 etc., and the Pittances seem to be spending more than they visibly earned and may therefore have unreported income. (You may not be able to see this now, but we'll run through the computation an auditor makes during the audit later.)

From the face of the return there are at least *six* issues with good audit potential. Listed in order from the highest potential to the lowest, they are as follows: (1) casualty loss, (2) auto and entertainment, (3) contributions, (4) rental repairs and depreciation, (5) medical, and (6) the exemption for Martha. These would be the items that would be classified and the Pittances would be asked to prove. The possibilty of unreported income is also an issue, but one that is rarely classified. Instead, the auditor usually asks questions

Form **4684** Department of the Treasury Internal Revenue Service

Casualties and Thefts

▶ See separate instructions
▶ To be filed with Form 1040, 1041, 1065, 1120, etc.
Use a seperate Form 4684 for each different casualty or theft.

OMB No. 1545-0177 **1987** Attachment Sequence No. 35

Name(s) as shown on tax return: NOEL J AND ANNIE M PITTANCE

Identifying Number: 978-26-1330

SECTION A. - Personal Use Property

(Casualties and thefts to property NOT used in a trade or business or for income-producing purposes.)

1 Description of Properties (Show kind, location, and date of purchase for each)

Property A THEFT-PERSONAL BELONGINGS 12-27-87

Property B

Property C

Property D

OCCURRENCE 1

	Properties (Use a separate column for each property lost or damaged from one casualty or theft.)			
	A	B	C	D
2 Cost or other basis of each property	6,660			
3 Insurance or other reimbursement (Whether or not you submit a claim). See instructions NOTE: If line 2 is more than line 3, skip line 4	0			
4 Gain from casualty or theft. If line 3 is more than line 2, enter difference here and skip lines 5 through 13	0			
5 Fair market value before casualty or theft	6,660			
6 Fair market value after casualty or theft	0			
7 Subtract line 6 from line 5	6,660			
8 Enter smaller of line 2 or line 7	6,660			
9 Subtract line 3 from line 8	6,660			

10 Casualty or theft loss. Add amounts from line 9 for all columns	6,660
11 Enter the amount from line 10 or $100, whichever is smaller	100
12 Subtract line 11 from line 10	6,560
CAUTION: Use only one Form 4684 for lines 13 through 18.	
13 Add the line 12 amounts from all Forms 4684, Section A	6,560
14 Add the line 4 amounts from all Forms 4684, Section A	0
15 If line 14 is more than line 13, enter difference here and on Schedule D, and do not complete the rest of form. (See Instructions) Otherwise, enter zero and complete lines 16 through 18. If line 14 is equal to line 13, do not complete the rest of form	0
16 If line 13 is more than line 14, enter difference	6,560
17 Enter 10% of adjusted gross income (Form 1040, line 31). Estates and trusts, See instructions	4,438
18 Subtract line 17 from line 16. If zero or less, enter zero. Enter on Schedule A (Form 1040), line 18. Estates and trusts, enter on the "other deductions" line of your tax return	2,122

For Paperwork Reduction Act Notice, see Page 1 of separate instructions

Form **2106**

Department of the Treasury
Internal Revenue Service (X)

EMPLOYEE BUSINESS EXPENSES

▶ See separate instructions

▶ Attach to Form 1040

OMB No. 1545-0139

1987

Attachment Sequence No. **54**

Your name	Social security number	Occupation in which expenses were incurred
NOEL J PITTANCE	978-26-1330	STOCKBROKER

Part I Employee Business Expenses

STEP 1 Enter Your Expenses		Column A Other than Meals and Entertainment	Column B Meals and Entertainment
1 Vehicle expense from Part II, line 15 or line 22	1	5,393	
2 Parking fees, tolls, and local transportation	2		
3 Travel expense while away from home, including lodging, airplane, car rental etc. Do not include meals & entertainment	3		
4 Business expenses not included in lines 1 through 3. Do not include meals and entertainment	4	240	
5 Meals and entertainment expenses. See instructions	5		1,454
6 Add lines 1 through 5 and enter the total expenses here	6	5,633	1,454

Note: If you were not reimbursed for any expenses in step 1, skip lines 7 through 13 and enter the amount from line 6 on line 14.

STEP 2 Figure Any Excess Reimbursements to Report in Income			
7 Reimbursements for the expenses listed in step 1 that your employer did not report to you on Form W-2 or Form 1099 Note; If, in both columns, line 6 is more than line 7, skip lines 8 & 9 and go to line 10. You do not have excess reimbursements.	7	2,700	
8 Subtract line 6 from line 7. If zero or less, enter zero	8		
9 Add the amounts on line 8 of both columns and enter the total here. Also add this amount to any shown on Form 1040, line 7. This is an excess reimbursement reportable as income ▶	9		

STEP 3 Figure Fully Deductible Reimbursed Expenses			
10 Subtract line 7 from line 6. If zero or less, enter zero	10	2,933	1,454
11 Reimbursements or allowances for expenses in Step 1 that your employer identified to you, included on Form W-2 or Form 1099, and were not subject to withholding tax Note: The amount entered on line 11 should have also been reported as income on Form 1040.	11		
12 Enter the smaller of line 10 or line 11	12		
13 Add the amounts on line 12 of both columns. Enter here and on Form 1040, line 23. This is your fully deductible reimbursed expenses ▶	13		

STEP 4 Figure Expenses to Deduct as an Itemized Deduction on Schedule A (Form 1040)			
14 Subtract line 12 from line 10 Note: If both columns of line 14 are zero, do not complete the rest of Part I.	14	2,933	1,454
15 Enter 20% (.20) of line 14, Column B	15		291
16 Subtract line 15 from line 14	16	2,933	1,163
17 Add the amounts on line 16 of both columns and enter the total here. Also enter the total on Schedule A (Form 1040), line 20. (Qualified Performing Artists and handicapped employees, see instructions.) ▶	17		4,096

For Paperwork Reduction Act Notice, see Instructions.

Form 2106 (1987)

Part II Vehicle Expenses (Use either your actual expenses (Section C) or the standard mileage rate. (Section B)

Section A. - General Information		Vehicle 1	Vehicle 2
1 Enter the date vehicle was placed in service	1	07 / 10/ 86	/ /
2 Total mileage vehicle was used during 1987	2	25,000 miles	miles
3 Miles included on line 2 that vehicle was used for business	3	18,750 miles	miles
4 Percent of business use (divide line 3 by line 2)	4	75.000%	%
5 Average daily round trip commuting distance	5	miles	miles
6 Miles included on line 2 that vehicle was used for commuting	6	miles	miles
7 Other personal mileage (subtract line 6 plus line 3 from line 2)	7	6,250 miles	miles

8 Do you (or your spouse) have another vehicle available for personal purposes? ☒ Yes ☐ No

9 If your employer provided you with a vehicle, is personal use during off duty hours permitted? ☐ Yes ☐ No ☒ N/A

10 Do you have evidence to support your deduction? ☒ Yes ☐ No. If yes, is the evidence written? ☒ Yes ☐ No

Section B. - Standard Mileage Rate (Do not use this section unless you own the vehicle.)		
11 Enter the smaller of Part II, line 3 or 15,000 miles	11	miles
12 Subtract line 11 from Part II, line 3	12	miles
13 Multiply line 11 by 22 ½¢ (.225) (see instructions for a fully depreciated vehicle)	13	
14 Multiply line 12 by 11¢ (.11)	14	
15 Add lines 13 and 14. Enter total here and on Part I, line 1	15	

Section C. - Actual Expenses		Vehicle 1	Vehicle 2
16 Gasoline, oil, repairs, vehicle insurance,etc	16	2,479	
17 Vehicle rentals	17		
18 Value of employer-provided vehicle (applies only if included on Form W-2 at 100% fair rental value, see instructions)	18		
19 Add lines 16 through 18	19	2,479	
20 Multiply line 19 by the percentage on Part II,line 4	20	1,859	
21 Depreciation from Section D, column (f) (see instructions)	21	3,534	
22 Add lines 20 and 21. Enter total here and on Part I,line 1	22	5,393	

Section D. - Depreciation of Vehicles (Depreciation can only be claimed for a vehicle you own. If a vehicle is used 50 percent or less in a trade or business, the Section 179 deduction is not allowed and depreciation must be taken using the straight line method over 5 years. For other limitations, see instructions.)

	Cost or other basis (a)	Basis for depreciation (Business use only-see instructions) (b)	Method of figuring depreciation (c)	Depreciation deduction (d)	Section 179 expense (e)	Total column (d)+column (e) (enter in Section C, line 21) (f)
Vehicle 1	12,400	9,300	ACRS 38%	3,534		3,534
Vehicle 2						

Form **8283** (Rev. October 1987)

Department of the Treasury Internal Revenue Service

Noncash Charitable Contributions

▶ Attach to Your Federal income tax return if the total claimed value of all property contributed exceeds $500.

▶ See separate Instructions.

OMB No. 1545-0908 Expires 9-30-88

Attachment Sequence No. 55

Name(s) as shown on your income tax return: NOEL J AND ANNIE M PITTANCE

Identification number: 978-26-1330

Section A. – Include in Section A only items (or groups of similar items) which have claimed value of $5,000 or less per item or group and certain publicly traded securities (see instructions).

Part I Information on Donated Property

	1 (a) Name and address of the donee organization:	(b) Description of donated property (attach a separate sheet if more space is needed)
A	GOODWILL INDUSTRIES LOS ANGELES CA	FURNITURE CLOTHING BOOKS
B		
C		
D		
E		

Note: Columns (d), (e), and (f) do not have to be completed for items with a value of $500 or less.

	(c) Date of the contribution	(d) Date acquired by donor (mo., yr.)	(e) How acquired by donor	(f) Donor's cost or adjusted basis	(g) Fair market value	(h) Method used to determine the fair market value
A	09-12-87	VAR.	PURCHASED		1,500	COST OF SIMILAR
B						
C						
D						
E						

Part II Other Information

– Complete question 2 if you gave less than the entire interest in property listed in Part I. Complete question 3 if restrictions were attached to a contribution listed in Part I.

2 If less than the entire interest in the property is contributed during the year, complete the following:

(a) Enter letter from Part I which identifies the property ______ . (Attach a separate statement if Part II applies to more than one property.)

(b) Total amount claimed as a deduction for the property listed in Part I for this tax year ______ ; for any prior tax year(s) ______ .

(c) Name and address of each organization to which any such contribution was made in a prior year (complete only if different from the donee organization above).

Charitable organization (Donee) name

Number and street

City or town, state, and ZIP code

(d) The place where any tangible property is located or kept: ______

(e) Name of any person, other than the donee organization, having actual possession of the property. ______

3 If conditions were attached to the contribution listed in Part I, answer the following questions:

	Yes	No
(a) Is there a restriction either temporarily or permanently on the donee's right to use or dispose of the donated property?		X
(b) Did you give anyone (other than the donee organization or another organization participating with the donee organization in cooperative fundraising) the right to the income from the donated property or to the possession of the property, including the right to vote donated securities, to acquire the property by purchase or otherwise, or to designate the person having such income, possesion, or the right to acquire?		X
(c) Is there a restriction limiting the donated property for a particular use?		X

For Paperwork Reduction Act Notice, see separate instructions.

Form **4562**

Department of the Treasury
Internal Revenue Service (X)

Depreciation and Amortization

▶ See separate instructions
▶ Attach this form to your return

OMB No. 1545-0172

1987

Attachment Sequence No. 67

Name(s) as shown on return: NOEL J AND ANNIE M PITTANCE

Identifying number: 978-26-1330

Business or activity to which this form relates: STATEMENT OF RENTAL & OIL & GAS INCOME PAGE 01

Part I **Depreciation** (Do not use this part for automobiles, certain other vehicles, computers, and property used for entertainment, recreation, or amusement. Instead, use Part III.)

Section A. – Election to Expense Depreciable Assets Placed in Service During This Tax Year (Section 179)

	(a) Description of property	(b) Date placed in service	(c) Cost	(d) Expense deduction
1				
2	Listed property–Enter total from Part III, Section A, column (h)			
3	Total (add lines 1 and 2, but do not enter more than $10,000)			
4	Enter the amount, if any, by which the cost of all section 179 property placed in service this tax year is more than $200,000			
5	Subtract ln 4 from ln 3. If result is less than zero, enter zero. (See Instr for other limitations)			

Section B. - Depreciation

(a) Class of property	(b) Date placed in service	(c) Basis for depreciation (Business use only–see instructions)	(d) Recovery period	(e) Method of figuring depreciation	(f) Deduction
6 Accelerated Cost Recovery System (ACRS) (see instructions): For assets placed in service ONLY during tax year beginning in 1987					
a 3-year property					
b 5-year property					
c 7-year property					
d 10-year property					
e 15-year property					
f 20-year real property					
g Residential rental property					
h Nonresidential real property					
7 Listed property–Enter total from Part III, Section A, column (g)					
8 ACRS deduction for assets placed in service prior to 1987 (see instructions)					10,800

Section C. - Other Depreciation

9	Property subject to section 168(f)(1) election (see instructions)	
10	Other depreciation (see instructions)	

Section D. - Summary

11	Total (add deductions on lines 5 through 10). Enter here and on the Depreciation line of your return. (Part and S corp–Do NOT include any amts entered on line 5.)	10,800
12	For assets above placed in service during the current year, enter the portion of the basis attributable to additional section 263A costs. (See instructions for who must use.)	

Part II **Amortization**

(a) Description of property	(b) Date acquired	(c) Cost or other basis	(d) Code section	(e) Amortization period or %	(f) Amortization for this year
1 Amortization for property placed in service only for tax year beginning in 1987					
2 Amortization for property placed in service prior to 1987					
3 Total. Enter here and on Other Deductions or Other expenses line of your return					

See Paperwork Reduction Act Notice on page 1 of the separate instructions.

Form **4562** (1987)

during the interview designed to discover whether the income issue justifies further audit or is just a false alarm. The suggestion that a taxpayer failed to report taxable income carries an implication of fraud, and an auditor likes to be sure of her ground before raising the issue.

The six issues I chose may not be the six another auditor would choose. At every stage of an audit, the auditor is making value judgments based not only on her IRS training but on factors unique to her. Throughout the audit that follows, the opinions and judgments are mine alone, although they do reflect IRS policy and practice. They cannot be used as a universal standard, however, and no auditor can be held to any judgment but his own. This is a guideline, not a gospel.

Let's go through each issue and see why it was selected. Remember, the aim of the audit program is to motivate as many of you as possible to comply with the tax law. Thus an auditor wants to collect the most tax (motivation) in the least amount of time (as many of you as possible). The most effective way to do this is to hit large deductions that are traditionally hard to prove. Using this criterion, the casualty loss of $6,660 (Form 4684) is out in front by a long stretch. The amount of the deduction, $2,122 (Schedule A, line 18), is also large, so that disallowing all or part of the loss will probably result in a respectable amount of tax. But the most compelling reason to go after any casualty loss is that it is usually impossible to prove to the degree required by law. This is because persons don't anticipate disaster and so don't have receipts all bundled up waiting for it. That is why, as part of your record keeping, you must keep receipts for major purchases even though they are not currently deductible. It is impossible to foresee when they may be stolen or lost.

Auto and entertainment (Form 2106) are also large items on this return, and because of the strict requirements of proof for these items mentioned above, there is a better than even chance Noel cannot live up to the auditor's expectations. Only a handful of taxpayers keep adequate records in these areas, so an adjustment is virtually assured. The auditor is not looking here to see whether it is likely that Noel incurred the expense, but whether it is likely he can prove it. The auditor can disallow the entire amount Noel claimed, although personally convinced he spent every penny he says he did, if Noel cannot back up his statements. So, even though the auditor knows from experience that stockbrokers often incur automobile and entertainment expenses, the problem of proof makes this a fertile issue. The employer's reimbursement (Form 2106, line 7) also raises questions. Normally an employer's reimbursement is intended to cover the employee's expense, so an auditor would not expect to see expenses in excess of reimbursement, especially not in this amount. If an employer does reimburse, it is usually for all expenses he requires his employees to incur. Was Noel undertaking expenses that his employer did not expect of him and that would therefore be nondeductible?

The Pittances' contributions are another item they may have difficulty proving (whether or not they actually spent the money), and again, this is a prime consideration in deciding to audit this issue. Why is the problem of proof obvious? Look at Contributions on the Schedule A. The Pittances are deducting $1,500 "Other than cash," on line 15. This means that they donated property to a charitable organization (in this case, Goodwill—see Form 8283). This required them to place a value on the property, or, in other words, to guess. The fact that $1,500 is a nice, even number tends to bear this out. Anytime the taxpayer guesses, the IRS has a potential adjustment, and you'll see how and why below.

Rental depreciation (Schedule E) is always a good issue, because so few taxpayers understand the mechanics of determining their depreciable basis in rental property. Depreciation is an accounting concept, and it is that added note of complexity which makes taxpayers give up before they can learn how to compute it properly. Lack of taxpayer education consistently makes rental depreciation profitable to audit. The repairs are questioned because taxpayers commonly fail to distinguish between a repair (deductible in the year paid) and a capital expenditure (depreciated over the life of the property). The problem is not helped by the fact that the line between repairs and capital expenditures often blurs and the distinction is not always clear. Generally a capital expenditure adds to the value of property or prolongs its life; a repair maintains property in its ordinary good working condition. The amount of repairs shown in the Pittance return is reasonably high ($2,495). The auditor doesn't know whether this figure is made up of a lot of small repairs or is one large capital expenditure or is a mixture of both. The odds favor at least one large capital item, so the audit potential is good.

The Pittances' medical expense (Schedule A) and their exemption for Martha (Form 1040, line 6c) are lesser issues. Medical expense is usually easy to prove. Even persons who failed to keep receipts can generally solve that problem by getting duplicate receipts or a yearly statement from their doctors. Drug receipts are more difficult to reconstruct, but the amount claimed for drugs is often quite small. Medical insurance may be a payroll deduction and quite simply proved by going to the employer. Other medical insurance can be verified by canceled checks or by writing to the insurance company. Some of these policies are not deductible, but medical insurance is rarely classified unless other medical expenses also appear to warrant audit. Medical is an issue on the Pittance return because they had insurance but show no reimbursement for two doctor bills totaling $1,300 (Drs. Thomas and Dartoli), without any obvious explanation. The auditor would not be concerned about the amounts paid to the two dentists or the optometrist, because most insurance does not reimburse for these services. Besides the possibility of insurance reimbursement, the medical expense catches the eye because of the round, even numbers: $300, $1,000, $150, $250.

The exemption for Martha involves a smaller amount ($1,900) than most of the other issues classified and so automatically ranks lower. Neither is it unusual for parents to be supported by their children. In this case, however, the mother is not living with the Pittances, so it is likely she has some independent means of support. That support may be a husband, a savings account, a widow's pension, or good old social security. If she has taxable income, e.g., interest on a savings account, of more than $1,900, then she cannot be claimed as an exemption. If her income is all nontaxable, the Pittances would still have to be sending or giving Mom more than half of what it costs her to live all year. Nowadays that can run pretty high, and the Pittances are already spending a goodly sum to support themselves. Can they afford to support Mom, too? All this is speculation, of course, but the auditor is only trying to gauge whether the audit will be fruitful at this point. When all the facts come to light, there may indeed be no issue, but when a return is being classified, the laws of probability apply.

Why were those six issues picked to the exclusion of others? Some deductions are too small to bother with. This is relative, however. The Pittance return is like a banquet where there are more issues to pick from than there is adequate time to audit. If possible, an auditor likes to limit the audit to three or four juicy issues. Selecting six, as I did, is stretching the limit, although it seems warranted in this case. Because the auditor can't audit every item on a return (with some exceptions already noted), a few deductions are going to slide by and get home free. On the Pittance return, which is overripe with issues, some smaller deductions are going to escape audit where they might not on another return. A five-hundred-dollar expense, which would be overshadowed on the Pittance return, would loom large on one on which the highest deduction is six hundred dollars.

Most of the miscellaneous expenses (Schedule A) are "small" on Noel and Annie's return. I would like to know what S.A.C.S.B. stands for, but I'm not going to audit it to find out. I can always make that part of the conversation in the interview. Home mortgage interest (line 19) and real estate taxes (line 16) are high but not out of line for Southern California today. Unless I doubt that the Pittances actually own a home, there is no reason to go into it. (Interest and taxes can almost always be easily verified if paid, which means they have low audit potential.)

The child-care expense, of $2,000 (Form 2441), computes to one hundred sixty-seven dollars per month, which does not seem unreasonable for the care of one (or two) children outside the home. Both Noel and Annie work and, on the face of the return, qualify to take the child-care credit. Two children claimed as exemptions on a joint return would not be classified unless fraud were suspected (usually as a result of information provided by an informant). Please note that although child care has been eclipsed as an issue on this return, it is more often than not classified for audit, because the expense is normally high in relation to other deductions on a return and because too many taxpayers pay cash and so encounter problems of proof.

Now that we have identified our issues, let's begin the audit.

THE AUDIT

Noel and Annie Pittance are a couple in their early thirties. They are shy, eager, nervous. To put them at ease and to gather useful background information, the auditor asks a few preliminary questions. They have never been audited before. Noel works for the brokerage firm of Davis, Gerrar, Fineman, Inc., on a commission basis. Annie is a licensed vocational nurse (LVN) at St. Luke's Hospital. She works the day shift, from 7 A.M. to 3 P.M. Nadine, their daughter, is eight years old and in the third grade. Martin is four and is cared for by Barbara Lawson during the day. Noel began working at Davis two years ago, after working his way through business school at night as a real estate appraiser. Annie has been an LVN for nine years.

Noel admits that most of the brokers in his firm buy and sell stock regularly. He has been slowly accumulating a portfolio and bought five thousand dollars' worth of stock in 1987. To date he has not sold any stock; he wants more experience as a broker before he begins active trading. Noel cannot remember receiving any other taxable income in 1987 than the amounts shown on the return. Asked whether they had any nontaxable income in that year, Noel says they might have. He cannot be more specific. They had about one hundred dollars cash on hand throughout the year. S.A.C.S.B. stands for the Society of American Commissioned Stock Brokers.

As part of the background information, the auditor is trying to pin down the Pittances' sources of income. She will use their statements later in the audit to determine whether to pursue unreported income as an issue.

CASUALTY/THEFT LOSS

The Pittances were burglarized on December 27, 1987. They had taken Nadine and Martin to Disneyland and returned to find their home broken in to and almost all of their valuables missing. They had no insurance coverage for their household belongings. Noel has a police report for the theft (shown here). They have no receipts for any item over six months old. However, some of the stolen items were Christmas presents, newly purchased, for which they still have receipts.

The police report confirms that the Pittances actually sustained a burglary. The auditor examines the entire report, but she is primarily interested in four facts: (1) the date of the burglary, (2) evidences of a burglary, (3) what items the Pittances reported stolen, and (4) whether any of the stolen property was recovered.

Page____ of_____ 03.01.0 (R.3/87)

Los Angeles Police Department

PRELIMINARY INVESTIGATION of Burglary

☐ Combined EVID Report ☐ MULTIPLE DRS ON THIS REPORT

SHOTS FIRED ☐

PRELIMINARY CASE SCREENING

- ☒ SUSPECT/VEHICLE NOT SEEN
- ☒ PRINTS OR OTHER EVIDENCE NOT PRESENT
- ☒ MO NOT DISTINCT
- ☐ PROPERTY LOSS LESS THAN $5000
- ☒ NO SERIOUS INJURY TO VICTIM
- ☐ ONLY ONE VICTIM INVOLVED

INVEST DIV: — DR: 872485564

VICTIM

LAST NAME, FIRST, MIDDLE (FIRM IF BUSINESS)	SEX	DESC	AGE	DOB
Pittance, Noel J.	M	C	33	2/18/54

ADDRESS	ZIP	PHONE
R- 726 Date Palm Vista, Hollywood	90028	467-1248
B- 9200 City Plaza, Los Angeles	90053	748-6001

DR. LIC. NO. (IF NONE, OTHER ID & NO): E04824330 — OCCUPATION: Broker

PREMISES (SPECIFIC TYPE): Residence

ENTRY 459/BFV: ☒ FRONT ☐ REAR ☐ SIDE ☐ ROOF ☐ FLOOR ☐ OTHER

POINT OF ENTRY: Front Door — POINT OF EXIT: Kitchen

METHOD: Pried Door, Window Rmvd

INSTRUMENT/TOOL: Crowbar

USE OF FORCE ☐

LOCATION OF OCCURRENCE: 726 Date Palm Vista — SAME AS V'S ☒ RES. ☐ BUS. — R.D. — PRINTS BY PREL INV ATTEMPT Y N OBTAINED Y N

DATE & TIME OF OCCURRENCE: 12-27-87 0945-1830 Hrs — DATE & TIME REPORTED TO PD: 12-27-87 2145 Hrs

TYPE PROPERTY STOLEN/LOST/DAMAGED ☐ 3.4 GIVEN: Personal Articles — STOLEN/LOST: $ 5960 — RECOVERED: $ — — EST. DAMAGED ARSON/VAND. $

VICT'S VEH. (IF INVOLVED) - YEAR, MAKE, TYPE, COLOR, LIC. NO. — NOTIFICATIONS (PERSON & DIVISION) — CONNECTED REPORTS (TYPE & DR)

MO IF LONG FORM, LIST UNIQUE ACTIONS. IF SHORT FORM, DESCRIBE SUSPECT'S ACTIONS IN BRIEF PHRASES, INCLUDING WEAPON USED. DO NOT REPEAT ABOVE INFO. BUT CLARIFY REPORT AS NECESSARY IF ANY OF THE MISSING ITEMS ARE POTENTIALLY IDENTIFIABLE, ITEMIZE AND DESCRIBE ALL ITEMS MISSING IN THIS INCIDENT IN THE NARRATIVE

NARCOTICS STOLEN–NARC. DIV. ☐ — DOMESTIC VIOLENCE ☐

REPORTING EMPLOYEE(S)	INITIALS, LAST NAME	SERIAL NO.	DIV./DETAIL
	E. Duran	87654	Hwd

PERSON REPORTING SIGNATURE x — OR RECEIVED BY PHONE ☐

NOTE: IF SHORT FORM AND VICTIM/PR ARE NOT THE SAME, ENTER PR INFORMATION IN INVOLVED PERSONS SECTION.

Complete below sections if any Preliminary Case Screening boxes are not checked.

DSD (GAS)/CRASH ☐

SUSP'S VEHICLE YEAR — MAKE — MODEL — TYPE — COLOR (S) — VEH. LIC. NO. — STATE

Interior COLOR: 1 BUCKET SEATS 2 DAMAGED INSIDE

Exterior: 1 CUSTOM WHEELS 2 PAINTED INSCRIPT. 3 LEVEL ALTERED 4 RUST/PRIMER 5 CUSTOM PAINT 6 VINYL TOP

Body: 1 DAMAGE 2 MODIFIED 3 STICKER 4 LEFT 5 RIGHT 6 FRONT 7 REAR

Windows: 1 DAMAGE 2 CUST TINT 3 CURTAINS 4 LEFT 5 RIGHT 6 FRONT 7 REAR

	SEX	DESC.	HAIR	EYES	HEIGHT	WEIGHT	AGE	CLOTHING	NAME, ADDRESS, DOB, IF KNOWN; NAME, BKG. NO., CHARGE, IF ARRESTED.
S-1									
S-2									

PERSONAL ODDITIES (UNUSUAL FEATURES, SCARS, TATTOOS, ETC.) — Weapon (VERBAL THREATS, BODILY FORCE, SIMULATED GUN, ETC. IF KNIFE OR GUN, DESCRIBE FULLY)

FIREARM STOLEN/LOST - DHD & R&I CRIME/PROPERTY TT SPVR. ☐

INVOLVED PERSONS W-WITNESS R-PERSON RPTG. S-PERSON SECURING (459) D-PERSON DISCOVERING (459) P-PARENT

NAME	SEX	DESC	DOB	ADDRESS	CITY	ZIP	PHONE
DR. LIC. NO. (IF NONE, LIST OTHER ID & NO.)				R- / B-			
				R- / B-			

NARRATIVE 1) LIST ADD'L SUSPS., VICTS., & INVOLVED PERSONS. 2) RECONSTRUCT OCCURRENCE, INCL. ALL ELEMENTS OF CORPUS DELECTI. 3) IF NOT USING EVID. CONTINUATION FORM, DESCRIBE EVIDENCE INCLUDE PRINTS. STATE LOCATION FOUND AND BY WHOM. GIVE DISPOSITION. 4) SUMMARIZE OTHER DETAILS, INCL. WHEN & WHERE PERSONS WITH NO PHONE CAN BE LOCATED. 5) INDICATE TYPE OF TRANSLATOR NEEDED FOR ANY INVOLVED PERSON. 6) LIST ITEMS MISSING.

ITEM # — QUAN. — ARTICLE — SERIAL # — BRAND — MODEL # — MISC. (COLOR, SIZE, INSCRIPTIONS, CALIBER, ETC.) — DOLLAR VALUE

Vict. states he and family left home on 12-27-87 0945 Hrs for Disneyland. Vict. returned at 1830 Hrs and home had been broken into and articles of value were missing. Vict. did not give permission to anyone to use or remove prop. Ofcrs. invest. revealed signs of force entry. Neighbors reported no susp. activity or sounds of break-in. Vict. states the following items have been removed: Computer, Stereo, TV, Tape Recorder, Misc. Cash, Camera, Tea Set, Misc. Records, Men's Watch, Costume Jewelry, Misc. Bottles of Wine, 10-Speed Bicycle

EXTRA COPY TO: ______

VICTIM INDEMNIFICATION INFORMATION (IF APPLICABLE):

IS ANY OF THE VICTIM'S PROPERTY MARKED WITH AN OWNER APPLIED IDENTIFICATION NUMBER? IF "YES", EXPLAIN IN NARRATIVE. YES ☐ NO ☒

APPROVAL AND REVIEW	SUPERVISOR APPROVING	SERIAL NO.	DETECTIVE SUPERVISOR REVIEWING	SERIAL NO.
	Sgt. Schappel	12345		
	DATE & TIME REPRODUCED	DIVISION / CLERK		Category ______

The date the theft was discovered determines in what tax year the loss is deductible. According to the police report, the break-in was discovered and reported on December 27, 1987, so the loss is being claimed in the right year. The date raises another question, however. An auditor is always more comfortable with a loss that occurs early in the tax year. A loss in December has the look of last-minute tax planning, all the more so the closer the loss comes to December 31. All it takes is a telephone call to obtain that important police report. The police come out, the taxpayer tells them he has been robbed, they leave, and he has an instant deduction. In December, a taxpayer's fancy sometimes turns to thoughts of lower tax. In a few cases, these thoughts next turn to theft loss. Obviously, casualty and theft losses know no season, and many legitimate losses occur in December, but you should be aware that a year-end loss may make your auditor wary.

That is why evidences of a burglary are important. The Pittances reported a burglary, so the police should have found signs of a breaking and entering. Looking at the Pittance police report, we see that the front door showed evidence of having been pried with a crowbar and that the kitchen window had been removed frame and all. These signs of forcible entry corroborate the Pittances' oral testimony that a burglary occurred. The auditor is now reasonably satisfied that there was a loss.

The auditor must now determine the amount of the loss. To do this, she needs to know what items were stolen. When the police arrived, the Pittances had taken stock of their loss and were able to tell the police what articles were missing and their value. This information is included on the police report. Sometimes, in the confusion and shock of a theft, a taxpayer will give the police an incomplete list; often it is several days before he discovers every item that is missing. At that point he should, and usually does, amend the police report so that the police have a complete list of the items stolen. The auditor will accept this amendment to the police report as proof that those additional items were stolen if the amendment was made within a reasonable time after the theft and if the items that were overlooked originally were of a kind whose loss might not be immediately apparent (for example, jewelry kept in a drawer, but not your console TV set or your couch). An amendment made after you received your notice of audit will not be accepted. There was no amendment to the Pittances' police report. The value of any item not reported stolen would probably not be allowed, and the auditor will compare the police report against any list of stolen articles the Pittances submit.

Finally, the auditor looks to see if the police recovered any of the stolen items. If there was a recovery and the articles were not damaged, only a partial loss or no loss would have been incurred. There is no indication on the police report submitted by Noel and Annie whether the police later got their man. Noel and Annie swear they have never laid eyes on their valuables again. The auditor knows that recovery in such cases is rare. Unless she requires other information anyway or has serious doubts about the Pittances' credibility, the auditor will not ask them to prove their oral testimony by getting a corroborating statement from the police.

The auditor now believes that a theft loss did indeed occur, and she is willing to allow a deduction. She knows what items were stolen. Her next step is to determine the amount of the loss. The amount of a theft loss is the *lesser* of: (1) the fair market value (FMV) of the item or (2) the taxpayer's adjusted basis in the property (usually what the item cost). As most property ages, it depreciates in value, so that it is not worth as much in the marketplace when it is a year old as when it was new. The "fair market value" of an item (what a willing buyer would pay a willing seller in the open marketplace) is therefore usually smaller than the taxpayer's basis (cost) and is used as the measure of the taxpayer's loss. Fair market value is generally abbreviated as FMV. If an item, such as a piece of jewelry or a painting, appreciates in value as it gets older, then the amount of the loss would be the taxpayer's basis (cost), rather than the higher FMV.

Annie gives the auditor a list of the items taken plus what receipts they have. The list shows what each item cost, its age, and what FMV the Pittances placed on it. This fair market value matches the amounts they gave the police for inclusion on the police report. The auditor copies the list and adds two columns of her own: (1) whether there is a receipt showing the Pittances' basis in the item and proving that they did indeed own it and (2) whether the item was reported stolen to the police. The completed list appears as follows:

Item	Cost	FMV Claimed	Age	Receipt?	Reported?
(1) Cash	$500	$500	—	—	yes
(2) Garnet diamond ring	450	700	5 years	no	no
(3) Pentax SF1	295	295	new	yes	yes
(4) Records—approx. 30	240	175	various	no	yes
(5) Stereo	600	500	3 yrs	no	yes
(6) Watch—men's quartz	250	250	new	no	yes
(7) Bicycle	125	125	new	yes	yes
(8) Assorted costume jewelry	?	110	various	no	yes
(9) 19″ portable color TV set	395	350	1 yr	no	yes
(10) Silver tea service	730	775	6 mos	yes	yes
(11) Mini-cassette recorder	80	80	new	no	yes
(12) Apple II computer	2,675	2,675	new	yes	yes
(13) Wine	125	125	various	no	yes
Total		$6,660			

The fair market value claimed by the Pittances is an estimate. They say they had never had any of the items appraised, nor did they do any research to find out the FMV of the older items. In effect, the Pittances are telling the auditor their figures are incorrect. They have no basis for the FMV they show; they picked them out of the air as a best guess when the police asked them to come up with numbers—*any* numbers—to put down on the police report.

By now you should know that the Pittances are not going to win this guessing game. The burden of proof is on them, and they cannot *prove* their estimates are right. I have said that in a case like this the auditor's guess is as good as the taxpayer's. Actually, because of the burden of proof, the auditor's guess is better.

The auditor will go down this list, item by item, and decide what she believes the fair market value should be. Quite often she has no more idea than the taxpayer does what the FMV was at the time an article was stolen. She hasn't even seen it; she has only the taxpayer's description. She doesn't know if it was in mint condition or looked as if it had been run over by a truck. But she doesn't have to prove that her guess is right. Because the taxpayer has failed to prove the true amount of his loss, he can dispute the auditor's finding only by proving it is wrong. The FMV determined by the auditor is strictly subjective. It is a personal judgment based on constant exposure to casualty and theft losses claimed on returns and the knowledge that almost all taxpayers tend to overvalue their property. In a society that values the new, used property (unless it is an antique) does not command high prices in the marketplace. Even with inflation, the fair market value of property several years old is seldom as high as most taxpayers think it is.

Auditors' judgments of fair market value will vary. The Pittances' auditor has made adjustments as shown below. The column labeled "Loss Allowed" reflects her judgment of the fair market value (or the lesser basis in the case of the silver tea service [10]). No loss has been allowed for the garnet diamond ring (2), because it was not included on the police report and there was no amendment. The column labeled "Adjustment" shows the difference between what the Pittances claimed on their tax return and the amount allowed by their auditor.

Item	*Cost*	*FMV Claimed*	*Loss Allowed*	*Adjustment*
(1) Cash	$500	$500	$100	$400
(2) Garnet diamond ring	450	700	0	700
(3) Pentax SF1	295	295	295	0
(4) Records—approx. 30	240	175	90	85
(5) Stereo	600	500	240	260
(6) Watch—men's quartz	250	250	125	125
(7) Bicycle	125	125	125	0
(8) Assorted costume jewelry	?	110	50	60
(9) 19″ portable color TV set	395	350	250	100
(10) Silver tea service	730	775	730	45
(11) Mini-cassette recorder	80	80	80	0
(12) Apple II computer	2,675	2,675	2,675	0
(13) Wine	125	125	40	85
Total		$6,660	$4,800	$1,860

Although the Pittances reported five hundred dollars cash stolen, the auditor has only allowed them one hundred dollars. The fair market value of five hundred dollars cash is five hundred dollars, so why was this adjustment made? Unless the Pittances can show that they had five hundred dollars lying around the house, they are going to lose at least part of the amount they claimed. This will happen whenever a taxpayer claims a loss of cash in a substantial amount. It is the exception, not the rule, to keep hundreds of dollars in the house or on one's person, instead of in a bank. Therefore it is more likely the Pittances did not have that much cash in the house than that they did. If Noel or Annie can show a substantial withdrawal of cash from a bank account that week or prove they received a check for which there is no corresponding deposit on their bank statements, they may be able to change the auditor's mind. For the present, one hundred dollars has been allowed, because, at the beginning of the audit, Noel said they always kept about one hundred dollars cash on hand at all times.

Items (3), (7), and (12), which are new (Christmas presents) and for which the Pittances have receipts, have been allowed at their proven cost basis. The fair market value should approximate the cost when an item is brand-new. The cassette recorder (11) has also been allowed as claimed, even though the Pittances do not have a receipt. The item is included on the police report, the amount seems to closely reflect the cost of such an item, and other articles have been allowed without receipts. The Pittances' oral testimony is being accepted here based on the auditor's overall belief in their credibility.

The auditor, having accepted the fact that a theft occurred, has been willing to allow losses for items that the Pittances cannot prove they ever owned: (4), (5), (6), (8), and (9). This is a case in which the auditor can allow reasonable amounts based on the taxpayers' oral testimony if she believes they are telling the truth. The auditor is not obligated to make any allowance, however, for any item if the taxpayer cannot verify his basis or ownership. If the Pittances' auditor had decided to take this stand, she would have allowed only a loss for the articles the Pittances kept receipts for: the Pentax camera, the bicycle, the silver tea service, and the computer. The total loss allowed in that case would have been only $3,825, instead of $4,800. Because whether to accept the Pittances' oral testimony is entirely within the auditor's discretion, either amount could be allowed and upheld. This is why you must win your auditor's confidence. The Pittances were able to do so here because they did have solid documentation to prove the theft, in addition to four receipts that matched the amounts claimed on their return. The Pittances took a loss of $6,660 and have been allowed $4,800. However, because ten percent of the Pittances' adjusted gross income must be deducted from the allowable loss, the auditor will wait until the audit is completed to compute the correct deduction.

AUTOMOBILE AND ENTERTAINMENT EXPENSE

Noel has brought in a letter (reproduced here) from his employer, Davis, Gerrar, Fineman, Inc., stating he is required to use his automobile for business and expected to entertain old and prospective clients. He receives no reimbursement for entertainment. He was reimbursed a flat rate of $225 per month for using his automobile for business purposes.

When an employee claims business expenses, a letter such as this one from Noel's employer is essential. The letter should state the employee's duties, what expenses he is required to incur for business, which of those expenses are reimbursed, and at what rate or amount. Reimbursement or lack of it must be covered in the letter; it is not enough for the employer to say that the taxpayer is required to use his car or entertain for business without mentioning whether reimbursement is available. If the letter is silent on this subject, the taxpayer will be considered to have been reimbursed.

The letter from Noel's employer is adequate to show that any expenses he paid for automobile or entertainment in excess of his reimbursement will be deductible. It does not prove he actually had any expense. Noel himself is required to keep records to verify the amounts. The reimbursement he received is no clue to how much he spent, because it is a fixed amount. No matter what Noel's actual expense is, he receives $225 per month. He may have spent more, but he could also have spent less.

Let's audit Noel's automobile expense first, then move on to entertainment. The back of the Form 2106 (appearing at the beginning of this chapter) shows the auditor how Noel computed his deduction of

November 3, 1988

To Whom It May Concern:

Re: Employee Noel J. Pittance

Title: Commission Broker

Duties: Mr. Pittance was responsible for maintaining relationships with the major accounts of this corporation, as well as being assigned the responsibility of obtaining new accounts.

In such capacities, Mr. Pittance was required to use his own automobile for business purposes. Toward the expenses incurred through the use of his auto, Mr. Pittance was reimbursed $225.00 per month by this corporation, a total of $2,700 for 1987. It was understood that Mr. Pittance's auto expenses might exceed this amount; however, due to his position and compensation, Mr. Pittance was expected to be responsible for such additional amounts.

With regard to entertainment expenses, all major expenses were paid by Mr. Pittance. It was expected that Mr. Pittance would pay for entertaining expenses, in order to maintain current accounts and bring in new ones.

Allen H. Fineman
Executive Vice-President

$5,393 before reimbursement. Using the actual-expenses method gave him a larger deduction than using the mileage rate. The actual-expenses method tallies up all of the automobile's operating expenses for the year plus depreciation. The percentage of miles driven for business use (75 percent in Noel's case) is then multiplied by the total expenses to arrive at the cost of operating the car for business.

To use this method as Noel has, receipts must be kept for all operating expenses, in addition to a record of the business miles driven. When asked for his receipts, Noel hands over the contract of sale for his Honda and two repair bills totaling $140. He has no gasoline receipts, because he pays cash and didn't realize he could get a receipt unless he used a credit card. He could probably dig up the canceled checks for his insurance payments if he had to.

Without adequate receipts, Noel's allowable deduction will have to be computed using the mileage rate instead. This rate is $.225 per mile. The auditor must now determine how many business miles Noel drove. This should be easy, because the law requires Noel to keep a log or diary setting down how many miles he drove and for what business purpose. All the auditor has to do is total Noel's entries. Where is the log? Noel admits somewhat sheepishly that he doesn't have one, but he sure will from now on.

At this point the auditor can say, "No log, no deduction," write a fat zero next to "Amount Allowed," and move on to entertainment. But she won't. Why not? Because Noel's employer has confirmed the fact that he did drive for business. The auditor is fairly convinced Noel incurred some expense, and automobile is another area where she is allowed to accept oral testimony. It will take a little longer, it will be less exact, and Noel will probably lose on the deal, but his business miles can be reconstructed by asking the right questions.

Noel has produced two repair bills for his Honda, which is a stroke of fortune for his auditor, if not necessarily for Noel. An auditor can perform miracles with two repair bills. I exaggerate, but they do come in mighty handy. This is because it is industry practice to write the odometer reading on a repair bill. Given two mileage readings spaced somewhat far apart and a faint knowledge of ratio and proportion, an auditor can be reasonably certain of the total miles a taxpayer drove during the year. From there it is possible to compute the business and the personal miles and come up with a number that only does a slight injustice to reality.

HONDA PARTS AND LABOR WARRANTY: 90 DAYS OR 4000 MILES.
WARRANTY VALID ONLY AT AUTHORIZED HONDA DEALER.

COST	QTY	PART NO	DESCRIPTION	SALE AMOUNT

CROSS REFERENCE
REPAIR ORDER NO.

TOTAL

SUBLET	P O NO	INV NO	CUSTOMER INITIAL

SUBLET TOWING

WE RECOMMEND THE FOLLOWING REPAIRS

ALL PARTS REMOVED WILL BE DISCARDED UNLESS INSTRUCTED OTHERWISE
SAVE ☐ DISCARD ☐

OUR LABOR RATE IS $39.00 PER FLAT RATE HOUR.

I acknowledge that I was informed that the above repairs are necessary, but I declined to have them done.
X

HONDA AUTOMOBILES

KLEIN-FOREMAN MOTORS
5511 VAN NUYS BOULEVARD
VAN NUYS, CALIFORNIA 91401
873-1776 • 786-1314

B.A.R. # AM-83843

KEY NO

TIME PROMISED AM PM

SELLING DEALER

RO#
WRO#

DATE 12/03/86

CUSTOMER'S NAME: NOEL PITTANCE
ADDRESS: 726 DATE PALM VISTA
CITY: HOLLYWOOD
ZIP CODE
ADVISOR
COLOR
DELIVERY DATE

YEAR	LICENSE NO	TYPE OR MODEL	SERIAL NO
86	1RVU261	ACCORD	

PHONE-RES.	PHONE-BUS.	MILEAGE	ENGINE NO
	748-6001	21,628	

I hereby authorize the repair work to be done along with the necessary material, and hereby grant your employees permission to operate the vehicle herein described on streets, highways or elsewhere for the purpose of testing and/or inspection. **SUBJECT TO CONDITIONS ON REVERSE SIDE OF THIS CONTRACT. PLEASE READ REVERSE SIDE.**
CUSTOMER ACKNOWLEDGES RECEIPT OF A COPY HEREOF

WE RESERVE THE RIGHT TO REFUSE SERVICE TO ANYONE.

Do not do more than the estimated work. If necessary to do more to complete the job properly, please call me at ______. I understand that if we have not made contact the job will be stopped until proper authorization is received.

CUSTOMER'S AUTHORIZATION X

PLEASE READ YOUR PINK COPY.

TIME UNITS	REPAIR ORDER - LABOR INSTRUCTIONS	LABOR CHARGE
	CHECK FLUID LEVELS	
	CHANGE OIL	
	CHANGE OIL FILTER CART	
	CHG TRANS & DIFF OIL	
	CHANGE AIR CLEANER	
	CHANGE FUEL FILTER	
	ADJ BRAKES	
	ADJ CLUTCH	
	ADJ VALVES	
	CHANGE COOLANT	
	REPLACE PLUGS	
	ELECT TUNE TIMING & DWELL	
	COMPRESSION 1 / 2 / 3 / 4 / ☐ MAINTENANCE SERVICE MILES	
	56 BATTERY	59 99
	TOW CAR TO STATION	25 00

QTS. OIL
MAN TRANS OIL @
AUTO. TRANS. OIL
TOTAL OIL & FLUID

ALL SHOP WORK
CASH ____
CHECK ____ CREDIT CARD ____

ORIGINAL ESTIMATE $ | REVISED ESTIMATE $ | CONTACT VIA IN PERSON ☐ PHONE ☐

DATE | PERSON CONTACTED | CUSTOMER'S DRIVER'S LICENSE #

TIME | I acknowledge notice and oral approval of an increase in the original estimated price X

INTERNAL SUMMARY

ACCT	CHARGE	COST

SS #

* SHOP SUPPLIES	
MECH. LABOR/LUBE	25 00
RADIO LABOR	
PARTS	59 99
ACCESS.	
OIL AND FLUID	
SUBLET	
SALES TAX	3 90
TOTAL AMOUNT	88 89

ACCOUNTING COPY

Reynolds + Reynolds LITHO IN U.S.A. 1287 L80000

HONDA PARTS AND LABOR WARRANTY: 90 DAYS OR 4000 MILES.
WARRANTY VALID ONLY AT AUTHORIZED HONDA DEALER.

KLEIN-FOREMAN MOTORS
5511 VAN NUYS BOULEVARD
VAN NUYS, CALIFORNIA 91401
873-1776 • 786-1314

HONDA AUTOMOBILES

KEY NO

BAR # AM-83643

TIME PROMISED AM PM

RO#

WRO#

COST	QTY	PART NO	DESCRIPTION	SALE AMOUNT

CROSS REFERENCE REPAIR ORDER NO. ____ TOTAL

SUBLET	PO NO	INV NO	CUSTOMER INITIAL

SUBLET TOWING

CUSTOMER'S NAME: NOEL PITTANCE
ADDRESS: 726 DATE PALM VISTA
CITY: HOLLYWOOD
ZIP CODE
YEAR: 86 LICENSE NO: 1RVU266 TYPE OR MODEL: ACCORD SERIAL NO
PHONE-RES PHONE-BUS MILEAGE: 34,979 ENGINE NO: 13629R7D3

SELLING DEALER
ADVISOR
COLOR
DELIVERY DATE

DATE: 8/28/87

I hereby authorize the repair work to be done along with the necessary material, and hereby grant your employees permission to operate the vehicle herein described on streets, highways or elsewhere for the purpose of testing and/or inspection. **SUBJECT TO CONDITIONS ON REVERSE SIDE OF THIS CONTRACT. PLEASE READ REVERSE SIDE.**
CUSTOMER ACKNOWLEDGES RECEIPT OF A COPY HEREOF

WE RESERVE THE RIGHT TO REFUSE SERVICE TO ANYONE.

Do not do more than the estimated work. If necessary to do more to complete the job properly, please call me at ____________. I understand that if we have not made contact the job will be stopped until proper authorization is received.

CUSTOMER'S AUTHORIZATION X

PLEASE READ YOUR PINK COPY.

TIME UNITS — REPAIR ORDER - LABOR INSTRUCTIONS

COMPRESSION 1/ 2/ 3/ 4/ ☐ MAINTENANCE SERVICE

	LABOR CHARGE
CHECK FLUID LEVELS	
CHANGE OIL	
CHANGE OIL FILTER CART	
CHG. TRANS & DIFF OIL	
CHANGE AIR CLEANER	
CHANGE FUEL FILTER	
ADJ BRAKES	
ADJ CLUTCH	
ADJ VALVES	
CHANGE COOLANT	
REPLACE PLUGS	
ELECT TUNE TIMING & DWELL	
MILES	
CERT. CAR CARE	15 50
CHANGE ENG OIL	28 00
REP ENG OIL FILTER CART	7 50

QTS. OIL @
MAN. TRANS. OIL @
AUTO. TRANS. OIL
TOTAL OIL & FLUID

ALL SHOP WORK
CASH ____
CHECK ____ CREDIT CARD ____

ORIGINAL ESTIMATE $ REVISED ESTIMATE $ CONTACT VIA: IN PERSON ☐ PHONE ☐
DATE PERSON CONTACTED CUSTOMER'S DRIVER'S LICENSE #
TIME I acknowledge notice and oral approval of an increase in the original estimated price
X

WE RECOMMEND THE FOLLOWING REPAIRS

INTERNAL SUMMARY

ACCT	CHARGE	COST

* SHOP SUPPLIES	
MECH. LABOR/LUBE	
RADIO LABOR	
PARTS	
ACCESS.	
OIL AND FLUID	
SUBLET	
SALES TAX	
TOTAL AMOUNT	

ALL PARTS REMOVED WILL BE DISCARDED UNLESS INSTRUCTED OTHERWISE
SAVE ☐ DISCARD ☐

OUR LABOR RATE IS $39.00 PER FLAT RATE HOUR.

I acknowledge that I was informed that the above repairs are necessary, but I declined to have them done.
X

SS #

Reynolds + Reynolds LITHO IN U.S.A. 1287 L80888

ACCOUNTING COPY

Noel's repair bills are shown here. One repair bill is dated December 3, 1986; the other is dated August 28, 1987. That is a nine-month spread, and it should reflect the pattern of Noel's driving. The auditor would use them if they were only weeks apart, however, because it is all she has to work with. In December 1986, the mileage on Noel's car was 21,628 miles; in August it was 34,979. Subtracting the earlier reading from the later one, the auditor knows Noel drove 13,351 miles in a nine-month period. By multiplying 13,351 times 12/9, the auditor projects that the total miles driven by Noel for twelve months was 17,801. Looking at the form 2106, Part II, line 2, we see that Noel estimated his total mileage at 25,000 miles. From the repair bills he presented, that figure seems to be about 7,000 miles too high.

The auditor has now arrived at the total number of miles driven (17,801)—this includes driving for all purposes, both business and personal. Only the number of business miles is deductible. If the auditor can determine how much (nondeductible) personal driving Noel did and subtract that amount from the total miles driven, the remainder will be the number of business miles.

Driving to and from the office every day is commuting and is considered personal. The auditor notes that Noel has not filled in this requested information on Form 2106 (Part II, lines 5 and 6). This could be mere carelessness on his part, but it could also be an attempt to cover the fact that business use is actually less than 75 percent.

Noel says he goes to the office at seven every morning, when the stock market opens. At noon, when the market closes, he makes the rounds of his clients, either taking them out to lunch or visiting them at their homes or offices. He then returns to his office before going home. He says he lives three miles from his office.

If Noel's home is three miles from the office, he commutes six miles each day, five days a week, or a total of thirty miles each week. Noel says he took two one-week vacations in 1987. He therefore worked fifty weeks. His total commuting for the year was thirty miles per week times fifty weeks, or fifteen hundred miles.

The auditor asks if Noel used the Honda on his vacation, and Noel says yes, Annie and he drove to Las Vegas both times they were off: Las Vegas is 294 miles one way from Hollywood. Two round trips equal 1,176 miles (294 miles × 4), to be added to the

1,500 miles Noel commutes. What about other personal driving around town? Annie uses her own car to do the shopping, to take Nadine to school and Martin to the sitter, and to go to church. Noel has no idea how much personal driving he does. The auditor settles for 1,100 miles.

Noel's personal driving in 1987 has now been estimated at 3,776 miles (1,500 miles commuting, 1,176 miles to Las Vegas, and 1,100 miles for other personal driving). None of this mileage is deductible and must be subtracted from the total miles driven that year to arrive at business mileage. The total miles driven were 17,801 minus 3,776 personal miles equals *14,025 business miles.*

The auditor is going to use the mileage rate to compute the allowable deduction. Noel therefore can deduct $.225 per mile times 14,025 miles or $3,156.

Noel points out, however, that he forgot to take a deduction for parking fees (Form 2106, Part I, line 2). He kept no record of how much he spent, but "obviously I had to spend something." The auditor allows $120, about $10 a month. This amount is purely arbitrary, because Noel has no records. The auditor knows parking is a real and often high expense. She is willing to make an allowance, but without any records, she is not inclined to be overly generous. Noel's compliance with the record-keeping requirements for automobile expense has been extremely lax. The amounts shown on the Form 2106 apparently resulted from sheer guesswork, because he has no receipts to back up any of the numbers. Because of the lack of evidence, the auditor has also resorted to guesswork, and she knows that the 14,025 figure for business miles may just as easily be too high as too low. Thus she may be giving Noel more than he actually deserves, even though the amount is substantially less than he claimed. With this in mind, the auditor is going to minimize any credit she gives Noel for parking fees.

Noel's total allowable deduction is now $3,276 ($3,156 mileage plus $120 parking). Noel claimed expenses of $5,393. The auditor's adjustment, on which the Pittances will owe additional tax, is $2,117.

Noel's entertainment expense (Form 2106, Part I, line 5) is also being questioned. We have already seen the letter from his employer stating he is expected to entertain and that he receives no reimbursement. Because Noel works on commission, the entertainment of clients and prospective clients can have a direct effect on his commission and may increase his total earnings. For these reasons, the auditor agrees that whatever entertainment expense Noel can prove he incurred will be allowed as a deduction.

The record-keeping requirements for entertainment expense are governed by the Internal Revenue Code, section 274. A taxpayer must substantially comply with these rigid requirements or he will not be entitled to a deduction. Entertainment is one of the few deductions concerning which the auditor has no discretion to allow reasonable amounts based on the taxpayer's oral testimony. *Proof is everything.*

What proof is required? In order to meet the "adequate records" requirement of section 274(d), a taxpayer must keep an account book, a diary, or receipts in or on which *five* elements of each entertainment expense are recorded: (1) the amount, (2) the date, (3) the place, (4) the business purpose of the entertainment, and (5) the name of the person entertained and his business relationship to the taxpayer. These elements must be recorded at or near the time of the expense, not later, when your memory may be fuzzy.

Although the Code does not require you to keep receipts for individual expenses under twenty-five dollars, if you are recording your expenses in a diary, it is nevertheless wise to keep them. An auditor may ask to see receipts in order to verify that your diary is accurate. Diaries are easy to create—all a taxpayer needs is a pen and a notebook—and auditors prefer independent verification that the entries have some basis in fact. Unless an auditor is satisfied that the diary or other account book is genuine and timely kept, she does not have to allow the deduction, no matter how perfectly the five elements are set down.

Noel has kept records, but they are a motley assortment: a calendar/diary showing some of the elements, some credit-card slips, and some restaurant stubs. The diary appears to have been maintained at the time, and the auditor believes it is genuine. Two weeks' entries are shown here. The diary shows the date, the name of the person entertained, and the amount. Now and then the name of the restaurant appears, but not consistently. With a few excep-

MONDAY MARCH 24
thru
SUNDAY MARCH 30

february

S	M	T	W	T	F	S
					1	2
3	4	5	6	7	8	9
10	11	12	13	14	15	16
17	18	19	20	21	22	23
24	25	26	27	28	29	

march

S	M	T	W	T	F	S
						1
2	3	4	5	6	7	8
9	10	11	12	13	14	15
16	17	18	19	20	21	22
23/30	24/31	25	26	27	28	29

april

S	M	T	W	T	F	S
		1	2	3	4	5
6	7	8	9	10	11	12
13	14	15	16	17	18	19
20	21	22	23	24	25	26
27	28	29	30			

may

S	M	T	W	T	F	S
				1	2	3
4	5	6	7	8	9	10
11	12	13	14	15	16	17
18	19	20	21	22	23	24
25	26	27	28	29	30	31

Monday March 24 84/282

8 VIC MARTIN
STUDIO GRILL
9 $15.15
10
11
12
1
2
3
4
5
evening

Tuesday March 25 85/281

8
9
10
11
12
1
2
3
4
5
evening

Wednesday March 26 86/280

8 1130
MS KELLER
9 $23.56
10
11
12
1
2
3
4
5
evening

Thursday March 27 87/279

8 DRINKS 7 50
9 BILL BERRY
10 YAMASHIRO'S
11 8 25
12
1
2
3
4
5
evening

Friday March 28 88/278

8 EXCHANGE
9 930
10
11
12
1
2
3
4
5
evening

Saturday March 29 89/277

Sunday March 30 90/276

AT-A-GLANCE®

september						
S	M	T	W	T	F	S
	1	2	3	4	5	6
7	8	9	10	11	12	13
14	15	16	17	18	19	20
21	22	23	24	25	26	27
28	29	30				

october						
S	M	T	W	T	F	S
			1	2	3	4
5	6	7	8	9	10	11
12	13	14	15	16	17	18
19	20	21	22	23	24	25
26	27	28	29	30	31	

november						
S	M	T	W	T	F	S
						1
2	3	4	5	6	7	8
9	10	11	12	13	14	15
16	17	18	19	20	21	22
23/30	24	25	26	27	28	29

december						
S	M	T	W	T	F	S
	1	2	3	4	5	6
7	8	9	10	11	12	13
14	15	16	17	18	19	20
21	22	23	24	25	26	27
28	29	30	31			

MONDAY OCT. 20 thru SUNDAY OCT. 26

Monday Oct. 20 294/72

8 ERNEST TUBBS

9 $12.37

10

11

12

1

2

3

4

5

evening

Tuesday Oct. 21 295/71

8 CALL JIM

9

10

11

12

1

2

3

4

5

evening

Wednesday Oct. 22 296/70

8

9

10

11

12

1

2

3

4

5

evening

Thursday Oct. 23 297/69

8

9

10

11

12

1

2

3

4

5

evening

Friday Oct. 24 298/68

8 EL CHOLLO

9 RON CALLAHAN

10 $36.85

11 5:30

12

1

2

3

4

5

evening

Saturday Oct. 25 299/67

Sunday Oct. 26 300/66

AT-A-GLANCE®

tions, then, the diary shows only three of the required elements. Based on the diary alone, Noel would not be allowed any deduction for entertainment expense.

The credit-card slips and restaurant stubs provide a fourth required element, however: the place. By matching the dates on these receipts with the diary entries, the auditor can tell where the person named in the diary was entertained. The receipts also confirm the auditor's initial impression that the diary is accurate, because she can cross-check the dates and amounts on the receipts against the diary.

Four out of the five elements have now been met. But the Code says five, and four is not good enough. Noel could have gotten a zero deduction with a lot less fuss; he didn't have to bother with keeping records at all. The Code does provide a measure of grace, however, by allowing deductions where the taxpayer has *substantially complied* with the requirements of adequate records but has failed to establish a particular element of an expense. Noel may be redeemed after all.

There is no set definition of "substantial compliance." Whether Noel has substantially complied is a decision the auditor must make after considering the facts and circumstances of each case. If, in the auditor's judgment, Noel's records show substantial compliance, he will be permitted to establish the missing element, in this case the business purpose, by whatever evidence the auditor deems adequate.

Noel's auditor decides to accept his diary entries if Noel indentifies each of the named persons by occupation or job title and tells her whether each was already a client or merely a prospect, and if the latter, whether that person ever became a client. In listening to Noel's oral testimony, the auditor will try to pick out hesitation, inconsistency, or other evidence that he is not telling the truth.

Noel is able to convince his auditor that he had a legitimate purpose for wining and dining all the named individuals. The auditor now totals the amounts entered in the book and discovers that they add up to $954. Noel has claimed $1,454 on his tax return, and the auditor wants to know why there is a $500 discrepancy. Noel explains that he spends money almost every day that it is impossible for him to keep track of: doughnuts, coffee, drinks for clients. He knows that he probably spent more than $500, but that was all he put down because he didn't want to seem too unreasonable. "Everybody knows you've got to spend money to make money," Noel says, "and $500 doesn't seem too high when you look at how much I earned." The auditor is unmoved by the logic of his argument. Noel has not satisfied any of the five required elements. Noel is allowed only the $954 he has verified. Only 80 percent of this amount, or $763, is deductible. There is a $400 ($500 × 80 percent rule) adjustment to the amount Noel claimed for entertainment expense.

CONTRIBUTIONS EXPENSE

As we have already noted, Contributions (Schedule A) is going to present problems of proof for the Pittances, and the auditor begins the audit of this expense reasonably sure she will be able to make adjustments. This knowledge has been reinforced by the relatively large adjustments to Noel's automobile and entertainment expense. The substantial adjustments in those areas plus some overvaluation on the theft-loss deduction have combined to make the auditor increasingly skeptical about the accuracy of the Pittances' tax return. This may begin to affect her acceptance of their oral testimony where receipts are missing.

The Pittances have several canceled checks, a statement from their church, and a receipt from Goodwill for articles of furniture and clothing that they donated. Annie also has pay stubs to show her payroll deductions for United Way.

The auditor first adds up the canceled checks. There are checks for one hundred dollars to the Disabled Veterans, ten dollars to the Boy Scouts, and twenty dollars to the Heart Association. All are qualified organizations, the checks are genuine, and Martin is too young for the donation to the Boy Scouts to have been a membership fee. The one hundred thirty dollars' worth of checks are allowed. Next the auditor examines the pay stubs, which show ten dollars being withheld for charity every pay period, for a total of two hundred sixty dollars. This is also allowed without question.

The church statement submitted by the Pittances is shown here. It

Greater New Bethlehem
Congregational Church
1719 West Lime St.
Los Angeles, CA.

To Whom It May Concern:

The gift of offering and tithes given to the church by Mr. and Mrs. Pittance was \$220.00. This was for the year of 1987.

Our church records show the same information sent to your office.

Very truly yours
Rev. Malcolm R. Smith

confirms that the church records show contributions of two hundred twenty dollars from Mr. and Mrs. Pittance in 1987. The statement is signed by the church's minister. After a careful examination, the auditor tells the Pittances the statement is not acceptable. Why? Look at the letterhead. What letterhead? It is highly unusual for a church not to have printed letterhead stationery. The Pittances' statement with the name of the church written in by hand is therefore suspect. The auditor wonders if it isn't a crude attempt from a do-it-yourself receipt kit.

The Pittances swear the statement is authentic, and the auditor decides to call the minister for confirmation. The minister says he remembers writing the statement, and the reason it is not on regular church stationery is because the supply in his desk had run out and he was too busy at the moment to replace it. Because of the minister's corroboration, the two hundred twenty dollars is allowed. (Note: Whenever possible, make sure duplicate receipts or statements look official and authentic. If the auditor had been unwilling to make that phone call, the Pittances would have had to go back to the church and ask for a new statement on letterhead paper.)

The amount of contributions for which the Pittances have receipts has now been verified in full. From here on out, the Pittances must rely on their wits and whatever credibility they have built up with the auditor. The audit is moving into the region where the Pittances have no tangible proof.

Annie explains that the donation to KCET was made during one of the station's fund-raising drives. Because they enjoy public television, they give every year. The station is close to where they live, and they drive over and give seventy-five dollars cash. The auditor asks if they got anything in return, and Annie says they got a book for donating. She is able to name the book and its author, and the auditor decides that they really did make the donation. However, the value of the book must be subtracted from the amount given. Annie and the auditor settle on twelve dollars as the value of the book, and the balance of sixty-three dollars is allowed as a deduction.

Similarly, when the Muscular Dystrophy telethon is held every year, the Pittances take Nadine and Martin down to the television studio to see the show. They give the children fifty dollars to take down to one of the circus clowns who pass a bucket around, and the

GOODWILL *Industries*
of Southern California

MAIN PLANT
342 SAN FERNANDO RD.
LOS ANGELES, 90031
(213) 223-1211

DATE PROMISED / /

NAME
NOEL AND ANNIE PITTANCE

ADDRESS
726 DATE PALM

CITY
HOLLYWOOD, CA

CROSS STREET

PHONE NO.	OPERATOR	DATE RECEIVED
467-1248		6 / 27 / 87

MAP
PAGE # DISPATCH #

SPECIAL INSTRUCTIONS: OUTSIDE ☐ REAR ☐ FRONT ☐

365514

APPLIANCES-SM		FURNITURE	X	STOVE	
BOOKS	X	HIDE-A-BED		TOOLS	
BOX SPRINGS		HOUSEWARES		TOYS & GAMES	
CARPETING		MATTRESS		TV, RADIO, STEREO	
CLOTHING & SHOES	X	OFFICE FURN. & EQ.		WASHER	
DRYER		REFRIGERATOR		WHEEL TOYS	

Thank You

John Garner 6-27-87
DRIVER/ATTENDANT DATE PICKED UP

TIME

YOUR CONTRIBUTION IS TAX DEDUCTIBLE WITH YOUR FAIR ESTIMATE OF ITS VALUE. SAVE THIS RECEIPT

CUSTOMER COPY

Ⓟ M

clown gives them each a balloon and a button with Jerry Lewis's picture on it. Short of asking Annie to describe the clown's costume, the auditor believes her testimony could not be any more complete, and the fifty dollars is allowed.

The thirty dollars paid to the Los Angeles County Museum turns out to be amounts paid for admission and not deductible. The total amount of church contributions claimed is five hundred twenty dollars. This is a round three hundred dollars more than indicated on the submitted church statement.

"That's only the amount the church records show," Noel says, "but they don't have a record of everything we gave, just what we put in the envelope. Lots of times, we just drop money in the plate without using the envelope."

"And there's the money we give Nadine for Sunday school, plus what I spend to bake cookies," Annie adds.

The auditor decides it is plausible the Pittances spent small amounts that didn't find their way into the church records. Without receipts, she does not have to allow the Pittances anything, and as we have noted, she has reason to doubt the accuracy of the return. She allows an additional fifty dollars as reasonable, if not overly generous, instead of the three hundred dollars claimed.

The last contribution claimed is for property donated to Goodwill. The Pittances have a receipt for this contribution, shown here. The receipt tells the auditor that a donation was made—period. It does not tell exactly what property was given or its value. As with the Pittances' theft loss, the value of the property has been estimated by them without an appraisal. As with the theft loss, the auditor will make her own estimate of the fair market value of the items donated, and this will be the amount that is allowed.

The Pittances have compiled a list of the articles they gave away. They have no receipts for the purchase of these items, but unlike the theft loss, there is no real question whether the articles existed. The receipt from Goodwill confirms this. Without the purchase receipts, the Pittances' basis cannot be established, but, for all the items donated, the fair market value, not the basis, is the allowable deduction.

Listing all the articles, plus the Pittances' estimate of their cost, age, and fair market value, the auditor goes through the same process she used to determine the amount of the theft loss:

Item	*Cost*	*Age*	*FMV Claimed*	*FMV Allowed*	*Adjustment*
Sofa	$799	4 yrs	$500	$300	$200
Coffee table	200	3 yrs	150	75	75
2 lamps	95	2 yrs	65	45	20
2 men's suits	360	3 yrs	275	120	155
4 dresses	260	various	120	80	40
1 wool coat	240	5 yrs	150	90	60
2 boxes of books	400	various	200	75	125
3 pairs running shoes	60	various	40	10	30
Total			$1,500	$795	$705

The auditor's judgment of fair market value is uniquely her own. The IRS provides no official guidelines. Some auditors and groups do their own research to come up with approximate figures, and their experience in other cases helps. But in every case where the taxpayer cannot supply a competent figure himself, the result is going to be the auditor's best guess, and that guess will almost certainly be less than the taxpayer claimed.

When taxpayers give items to Goodwill, the Salvation Army, and others, the biggest audit adjustments are to the values placed on articles of clothing. The measure of the deduction is fair market value, and used clothing sells for very little in the market. Some used clothing, like underwear, has almost no fair market value. Ask yourself what you would pay for a similar piece of used clothing at a thrift shop or garage sale.

Of the $2,565 claimed for contributions by the Pittances, they have verified or been allowed $1,568. The audit adjustment is $997.

RENTAL DEPRECIATION AND REPAIRS

The duplex owned by the Pittances is over four years old. When they purchased the property in 1984, they decided what their basis in the building should be and what depreciation method to use. Having determined these figures, they set up the depreciation schedule shown below. They have been using this schedule since 1984. The auditor wants to verify two things: whether $135,000 is the

Depreciation

(a) Class of property	(b) Date placed in service	(c) Basis for depreciation (Business use only—see instructions)	(d) Recovery period	(e) Method of figuring depreciation	(f) Deduction
Residential rental property	07-16-84	135,000	18	ACRS	10,800

correct basis and whether the Pittances have chosen the correct depreciation method.

The allowable recovery period and percentage depend upon the date rental property is placed in service. The auditor can quickly verify that the recovery period for real estate placed in service on July 16, 1984, is eighteen years. An official depreciation table tells her the correct recovery percentage should be 8 percent. So far the Pittances have maneuvered through some trickly legal ground successfuly.

To compute the Pittances' basis in their duplex, the auditor asks to see the escrow papers (or contract of sale) showing the purchase price of the property and the 1984 real-estate tax bill indicating the appraised values of the land and building in the year of purchase (or a qualified appraisal by a private firm). The Pittances have brought both of these documents as requested.

According to the escrow papers, the duplex cost $180,000. This price includes both the building and the land, but only the building can be depreciated. It is the basis of the building alone that must be calculated. The real-estate tax bill is used for this purpose.

The Pittances' tax bill is reprinted here. It contains a box with the heading "Assessed Value." Inside that box, the auditor sees that in 1984 the assessed value of the land was 15,225 and the assessed value of the building (improvements) was 28,275. The total assessed value of both was 43,500. These are not dollar amounts, and the auditor is not interested in whether the assessed values agree with what the Pittances paid for the property. She uses these figures to determine the value of the building relative to the land. The total assessed value is 43,500, of which 28,275, or 65 percent, is allocable to the building.

If the building accounts for 65 percent of the property's assessed value, then the cost (or basis) of the building alone, exclusive of land, was 65 percent of the total purchase price, or $117,000 ($180,000 × .65). This amount is the basis the auditor will use to compute the allowable depreciation, instead of the $135,000 used by Noel and Annie.

1984

1st INSTALLMENT

2nd INSTALLMENT

JOINT CONSOLIDATED TAX BILL

CITIES, COUNTY, SCHOOLS AND ALL OTHER TAXING AGENCIES IN LOS ANGELES COUNTY

SECURED PROPERTY TAX FOR FISCAL YEAR JULY 1, 1984 TO JUNE 30, 1985

RICHARD B. DIXON, TREASURER-TAX COLLECTOR
225 N. Hill Street, Los Angeles, California
P.O. Box 2102 Term. Annex Los Angeles, CA 90051

TELEPHONE INFORMATION
SEE PARAGRAPH 1 ON
REVERSE SIDE

OWNER OF RECORD AS OF MARCH 1, 1984

AVERY

ASSESSOR'S ID. NO.

2633 039 019

PITTANCE, NOEL J. AND
ANNIE M.
1890 MANGO DRIVE
LOS ANGELES, CA 90068

PROPERTY LOCATION AND/OR PROPERTY DESCRIPTION

1890 MANGO DRIVE LOS ANGELES
TRACT NO. 009 LOT 23

ACCOUNT NO	SEQUENCE NO	REG.	DIVISION INDEX	ASSESSOR'S ID. NO. MAP BOOK	PAGE	PARCEL	TRA
	1004468	03		2633	039	019	0013

LOCALLY ASSESSED VALUES IN THIS COUNTY ARE DETERMINED BY THE LOS ANGELES COUNTY ASSESSOR AT FULL VALUE EXCEPT AS OTHERWISE PROVIDED BY LAW.

	ASSESSED VALUE	EXEMPT. TYPE	EXEMPTION VALUE	NET ASSESSED VALUE
1. LAND	15225			
2. IMPROVEMENTS	28275			
3. FIXTURES				
4.				
5. TOTAL REAL PROPERTY	43500	HOME		43,500
6.				
7.				

ASSESSED VALUE OF REAL PROPERTY	43,500	
HOMEOWNER'S EXEMPTION..............		
TOTAL APPLICABLE TAX RATE..............	2.86933	
GROSS TAXES BEFORE APPLICATION OF HOMEOWNER'S EXEMPTION		1248.16
TAX REDUCTION ATTRIBUTABLE TO STATE-FINANCED HOMEOWNER'S TAX RELIEF PROGRAM***SEE PARAGRAPH NO. 7 ON REVERSE SIDE		.00
TOTAL TAX AFTER ALLOWANCE FOR HOMEOWNER'S EXEMPTION............		1248.16
PERSONAL PROPERTY, DIRECT ASSESSMENT OR SPECIFIC LAND LEVY		.00
TOTAL TAXES DUE		1248.16

YOUR CANCELLED CHECK IS YOUR RECEIPT

KEEP THIS UPPER PORTION OF THE BILL FOR YOUR RECORDS

SEE REVERSE SIDE FOR IMPORTANT INFORMATION

DETACH - HERE

DETACH DETACH

ADDRESS CHANGE FORM

IF YOUR MAILING ADDRESS IS DIFFERENT FROM THAT ABOVE FILL IN THE BOXES ON THIS FORM, DETACH AND RETURN WITH YOUR PAYMENT.

2633 | 039 | 019 | PITTANCE

NAME PITTANCE, NOEL J.

HOUSE NUMBER, STREET NAME AND UNIT NUMBER

CITY	STATE	ZIP CODE

CURRENT DATE

The auditor has not changed the recovery percentage, but she has changed the basis, which means a new schedule of depreciation will have to be set up for the Pittances, and their depreciation recomputed. The original basis should have been $117,000, but a higher figure was used, and $28,350 depreciation has already been taken in prior years. This is $3,780 more than would have been claimed if the correct basis had been used ($28,350 − $24,570 correct depreciation). The auditor must, therefore, reduce the new basis by the excess depreciation taken. Seventy-nine percent of the basis remains to be recovered. To recoup the excess depreciation, the auditor must decrease the $117,000 basis by $4,785 ($3,780 = 79% of $4,785). This adjusted basis will be depreciated over the remaining fifteen-year life of the building. Multiplying $112,215 times 8 percent, the correct recovery percentage, results in a depreciation deduction of $8,977. Because the Pittances claimed depreciation of $10,800, there is an audit adjustment here of $1,823.

Rental repairs were classified because of the possibility that the Pittances may have mistakenly deducted a capital expenditure as a repair. The auditor now discovers that this is exactly what happened.

In July 1987, Noel decided to put in a patio running the length of the duplex in the back. Because a patio adds to the value of the property, it must be considered a capital expenditure. Instead of deducting the entire expense in 1987 as a repair, the Pittances must deduct the cost of the patio over the remaining life of the building. It will be depreciated in the same way the building is.

First, however, the cost of putting in the patio must be established. The auditor asks for all documents relating to the patio, and Noel hands over four: (1) a receipt from Quarry Masters showing the purchase of flagstone for 1890 Mango Drive at a cost of one thousand dollars; (2) a receipt, with canceled check attached, from Potter's Building Supply for one hundred dollars' worth of mortar mix; (3) a receipt from Jack Clayton for four hundred dollars; and (4) a canceled check made out to Stan Brogan for two hundred fifty dollars (the latter two shown here). Noel says they also paid about two hundred dollars cash to neighborhood children for digging up the grass and smoothing out the ground.

The receipts for the flagstone and mortar present no difficulties. They specify the items purchased, they show the amounts paid, the date matches Noel's testimony, and the delivery address for the

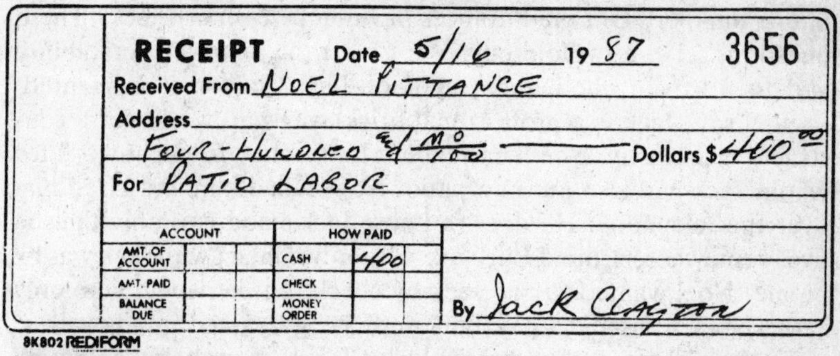

RECEIPT Date 5/16 19 87 3656

Received From NOEL PITTANCE

Address

FOUR-HUNDRED & NO/100 Dollars $ 400 00

For PATIO LABOR

ACCOUNT			HOW PAID	
AMT. OF ACCOUNT			CASH	400
AMT. PAID			CHECK	
BALANCE DUE			MONEY ORDER	

By Jack Clayton

8K802 REDIFORM

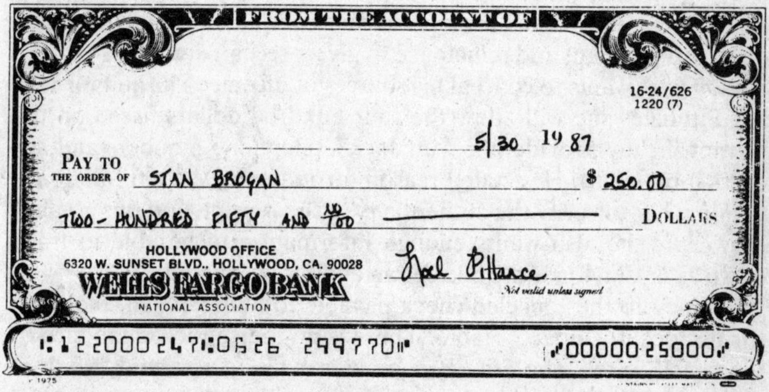

FROM THE ACCOUNT OF

16-24/626
1220 (7)

5/30 19 87

PAY TO THE ORDER OF STAN BROGAN $ 250.00

TWO-HUNDRED FIFTY AND NO/100 DOLLARS

HOLLYWOOD OFFICE
6320 W. SUNSET BLVD., HOLLYWOOD, CA. 90028
WELLS FARGO BANK
NATIONAL ASSOCIATION

Noel Pittance

Not valid unless signed

⑆1220002471⑆0626 299770⑈ ⑈0000025000⑈

flagstone is the duplex, so that the auditor knows the patio was not for the Pittances' personal residence. The receipt from Jack Clayton is of the type bought in stationery stores. An auditor is somewhat wary of a receipt like this, because it could easily have been fabricated by the taxpayer himself. The use of such receipts by private individuals is common, however, and the auditor knows a labor expense would normally be incurred (unless Noel laid the patio himself).

The auditor is willing to accept the receipt if she can be convinced it is genuine. Jack Clayton's signature differs from the handwriting of either Noel or Annie on the front of the 1040, which proves only that if the receipt is a fake it is not an obvious one. The auditor wants to know who Jack Clayton is. Does he lay patios for a living, or is this how he picks up money in his spare time? How did the Pittances find out about him? What are his address and his telephone number? Did the Pittances pay him by cash or check? These questions serve a twofold purpose: to test the taxpayer's credibility and to discover whether an audit of Jack Clayton is warranted.

Noel says Jack is a professional bricklayer who works for a construction company. Noel heard about him from a friend at work for whom Jack had also put in a patio. Noel called him and hired him over the telephone. He doesn't know Jack's address, only that he lives somewhere around Burbank. His only contact with Jack was by phone. Noel wanted to pay Jack by check, but he would take only cash; Noel refused to pay him until he got a receipt, however.

To the auditor, it sounds as if Jack Clayton is probably operating a profitable, to date tax-exempt business on the side. The insistence on a cash payment and reluctance to give a receipt are indicative of a person who wants to conceal his sources of income. The auditor tells the Pittances she will allow the four hundred dollars based on the receipt if they provide her with Jack's telephone number (and address if possible). Her stated reason for requiring the information is to allow her to verify the authenticity of the receipt, and this is valid. However, she also wants enough information to be able to track down Jack Clayton if she decides an audit is warranted.

Coming to the canceled check payable to Stan Brogan, the auditor decides it is unacceptable. There is no indication on the face of the check to tell who Stan Brogan is or why he was paid two hundred and fifty dollars. Noel says he helped put in the mortar, but the auditor has already found enough discrepancies on the return and feels she has been generous enough. She could accept the Pittances' oral testimony, but at this point she decides to stand her ground and require adequate proof. As with Jack Clayton, she wants Brogan's address and telephone number. She also wants a statement from Brogan that the two hundred and fifty dollars paid to him in 1987 was for work on the patio. If she receives this information, she will allow the two hundred fifty dollars. The Pittances might have been able to avoid the auditor's doubt if they had made a memo entry on the check at the time it was written, stating what the payment was for. The auditor would probably still have requested Brogan's address and telephone number, however, so that she could locate him for audit if need be. This information is generally requested whenever a taxpayer is paying a private individual what amounts to taxable wages. The most common example is child-care payments made to a private sitter. Any taxpayer asked to prove these payments should bring the sitter's address and social security number, if known, to the audit. A written receipt from a sitter without this information will probably not be accepted.

Finally, there is the two hundred dollars Noel claims was paid in cash to the neighborhood children and for which he has no receipts. Without any evidence other than Noel's word to support this estimate, no allowance will be given.

If the information about Jack Clayton and Stan Brogan is forthcoming, the Pittances will have verified $1,750 as the total cost of the patio. The auditor will depreciate this amount over the eighteen-year life of the building and give Noel and Annie a deduction of one hundred five dollars for the improvement, based on a recovery percentage of 6 percent.

The balance of the rental repairs are verified by two receipts from Kenner Plumbing, one for one hundred sixty dollars and the other for three hundred ten dollars. Noel says the smaller amount was to fix a leaky faucet and the larger was to replace a section of water pipe that broke. Neither of these expenses is a capital expenditure, because they do not add to the value of the property or prolong its life, and the auditor allows them in full as repairs.

Noel has one last receipt, from M & C Hardware. The item purchased is described on the receipt only as MT308GB. The total price is $75.49, but the receipt shows only $5.49 paid. The date of the receipt is December 9, 1987. This receipt is inadequate to prove a deductible expense of $75.49. Why? The answer is probably obvious to most of you, even though you are not auditors. An auditor cannot tell from this receipt what Noel bought: was it a personal item for himself or his home instead of for the rental; was it a capital item, which should be depreciated, or a replacement part that can be classified as a current repair expense? An auditor also has no proof of payment. The receipt only proves $5.49 was paid. The item may have been on layaway and never purchased. If Noel did pay the balance, did he pay it in 1987 or 1988—if he waited a month to make the second payment, $70 should be deducted in the next tax year, 1988. No deduction will be allowed for this item unless Noel and Annie can produce more evidence.

If you have a receipt like the one from M & C Hardware, what should you do? Always write on the receipt at the time you get it

M&C HARDWARE

Date 12/9 1987

Mr NOEL PITTANCE

No.

Reg. No. Clerk — ACCOUNT FORWARDED

1	HT 3084B		70 88
2			
3	TAX		4 61
4			
5			75 49
6			
7			
8	PAID		5 49
9			
10			70 00
11			
12			
13			
14	002881- 8		
15			

Your account stated to date. If error is found return at once.

what the receipt is for. Put this information in a corner or margin, where it will be clear to the auditor that it is a memo to yourself and not as if you were trying to alter the receipt and make it something it's not. Do this any time you have a receipt, restaurant stub, or cash-register tape that lacks sufficient information for an auditor. Restaurant stubs are often completely blank, but if you fill them in at the time (don't forget all five elements if it is for entertainment), they should be acceptable. If a cash-register tape or restaurant stub lacks the date, add it, again making sure it is obviously written as a memo by you. If a receipt like Noel's only shows part payment, make sure the balance is paid by check, or if not, that you are given a second receipt marked PAID IN FULL.

After totaling up what the Pittances have verified or she has allowed for rental depreciation and repairs, the auditor finds that the allowable deduction for both items is $9,352. The Pittances had claimed $13,295 for both expenses, so there is an audit adjustment of $3,943. The Pittances are not doing too well.

EXEMPTION

Martha is Annie's mother, age sixty-seven, a widow, living in Oklahoma City in a house paid off nine years ago, before Annie's father died. Annie's father left her mother the house and a small savings account. He had been a self-employed small businessman, ill on and off for several years before he died, in 1983. His illness had used up most of his savings, and he had no retirement plan. His business died with him. In 1987, four years later, Martha was living on social security and interest from the savings account, plus whatever money Noel and Annie sent her.

Annie has a letter, written by her mother two weeks ago, that states that Noel and Annie provided over one half of her support in 1987 and are entitled to claim her as an exemption. The letter does not say how much money the Pittances sent Martha or how much she received in social security and interest. Standing alone, Martha's letter is not sufficient to allow the Pittances to claim the exemption. It requires independent evidence to back it up. Letters from relatives can be self-serving statements, because it is not usually difficult for a taxpayer to persuade a mother, father, brother, sister, son, or daughter to help him out in an audit. Blood is thicker than love for the IRS.

Even were the letter not potentially self-serving, it would still be inadequate, because there is no evidence that Martha is qualified to judge who is entitled to the exemption. She writes that Noel and Annie provided over one half of her support, and she is no doubt in a better position to judge this than the auditor, but the support test is only one of five tests that must be met before a person qualifies as an exemption. The auditor cannot rely on Martha's knowing and having applied all five of these tests; she must go through them individually herself.

The five dependency tests are as follows: (1) support test, (2) gross-income test; (3) member-of-household or relationship test; (4)

citizenship test, and (5) joint-return test. The auditor, however, is only really interested in the support test and the gross-income test. From the testimony Annie has already given, the auditor is fairly certain the other three tests are not in issue: a mother meets the relationship test, as a widow Martha would not be filing a joint return, and because of her long residency in Oklahoma City and with no reason to suspect otherwise, the auditor feels safe in assuming Martha is a U.S. citizen or resident.

The auditor's questions will be confined to determining whether Martha had nineteen hundred dollars or more of taxable income in 1987 and whether, as Martha says in her letter, the Pittances actually did provide over one half of her support. The first question she asks is how much social security Martha drew in 1987. Annie says she doesn't have an exact figure, but she believes it was about $525 per month. How much interest income did she have? Annie does not know, but she is sure it was less than fifteen hundred dollars. "Poor Father didn't leave much," she says.

At this point the auditor can disallow the exemption and move on to the next issue. Annie's lack of knowledge about her mother's interest income is fatal. The auditor has no assurance other than a vague belief on Annie's part that her mother's taxable income was less than nineteen hundred dollars. The gross-income test has not been met. Annie will have to prove the exact amount of interest her mother earned, probably by obtaining a copy of the year-end statement sent to Martha by her bank, before the auditor will be satisfied on this count.

Although she could disallow the exemption on account of the gross-income test, the auditor still wants to go into the support test and develop the facts needed to determine if this test was met. The auditor must have this information anyway if Annie proves that Martha's interest income was less than nineteen hundred dollars and the gross-income test is met. Furthermore, if the Pittances cannot show that they provided over one half of Martha's support, there will be no need for them to write for Martha's bank statement. If there is no chance the support test can be met, how much (or little) taxable income the mother had will be a moot question.

Continuing, then, the auditor asks how much money Noel and Annie sent to Martha. Annie produces twenty-five money orders in varying amounts totaling $5,400. This evidence is accepted reluc-

PURCHASER'S COPY OF PERSONAL MONEY ORDER DRAWN ON OFFICE SHOWN HEREON

90-3798/1222

April 21 19 87

PAID TO MARTHA WINN FOR $ **20.00**

NOT VALID OVER $500.00

***20 DOLS 00 CTS ***

CAPITAL BANK OF CALIFORNIA

MAIN OFFICE 1875 CENTURY PARK EAST, LOS ANGELES, CA 90067

#822

APR 21 1987

NOT NEGOTIABLE

The customer procuring the Personal Money Order form, corresponding in number and amount to that shown hereon, agrees to insert thereon in ink, the date, payee, his signature and address and assumes responsibility for all events made possible by his failure to do so.

SAVE THIS COPY FOR YOUR RECORD

PURCHASER'S COPY OF PERSONAL MONEY ORDER DRAWN ON OFFICE SHOWN HEREON

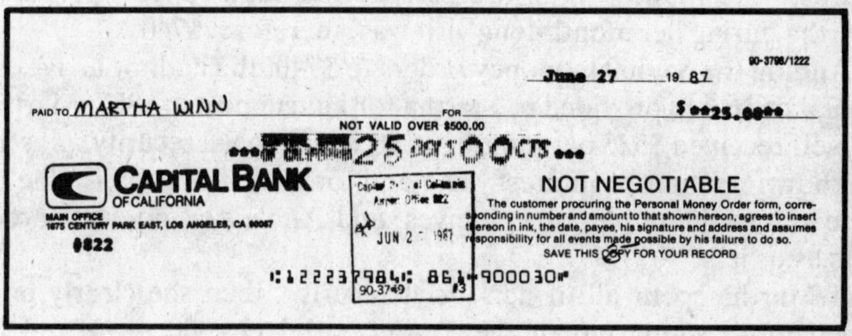
90-3798/1222

June 27 19 87

PAID TO MARTHA WINN FOR $ **25.00**

NOT VALID OVER $500.00

***25 DOLS 00 CTS ***

CAPITAL BANK OF CALIFORNIA

MAIN OFFICE 1875 CENTURY PARK EAST, LOS ANGELES, CA 90067

#822

JUN 2 1987

90-3749

NOT NEGOTIABLE

The customer procuring the Personal Money Order form, corresponding in number and amount to that shown hereon, agrees to insert thereon in ink, the date, payee, his signature and address and assumes responsibility for all events made possible by his failure to do so.

SAVE THIS COPY FOR YOUR RECORD

PURCHASER'S COPY OF PERSONAL MONEY ORDER DRAWN ON OFFICE SHOWN HEREON

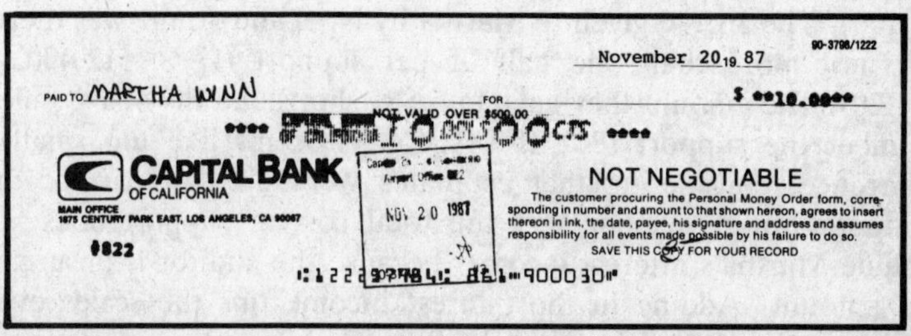
90-3798/1222

November 20 19 87

PAID TO MARTHA WINN FOR $ **10.00**

NOT VALID OVER $500.00

****10 DOLS 00 CTS ****

CAPITAL BANK OF CALIFORNIA

MAIN OFFICE 1875 CENTURY PARK EAST, LOS ANGELES, CA 90067

#822

NOV 20 1987

NOT NEGOTIABLE

The customer procuring the Personal Money Order form, corresponding in number and amount to that shown hereon, agrees to insert thereon in ink, the date, payee, his signature and address and assumes responsibility for all events made possible by his failure to do so.

SAVE THIS COPY FOR YOUR RECORD

tantly. Because money-order receipts are filled in by the purchaser, it is easy to use these stubs as evidence of payments that were never actually made. It is possible to leave them blank and fill them in at a later date, when proof of a specific expense is needed. For this reason, some auditors will not accept money-order receipts at all without other supporting evidence. If you must use money orders, at least make sure you fill them in completely at the time of purchase.

Besides the $5,400 the Pittances sent to Martha, they also provided support for her when she came to visit them in August for one month. During that time, Noel estimates, they spent $150 for her food, $300 medical expense, and $100 for recreation. Lodging must also be figured into the cost of support. The Pittances live in a four-bedroom house that cost $130,000 and was fifteen years old when purchased. Based on her knowledge of rents charged for similar housing in the area, the auditor judges that the fair rental value of the house would have been $800 per month. Martha's pro rata share of the fair rental value for one month would be $160. Her share of the utilities would be $30 according to Noel's oral testimony. Martha paid the round-trip airfare herself. The total support provided Martha during her month-long visit was, therefore, $740.

Adding the $5,400 in money orders to $740, the auditor arrives at a total of $6,140 provided to Martha for her support in 1987. Martha herself received $525 per month, or $6,300 in social security, plus an unknown amount of interest. The auditor asks if Martha is able to save any of the money she receives, and Annie says no, she barely gets by as it is.

If Martha spent all of her social security, then she clearly provided more support than the Pittances did ($6,300 compared to $6,140). Because she was unable to save any money, the total cost of her support must have been at least $12,440 ($6,300 plus $6,140). The $6,140 given to Martha by Noel and Annie was therefore not more than one half of her support (½ × $12,400 = $6,220). The amount they gave falls $81 short, and they have failed to meet the support test. If $81 dollars seems like too small a difference, considering that estimates were used in part of the computation, remember that the total cost of support does not include Martha's interest income, because the auditor is unsure of the amount. Adding in the interest income tips the scales even further in the IRS's favor, not the Pittances'.

The exemption for Martha is not allowed.

MEDICAL EXPENSE

The auditor's primary interest in examining the medical expense (Schedule A) is to discover if any of the claimed expenses were reimbursed by medical insurance. Her first step, then, is to find out what type of coverage the Pittances had. Free hospitalization for the entire family is one of the fringe benefits Annie receives as a nurse at St. Luke's Hospital. Doctors' expense is not provided, however, so Noel has $120 per month deducted from his paycheck for Blue Cross. He has his pay slips to verify that $1,440 is withheld yearly. Noel also has canceled checks, made out to American Assurance, totaling $300. He did not bring a copy of his insurance policy, but he says it pays $30 per day for every day he or Annie is disabled and cannot work. From Noel's description, the auditor believes this is disability insurance and not deductible. Blue Cross group insurance generally provides reimbursement for hospitalization and other medical expense and would therefore be deductible. The auditor allows a total of $1,440 for medical insurance.

To verify their drug expense, the Pittances have a mixture of canceled checks and receipts (two examples shown here). Annie says they also spent about $50 for other prescription drugs, but they didn't keep any receipts for these. The canceled checks are made out to Drug King, Payless Drugs, and Burnside Pharmacy in amounts totaling $83. None of these canceled checks, however, are acceptable as proof. Why? Because drugstores sell ballpoint pens, basketballs, blenders, and bicycles, as well as drugs and medicine. A canceled check payable to a drugstore is not evidence of what was purchased there. Only a receipt showing the prescription number is adequate to prove an expense actually was for drugs. The Pittances

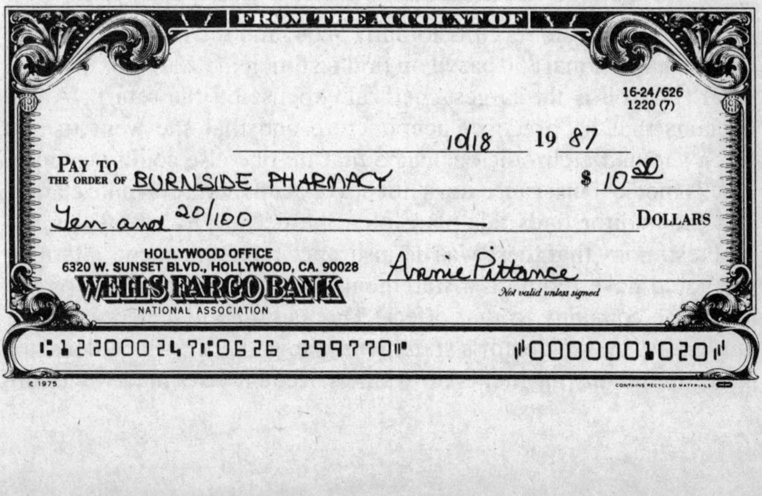

OscoDrug

PRESCRIPTIONS
Retain this receipt for tax and insurance purposes.

NAME: ANNIE PITTANCE
ADDRESS:
PHONE: DATE: 8-15-87

Rx # 758321
DOCTOR: MARWAN
PHONE: AMT.$ 11.19

Rx #
DOCTOR:
PHONE: AMT.$

do have acceptable receipts totaling $206, and the auditor agrees to allow an additional $50 based on oral testimony.

Dr. Dartoli is the largest medical expense on the return. Annie explains that he practices acupuncture and that she went to him when she had a chronic backache that no one else could diagnose. Noel's medical insurance does not cover acupuncture, Annie claims, and the auditor finds this plausible. She decides to accept Annie's oral testimony that there was no insurance reimbursement, although she could have required a statement from either the doctor or the insurance company to that effect. The auditor's judgment is borne out in part by the doctor's statement (shown here), which does not indicate that any payments on Annie's account were made by insur-

ACUPUNCTURE CLINIC

Dr. Dartoli

STATEMENT

MRS. PITTANCE
726 DATE PALM VISTA
LOS ANGELES, CA 90028

PLEASE RETURN THIS STUB WITH YOUR REMITTANCE. YOUR CANCELLED CHECK IS YOUR RECEIPT. $______

DATE	DESCRIPTION	CHARGES	CREDITS	BALANCE
12-30-87	Professional Services	$1000 -	$700	$300

PAY LAST AMOUNT IN BALANCE COLUMN ▲

REDIFORM® 8S 874

POLY PAK (50 SETS) 8P874

ance. However, this is not conclusive, because some doctors and hospitals record only that a payment was made and not the source. Examining the statement from Dr. Dartoli, the auditor notes that although the fees for his services totaled one thousand dollars, payments amounted to only seven hundred dollars. The statement date is December 30, so it would appear to cover all transactions on the account in 1987. The auditor does not know whether the balance of three hundred dollars was actually paid by insurance despite what

Annie said, whether it was paid in 1988, or whether it was never paid at all. No matter which may be true, seven hundred dollars was paid in 1987 and seven hundred dollars is what will be allowed.

Insurance did not cover Dr. Thomas's bill either, because the three hundred dollars was paid for Martha, Annie's mother, while she was visiting in August. Although the Pittances can verify this expense with a bill and a canceled check, it is not deductible, because the exemption for Martha was not allowed to them, for failure to meet the support test. The three hundred dollars paid to Dr. Thomas is not allowed.

The Pittances have canceled checks payable to Drs. Williams, Marwan, and Hillman for $660, $195, and $250, respectively. This totals $1,105, which is $60 more than is claimed on the tax return. Noel says his medical insurances does not cover dentists or optometrists. The auditor accepts this testimony and gives the Pittances credit for the full $1,105. She also accepts a canceled check for $70 payable to Western Radiology. Travel of $23 (256 miles at $ .09 per mile) is allowed as reasonable without question; it is too small to bother with auditing.

Seven and a half percent of the Pittances' adjusted gross income must be subtracted from the total allowable medical expense to arrive at the proper deduction. Because the auditor has made changes in the rental expense, the Pittances' adjusted gross income is now higher than it was when the original medical deduction was computed. The change in adjusted gross income will increase the final audit adjustment. However, the auditor has decided to wait before computing the correct medical deduction; she wants to make sure the Pittances have reported all of their taxable income first. If they have not, the adjusted gross income, and consequently the medical deduction, will change again, and the auditor does not want to duplicate effort by computing the deduction twice. The computation will be made later.

GAMBLING LOSSES

Noel says he and Annie faithfully buy one lottery ticket a week. However, the Big Spin has eluded them. Because gambling losses are not deductible unless used to offset gambling gains, the fifty-two dollars claimed will be disallowed by the auditor. This is called a statutory adjustment and is made automatically whenever a taxpayer takes a deduction not allowed by law. The Pittances were not asked to bring in any proof of this expense, because whether it was incurred or not is irrelevant.

TAXABLE INCOME

Before this audit started, the auditor had decided that it might be necessary to "probe" for unreported taxable income. This decision was not made because of any inside information; it was based upon an inspection of the tax return. If it turns out that the Pittances did indeed have income they failed to report on the tax return, the auditor will not know whether the income comes from moonlighting, stock transactions, savings accounts, or some other taxable source. She doesn't have to prove where the money is coming from, only that it must have been received. If the auditor arrives at this conclusion, the burden of proof will be on the Pittances to show that the auditor is incorrect.

One clue that there may be unreported income is evidence on the return that a taxpayer is spending more money than he claims to have earned. This is what has tipped off the auditor assigned the Pittances' return. Look at the complete return again. True, the Pittances have quite a bit of itemized expense, but $2,122 of it alone is a theft loss, which isn't really money spent. True, their rental loss is fairly high, but $10,800 of that is attributable to depreciation, and that is just a paper loss. The same is true for the automobile expense: $3,534 is depreciation on the Honda. And look at line 34 on page 2 of the 1040—even after all those deductions, the Pittances still have $17,149 left to spend. Add to that $14,334 in depreciation, and you have $31,483, more than some persons' total salary. This is just another case of an auditor harassing a taxpayer, right?

Not quite. Let's look at the return now with an auditor's eye. Do the Pittances really have $31,483 left to spend? The $31,483 is what remains of Noel and Annie's combined reported earnings after subtracting the money they spent for itemized expenses, rental expenses, and business expenses. But what *hasn't* been subtracted? Right on the return, the auditor can see five big items: (1) *$9,790* federal tax withholding (Form 1040, line 54); (2) *$4,241* FICA withholding (Form W-2, box 11); (3) *$2,000* child care (Form 2441)—this is deducted as a $400 credit from the tax on line 40 of the 1040; (4) *$4,217* subtracted from medical expenses ($3,329) and miscellaneous itemized deductions ($888), as adjusted gross income limitations (Schedule A, lines 3 and 23); and (5) *$1,225,* the amount by which total interest expense has been reduced (Schedule A, line 12b). These five items add up to $21,473 spent (or in the case of withholding, never received) in addition to the itemized, rental, and business expenses. What does that really leave the Pittances? $31,483 minus $21,473 equals $10,010. That's not a lot for a family of four (plus a mother) that is buying a house and making car payments and maybe even eating at regular intervals.

The audit so far has only confirmed her suspicions. Remember that income was not classified as an issue, because the auditor wanted to ask questions during the audit first before deciding to raise the issue. Also, the audit may have revealed that the Pittances did not spend what they claimed to, and in fact, the auditor will take any failure of proof into consideration when she finally does a complete comparison between expenses and income.

Two facts in particular brought out in the audit have served to convince the auditor that income needs some explaining. First, Noel's statement at the beginning of the audit that he purchased $5,000 worth of stocks that year, and second, the Pittances' money-order receipts showing $5,400 sent to Martha. These two expenses alone total $10,400, and as we have just seen, the Pittances only had $10,010 to spend, according to a rough computation from the return. This puts the Pittances $390 in the red without considering other expenses. There are no significant savings apparent from the return, nor do the Pittances rely heavily on credit card debt. The auditor now believes raising the issue is warranted.

An auditor reconstructs a taxpayer's income using what is known as an "indirect method." When a taxpayer is concealing income, there are no records for an auditor to examine, so she must arrive at an adjustment by a different route, or indirectly. By reconstructing the taxpayer's income and comparing it with the amount reported on the return, the correctness of the return can be proved or disproved.

There are three indirect methods available to the auditor: (1) source and application of funds, (2) bank-deposit analysis, and (3) net worth. For the Pittance return, the auditor is going to use source and application of funds, because it is the simplest method, and it can be computed from just the tax return and other facts developed during the audit. The basic premise of source and application of funds is to compare the Pittances' known income (source) against their known expenses (application). The auditor has already found out most of the information she needs from the audit, but she needs also to know more about the Pittances' personal living expenses, i.e., what they spent for food, clothing, recreation, personal driving, car payments, mortgage payments, utilities, and a variety of other day-to-day expenses.

In totaling up all the Pittances' expenses, the auditor will take care not to add in anything twice. For instance, the Pittances' monthly mortgage payment is $961. This includes payments on both principal and interest, but the home mortgage interest is already included on the return as an itemized expense (Schedule A, line 9). The auditor will add only the portion of the payment allocable to principal to the itemized expense, to avoid duplicating the interest.

For the items on the return that were audited, only the amounts that the Pittances verified they spent will be added to the computation. For example, although they claimed they paid Dr. Dartoli one thousand dollars, the Pittances only proved that they paid seven hundred dollars, so the auditor will use seven hundred dollars as an expense. If an item was not allowed by the auditor because it was not deductible, e.g., thirty dollars paid to the Los Angeles County Art Museum, but the Pittances proved the money was spent, it will be included as part of their total expenditures for the year. If an item was not classified, e.g., uniforms, the auditor will assume that the amount claimed was actually spent. Depreciation and the theft loss will not be included.

The auditor gives the Pittances a Form 4822 to fill out. On this form, the Pittances are asked to estimate their personal living expenses to the best of their recollection. They are told not to complete the section for itemized deductions, because the auditor will take these figures from the tax return and the audit. The figures Noel and Annie arrived at are shown here.

The auditor is now ready to begin her source and application of funds. The first step is to add up all of the Pittances' known sources of income:

Source	
Wages (W-2s)	$59,735
Interest income	68
Rental income	16,950
Employer reimbursement (auto)	2,700
Federal income tax refund (per Noel)	7,350
State income tax refund (per return)	726
Total known income	$87,529

Step 2 is to add all known expenses (application), using the figures determined during the audit, amounts not audited from the tax return, and amounts from the Form 4822 filled out by the Pittances:

Application	
Personal living expenses (from Form 4822)	$35,893
Itemized expenses:	
Medical	4,171
Taxes	4,248
Interest	14,177
Contributions (less items donated)	815
Miscellaneous (not including automobile and entertainment)	979
Automobile—Parking (balance included in personal living expenses above)	120
Entertainment/gifts	1,194
Rental expenses (excluding depreciation)	22,027
Child care	2,000
Money orders to Martha	5,400
Principal on rental mortgage (per Noel)	532
Total known expenses	$91,556

Form **4822** (Rev. 6-83)

Department of the Treasury - Internal Revenue Service

STATEMENT OF ANNUAL ESTIMATED PERSONAL AND FAMILY EXPENSES

TAXPAYER'S NAME AND ADDRESS

Noel J. and Annie M. Pittance
726 Date Palm Vista
Hollywood, CA 90028

TAX YEAR ENDED: 1987

Section		ITEM	BY CASH	BY CHECK	TOTAL	REMARKS
1. PERSONAL EXPENSES		Groceries and outside meals			$3600	$300 per month
		Clothing			900	
		Laundry and dry cleaning				
		Barber, beauty shop, and cosmetics			380	
		Education *(tuition, room, board, books, etc.)*				
		Recreation, entertainment, vacations			600	
		Dues *(clubs, lodge, etc.)*				
		Gifts and allowances			625	Christmas gifts
		Life and accident insurance				
		Federal taxes *(income, FICA, etc.)* FICA			4241	Per W-2
		Wittholding			9790	Per W-2
2. HOUSEHOLD EXPENSES		Rent				
		Mortgage payments *(including interest)*			858	$11534 - 10676 item. interest
		Utilities *(electricity, gas, telephone, water, etc.)*			560	
		Domestic help				
		Home insurance			450	
		Repairs and improvements			250	
		Child care				
3. AUTO EXPENSES		Gasoline, oil, grease, wash			1600	
		Tires, batteries, repairs, tags			188	
		Insurance			1780	
		Auto payments *(including interest)*			466	Noel's Honda $3540 - 3074 item. interest
		Lease of auto				
4. DEDUCTIBLE ITEMS		Contributions				
	Medical Expenses	Insurance				
		Drugs				
		Doctors, hospitals, etc.				
	Taxes	Real estate *(not included in 2. above)*				
		Personal property				
		Income *(State and local)*				
		Interest *(not included in 2. and 3. above)*				
	Miscellaneous	Alimony				
		Union dues				
5. PERSONAL ASSETS, ETC.		Stocks and bonds			5000	
		Furniture, appliances, jewelry			1200	
		Loans to others				
		Boat				
		Silver tea service			730	See theft loss
		Computer			2675	See theft loss
		TOTALS ▶			35893	

★ U.S. GOVERNMENT PRINTING OFFICE: 1983-381-541/5272

According to the auditor's calculations, the Pittances spent $91,556 and only received $87,529. This means there is a discrepancy of $4,027 ($91,556 minus $87,529) between the Pittances' reported taxable (and nontaxable) income and the amount they must have received. This difference must be explained or the auditor will add $4,027 to the Pittances' taxable income and they will be liable for tax on that amount.

The auditor shows the Pittances her computation and asks if they have any explanation for the difference. Because estimated figures have been used in portions of the source and application of funds, the auditor knows that $4,027 is not an exact amount. If the Pittances can explain most of the discrepancy, she will drop the issue.

Previously, Noel had stated that they may have received some nontaxable income in 1987, but he had not elaborated on that point. Now he says he believes 1987 was the year they borrowed $2,000 from his father. "Yes, it was that year," he says. "We needed help putting in the patio. We didn't have that much cash on hand."

The auditor asks if this was a loan, and Noel says that it was. The auditor points out that there is no interest expense to his father on the return. Noel says the loan was interest free, that his father didn't really care if he paid it back or not. The auditor is not willing to accept this explanation without proof; she asks Noel to get a statement from his father that the loan was made, a copy of the canceled check for $2,000, if available, and any canceled checks Noel has to show repayment.

This still leaves $2,027 unaccounted for. After several minutes' thought, Annie says she earned $1,500 working as a private-duty nurse in January of that year. She thought they had included it on the return, but maybe she forgot, because it was so early in the year. The auditor can find no evidence that the amount is on the return—there is only the one W-2 for Annie from St. Luke's Hospital. The private-duty nursing was for services performed through a nursing bureau for a private individual.

The auditor adds $1,500 to the Pittances' taxable income, and this becomes one of her audit adjustments. The auditor decides to also assert the negligence penalty because of the failure to report all taxable income. (Note: Failure to report taxable income may also be fraud. For a discussion of both fraud and negligence, see Chapter XV.)

One week later, the Pittances return. They have managed to find out the addresses of both Jack Clayton and Stan Brogan, who performed work on their patio. With this information, the auditor agrees to allow the labor expenses of $400 and $250 paid to these two men as part of the capital expenditure for the patio. The auditor had already computed this depreciation expense at $105.

Noel also has the requested statement from his father, confirming the loan of $2,000, plus the check payable to Noel for that amount. He has one check for $500 made out to his father, which he claims represents part of his repayment on the loan. This evidence is accepted by the auditor as proof of the loan.

The $2,000 loan plus the $1,500 earned by Annie sufficiently explain the difference of $4,027. As noted above, the auditor is working with estimates; once the Pittances have come up with sources of income totaling close to $4,027, the auditor has no further grounds to question their income, unless new information comes to light.

The auditor can now compute the Pittances' medical and theft loss deductions. She has made adjustments to their rental loss and taxable gross income, both of which affect the adjusted gross income and consequently the allowable medical expense and theft loss. The rental loss has been reduced by $3,738 and gross income has been increased by $1,500. These amounts, which total $5,238, are in effect being added back to the Pittances' adjusted gross income of $44,382 (Form 1040, line 30). Their new adjusted gross income is therefore $49,620 ($44,382 + $5,238). Using this figure, the auditor computes the medical deduction as shown on the form included here.

The Pittances claimed a medical expense of $1,159 on their return. Because seven and a half percent of their adjusted gross income now exceeds their allowable expenses, nothing is allowed. The adjustment is $1,159.

Medical and Dental Expenses **(Do not include expenses reimbursed or paid by others.)** (See Instructions on page 21.)					
	1a Prescription medicines and drugs, insulin, doctors, dentists, nurses, hospitals, insurance premiums you paid for medical and dental care, etc.	1a	3,501		
	b Transportation and lodging	1b	23		
	c Other (list—include hearing aids, dentures, eyeglasses, etc.) ▶LABORATORY	1c	70		
	2 Add lines 1a through 1c, and enter the total here	2	3,594		
	3 Multiply the amount on Form 1040, line 31, by 7.5% (.075)	3	4,962		
	4 Subtract line 3 from line 2. If zero or less, enter -0-. **Total** medical and dental ▶			4	0

The Pittances' casualty loss deduction suffers an identical fate. The auditor has allowed the loss of items with a fair market value of $4,300. However, this loss must be reduced by first $100, then by ten percent of adjusted gross income. Because ten percent of the Pittances' adjusted gross income is now $4,962, no deduction can be allowed for their $4,300 loss. The adjustment is $2,122, the amount claimed on form 4684.

The audit is now complete. It is time for the auditor to write up her final report, incorporating all the adjustments she has made. The Pittances' audit report appears in the next chapter, where you'll learn how to read and understand an audit report and what to do if you're unlucky enough to receive one.

XI. THE ENVELOPE, PLEASE

When all the evidence is in, your auditor will decide whether you are one of this year's winners. This determination may occur at the end of your first interview with the auditor or after you have submitted additional information requested by her. If you are in her office, she will explain the outcome to you, and you may ask questions. If not, you will find out the results through the mail; call your auditor is there is anything you don't understand.

There are three possible outcomes of an audit: (1) no tax due, (2) additional tax due, (3) a refund. If the wheel stops on (1) or (3), you are a winner. If it stops on (2), you have some decisions to make.

An audit that results in no additional tax is called a "no change" audit; that is, there is no change to the tax shown on your tax return. You get a no-change by verifying all of your deductions with those flawless records you have started to keep. You can also be given a no-change without perfect records if the tax result is negligible. When the audit is a no-change, there is nothing for you to do. Simply wait for a letter (DO 590) telling you that the "examination of your tax returns . . . shows no change is required in the tax reported. Your returns are accepted as filed."

No further action is required of you. Your audit is over. Pack your records away and go about your business. Just be sure you keep that no-change letter. Frame it if you want, but keep it handy. It may prevent you from being audited for the next two years. In Chapter IV, I told you about the IRS policy against repetitive audits, i.e., an audit on the same issues for which you received a no-change within the past two years. You may be asked to produce your letter if you claim a repetitive audit, but even if you aren't, the letter is insurance if another auditor wants a second look at that year.

Report of Individual Income Tax Examination Changes

Department of the Treasury
Internal Revenue Service

	Name of Taxpayer	Year	Form	Filing Status	In Reply Refer To:
1.	Noel J. and Annie M. Pittance	8712	1040	Joint	OE: 2114: EM

Name and Title of Person With Whom Changes Were Discussed	Date of Report	Social Security Number	Examining District
	11/19/88	978-26-1330	95

Income and Deduction Amounts Adjusted

2. Explanation Number (See attached)	3. Item Changed	4. Amount Shown on Return or as Previously Adjusted	5. Corrected Amount of Income and Deduction	6. Adjustment Increase (Decrease)
1101	Additional Income	$ 0	$1,500	$1,500
3301	Theft Loss	2,122	0	2,122
4007, 5430	Automobile/Entertainment	6,556	4,039	2,517
3620, 3608	Contributions	2,565	1,568	997
9408, 3823	Rental Depreciation/Repairs	13,295	9,557	3,738
4601, 9408	Medical	1,159	0	1,159
4109	Exemption	1,900	0	1,900
5203	Gambling Losses	52	0	52
8202	Self-employment Tax	0	0	0
8103	Negligence Penalty	0	0	0

Item		Line	Amount
A. Adjustment in income-increase (decrease) (See explanation of adjustments attached.)		7.	$13,985
B. Adjusted gross, taxable, or tax table income reported or as previously adjusted		8.	7,649
C. Corrected adjusted gross, taxable, or tax table income		9.	21,634
D. Tax figured with exemptions		10.	3,124
E. Credit for personal exemptions			
F. Tax credits (credit for the elderly, investment, foreign, etc.) (If adjusted, see explanation attached.)	Child Care Credit	11.	(400)
G. Other taxes (self-employment, alternative minimum, tax from refiguring prior year investment credit, etc.) (If adjusted, see explanation attached.)		12.	184.50
H. Corrected tax (line D less line E less line F plus line G)		13.	2,908.50
I. Tax shown on return or as previously adjusted		14.	624.00
J. Deficiency (increase in tax before credit adjustments—line H less line I)		15.	2,284.50
K. Overassessment (decrease in tax before credit adjustments—line I less line H)			
L. Adjustments to prepayment credits		16.	
M. Balance due – this does not include any interest charges (line J or K as adjusted by line L)		17.	2,284.50
N. Overpayment–this does not include any interest due you (line J or K as adjusted by line L)			
O. Penalties, if any (See explanation attached.)	IRC Section 6653(a)	18.	114.23

Consent to Assessment and Collection - I do not wish to exercise my appeal rights with the Internal Revenue Service or to contest in the United States Tax Court the findings in this report. Therefore, I consent to either:

(1) The immediate assessment and collection of the balance due shown on Line M, plus any interest due on this tax, and also any penalties shown on line O, or

(2) The overpayment shown on line N, plus any interest and adjusted by penalties shown on line O.

19. ______ Your signature ______ Date ______ Spouse's signature, if a joint return was filed ______ Date

(See notices on reverse side)

FORM 1902-B (Rev 10-84)

Approximately 20 percent of all audits are no-changes. The other 80 percent produce a change—for better or for worse. When the result is for better, there is a "statutory overassessment." When it is for worse, you owe a "statutory deficiency." In either case, you receive an audit report, which explains the changes made and totals up the new tax or refund.

THE AUDIT REPORT

The Pittances' audit report or Report of Individual Income Tax Changes (Form 1902-B or E) is shown here. It is extremely important that you be able to read and understand this report. For this reason, I'm going to run through the items of the report briefly, so that you will know the significance of each one. The numbers on the sample report correspond to the numbered explanations:

1. *Identification.* This block contains general information to identify the taxpayer, the tax year being audited, the return number (1040), your filing status, the name of your representative, the date of the report, your social security number, and the district in which you are being audited (95 is Los Angeles). Notice particularly the box that reads, "In Reply Refer To": "OE" is a general audit code, "2114" is the audit group the case is assigned to, and "EM" are your auditor's initials. If you cannot remember your auditor's name, give her initials instead, and you will be put in touch with her quickly.

2. *Explanation No.* These numbers correspond to explanations of the changes your auditor has made. The explanations will be attached to the report and are computer printed or hand-written on a Form 886-A. Usually these explanations are quite general. The auditor may also show her computations on the 886-A or for depreciation on a Form 1914. If you are present when the auditor writes the report and she explains the changes to you orally, you might not receive a written explanation.

3. *Item Changed.* The audit issues that were not verfied in full or that are not deductible are listed here. If the auditor determined you did not correctly report all of your income, it will also be listed.

4. *Amount Shown on Return.* The amount of income or expense you put on your return for each item changed is shown here.

5. *Corrected Amount.* The amount the auditor has determined is correct for each item changed goes here.

6. *Adjustment.* This amount is arrived at by subtracting column 5 from column 4. This is the difference between what you claimed on your return and what you were able to verify or which was allowable.

7. *Total Adjustment.* This is the total of all the adjustments, or changes, shown in column 6. If the total is a positive (plus) figure, you will owe additional tax. If it is a negative (minus) figure, you will probably receive a refund.

8. *Income Reported.* The taxable income shown on your return is entered here. If the service center made any corrections to your return due to math errors, the corrected figure will be used.

9. *Corrected Income.* Items 7 and 8 are added together to arrive at the correct taxable income, i.e., the amount it should have been, as determined by the audit.

10. *Tax.* A new tax is computed on your corrected taxable income (item 9), based on your filing status and number of allowable exemptions.

11. *Tax Credits.* These include investment credit, child-care credit, foreign-tax credit, retirement-income credit, and others. If, like the Pittances, you claimed a credit on your return, it will be entered here, either in the amount you claimed or as adjusted by the auditor. This figure is also subtracted from the tax (item 10).

12. *Self-employment Tax.* Annie Pittance admitted to the auditor that she received fifteen hundred dollars as a private-duty nurse in 1987. Because she had net income from self-employment in excess of four hundred dollars, she must pay self-employment tax (social security). If the auditor has adjusted your net self-employment income, she will recompute the tax and enter the corrected amount on this line. If no adjustment has been made, she will write in the amount on your return. This amount is added to the tax (item 10).

13. *Corrected Tax.* This is the total tax you owe as a result of the audit changes (but this is not necessarily the amount you have to pay).

14. *Tax Shown on Return.* The total tax on your return (after credits and self-employment tax) is entered on this line. Again, if the service center has made a correction, the corrected figure will be used.

15. *Deficiency/Overassessment.* Item 13 minus item 14 will either

result in a statutory deficiency (positive amount) or overassessment (negative amount). The statutory deficiency is used in computing any penalties.

16. *Prepayment Credits.* Any adjustments to your withholding, earned income, and other (rare) credits are shown on this line.

17. *Balance Due/Overpayment.* This is the bottom line: the amount of tax you must pay back (balance due) or the refund you will receive (overpayment). Interest will be computed on this amount, but the audit report does not show interest.

18. *Penalties.* Delinquency, negligence, and civil-fraud penalties are indicated here. If more than one penalty is involved, a breakdown should be shown. The Internal Revenue Code section for each penalty should be cited either on this line or on your attached explanation. Here the Pittances are being assessed a negligence penalty of 5 percent of the statutory deficiency (item 15).

19. *Signatures.* Sign and date the report here, if you agree to it. A signature line is included for each spouse if a joint return was filed.

DECISIONS TO MAKE

Two copies of the audit report will be given or mailed to you, along with the explanation of adjustments and any schedules needed to show the auditor's computations. The cover letter for the report (DO 915) briefly describes what action you should take and refers you to *Publication 5,* also enclosed, which outlines your appeal rights.

The audit report is not a bill. Your auditor is proposing adjustments to your tax return, which you may either accept or reject. So don't panic if the result is worse than you expected. The report is not necessarily final.

When you receive the report, you have *thirty* days to decide what action to take. Normally you will be sent a reminder about twenty days later, along with a Form 870, Waiver of Restrictions on Assessment. This waiver shows the amount of deficiency or overassessment and is merely a substitute audit report.

During the thirty-day period, you may do one of three things: First, you may submit any additional information you believe might change the auditor's decision. If your auditor has written the report because you failed to send in documents she requested, now is the obvious time to get on the ball and mail her what she asked for. In fact, she may have written the report just for that purpose—to light a fire under you—because once you have it, you are working against that thirty-day time limit. You are playing a whole new game, called "Beat the Clock."

If you do have new information to bring to light, your auditor will review it and either send you a revised report or a no-change letter that takes this information into account, or she will send you a Form 870, showing the same deficiency as before and explaining why. If you still owe additional tax, you now have ten days to decide what to do.

If you have no further information to help your cause, you may either agree or disagree with the audit report. After hearing or reading the auditor's reasoning or after consulting your representative if you have one, do you believe the report is fair and correct and that it is unlikely you will benefit by an appeal? If the answer is yes, you will probably want to agree with the auditor. Sign one copy of the report and mail it back in the envelope provided. If the statutory deficiency (item 15) is one thousand dollars or more and a joint return was filed, both spouses' signatures are required. Otherwise, one signature (either spouse) will do. Keep the other copy of the report for your records.

Because the report is not a bill, you do not need to pay at this time. You may, of course, if you want to, but you may also wait to be billed from your service center. Whether you pay now or not, your audit is *over,* once you sign and return the audit report. (For instructions on how to pay, see Chapter XIV.)

The Pittances decide they disagree. There are several choices open to them, and we deal with all of them in the next chapter. For the Pittances, the audit may be just beginning.

XII. STANDING ON YOUR RIGHTS

When you disagree with the audit report, you may be embarking upon the Service's administrative-appeals process. Or you may be headed straight for Tax Court. Which route you take is within your choice. Too many taxpayers, however, buy a one-way ticket to Tax Court without even being aware of it. After consideration, you may decide that Tax Court is the answer for you, but don't wind up there accidentally.

Accidents are prevented. Now that you have your audit report, you have thirty days from the date of the report to make your choice: submit more information, agree, or disagree. Thirty days in which you must do something. If your auditor does not hear from you before that time runs out, you are on your way to Tax Court with about as much intention as the guy who slips on a banana peel.

If you're not going to make the thirty-day deadline, let your auditor know, and arrange an extension of time. If you agree or intend to send in more documentation, do so promptly. And if you disagree, tell your auditor how you want the disputed issues resolved. Don't sit in brooding, hostile, or just plain lazy silence and let your appeal rights slip away.

When you fail to respond within thirty days, your auditor may presume you disagree, but unfortunately she doesn't know what you want to do about it. You have not told her. She has no option but to close your case "unagreed." Your file will be packed up and sent to the Notices, or 90-Day, Section. There is no point calling the auditor now. She does not have your tax return anymore. You are, inadvertently or not, bound for Tax Court.

There are two tracks you can take when you disagree with the audit results: (1) administrative appeal and (2) closed unagreed (Tax Court). Once you pick the track leading directly to Tax Court, there is no way to switch to the other track. This is not true of administrative appeal, as we'll see later in this chapter. Of the two tracks, administrative appeal is by far the most advantageous to you, the taxpayer, because it offers one more "way" station (appeal level where you can get your way) and because in the long run it ends at the same place: Tax (or district) Court. Administrative appeal is the scenic route; having your case closed unagreed is like taking the express train to court. Unless for some reason you want to skip all appeals, you must not let your case close unagreed.

Does that mean that you must go to Tax Court if your case is closed unagreed? No. You can't switch tracks, but you can get off before your destination. You never *have* to go to court. But it may be necessary if you don't want to pay the deficiency.

A word here about audit reports that are in error. Your unagreed case is subject to review at several points along the way to the Notices Section. It may be reviewed by the auditor herself, by the audit group manager, or by the Review Staff, whose function is to detect and correct mistakes of law or math. If an error is discovered, you will be sent a corrected or revised audit report, but this does not necessarily restore your appeal rights. In many cases, however, especially where the auditor must contact you again to clarify an issue, you will have the chance to agree or disagree to the new audit report and may start out on the other track (administrative appeal) if you still disagree.

An audit report that you have agreed to and signed is also subject to review and may be corrected. If the error was against you and you agreed to more tax than you really owed, the correct (smaller) amount will be assessed automatically. You will be sent a copy of the revised audit report for your information; you do not need to sign it. If the error was in your favor, that is, for less tax than you should owe, you will be sent a corrected audit report for your signature. You must agree to and sign for the higher amount or tell the auditor you disagree within the new time limit (usually ten days). If you fail to do either, your case will be closed unagreed even though you previously agreed to a lesser amount. Corrections to signed audit reports should be made by IRS within thirty days after your signature is received. In my experience, this rule is not always followed. If you receive a corrected report for greater tax more than a month after you originally signed, at least raise the issue. I have never seen this tested, but the outcome may be favorable to you.

STATUTORY NOTICE—NEXT STOP, TAX COURT

When your *unagreed* case file reaches the Notices, or 90-Day, Section, a Statutory Notice of Deficiency is issued. This sounds threatening, but you are in no imminent danger. The statutory notice, or 90-day letter as it is more often called, must be sent to your last known address by certified mail. It consists of a letter stating the amount of the deficiency and a statement showing how the deficiency was computed. The letter gives you 90 days from the mailing date of the letter (150 days if addressed to you outside of the United States) to file a petition with the United States Tax Court. (The procedures for filing a petition are covered in Chapter XIII.)

If you decide this is the end of the line and you are not going to file a petition, you are asked to sign the Statutory Notice Statement for the amount of tax your auditor determined as correct. By signing, you are only saving everyone time and money, because at the end of the 90- (or 150-) day period, the tax would have been assessed anyway, with or without your agreement. You will then receive a bill, and the tax must be paid. Only by petitioning the Tax Court can you prevent this automatic assessment.

That doesn't give you much choice, does it? Pay up or go to Tax Court. Fortunately it's not that black-and-white. During the ninety-day period, you can normally take another shot at resolving your case. The statutory notice gives you a name and number to call. If you have new documents or facts to present, call the person shown on the letter and ask to have your case sent back to the audit group. (Mailing your documents to the Notices Section will have the same effect.) Your file will be returned and usually assigned to the auditor who handled it before. The auditor will contact you either by letter or by phone and give you a chance to change her mind. If you have nothing new to add, don't expect a new determination. The auditor is liable to regard your renewed effort as a last-ditch attempt to postpone the inevitable and will probably ship it quickly back to Notices.

This is the major hazard once you receive a statutory notice: your auditor is under no obligation to hear you out a second time. In fact, the audit group may refuse to take your case back at all. This is rare in practice and is done only in extreme instances, in which the taxpayer has dragged the audit out as long as possible. Usually you will be allowed at least one opportunity to show your good faith.

The auditor's acceptance of your case when it returns from Notices does not extend or suspend the ninety-day period for petitioning the Tax Court. That keeps ticking away, and it is the framework in which you must operate. Your strategy must be planned around it. At the end of ninety days, the tax can be assessed, right out from under you so to speak. You can be a day or two away from the document you need and it will be a day or two too late. You are on the defensive now. You are forced to act and act quickly. The IRS is indifferent at this point. You are on your own.

Let's put this in better perspective. The ninety-day period is the time in which you must petition the Tax Court—if you want to go to Tax Court. Although the tax shown on the audit report you disagreed with can be assessed at the end of the ninety days, this is not necessarily done. If the auditor and you can reach a mutual agreement, your case can remain in the audit group past the ninety days, until the issue is resolved. You simply lose your right to go to Tax Court. If you know what the auditor needs to allow the deduction, however, and are confident you can satisfy her in the near future, you may not be interested in Tax Court. You anticipate no disagreement with the final audit results.

If the ninety days pass without your filing a petition with the Tax Court, you have let a door shut behind you. You are cut off from this means of appeal. You must weigh your chances of resolving the differences between yourself and the IRS. Is the likelihood of agreement good—within the time limit—or does it seem probable that, because of an IRS interpretation of the law or insufficiency of your verification, no agreement is possible?

My suggestion is to have your case sent back to the audit group and find out if resolution is possible. Once you are sure of the answer, make your decision. Don't petition the Tax Court until you give audit another try, because as soon as you petition, the IRS loses jurisdiction of your case. You will be locked into going to court even

Department of the Treasury
Internal Revenue Service

Date:

Tax Year Ended and Deficiency:

Person to Contact:

Contact Telephone Number:

Dear Taxpayer:

We have determined that there is a deficiency (increase) in your income tax as shown above. This letter is a NOTICE OF DEFICIENCY sent to you as required by law. The enclosed statement shows how we figured the deficiency.

If you want to contest this deficiency in court before making any payment, you have 90 days from the above mailing date of this letter (150 days if addressed to you outside of the United States) to file a petition with the United States Tax Court for a redetermination of the deficiency. The petition should be filed with the United States Tax Court, 400 Second Street NW., Washington, D.C. 20217, and the copy of this letter should be attached to the petition. The time in which you must file a petition with the Court (90 or 150 days as the case may be) is fixed by law and the Court cannot consider your case if your petition is filed late. If this letter is addressed to both a husband and wife, and both want to petition the Tax Court, both must sign the petition or each must file a separate, signed petition.

If you dispute not more than $10,000 for any one tax year, a simplified procedure is provided by the Tax Court for small tax cases. You can obtain information about this procedure, as well as a petition form you can use, by writing to the Clerk of the United States Tax Court at 400 Second Street NW., Washington, D.C. 20217. You should do this promptly if you intend to file a petition with the Tax Court.

If you decide not to file a petition with the Tax Court, we would appreciate it if you would sign and return the enclosed waiver form. This will permit us to assess the deficiency quickly and will limit the accumulation of interest. The enclosed envelope is for your convenience. If you decide not to sign and return the statement and you do not timely petition the Tax Court, the law requires us to assess and bill you for the deficiency after 90 days from the above mailing date of this letter (150 days if this letter is addressed to you outside the United States).

If you have any questions about this letter, please write to the person whose name and address are shown above, or you may call that person at the number shown above. If this number is outside your local calling area, there will be a long distance charge to you. If you prefer, you may call the IRS telephone number listed in your local directory. An IRS employee there will be able to help you, but the office at the address shown on this letter is most familiar with your case.

When you send the information we requested or if you write to us with questions about this letter, please provide your telephone number and the most convenient time for us to call if we need additional information. Please attach this letter to any correspondence to help us identify your case. Keep the copy for your records.

Thank you for your cooperation.

Sincerely yours,

Commissioner
By

Enclosures:
Copy of this letter
Waiver
Envelope

Form 5601 (Rev. 4-85)

though you might have been able to settle the matter more simply with the auditor.

Go as far as you can within IRS, leaving enough time to file a petition with the Tax Court if it becomes apparent the issue will probably not go your way. How far can you go in IRS after a statutory notice is issued? You can, as we have seen, get another hearing with an auditor in most cases. You may also be able to speak with the audit group manager. You also have a right to an appellate hearing if there is sufficient time remaining in the ninety-day period.

This is a lot to cram into ninety days. There are delays created in sending your case from one office to another and in scheduling mutually convenient appointment times. The IRS is not in the same hurry you are, although the case is considered priority work. Because of this, you must act promptly as soon as you receive the statutory notice. Don't create any delays yourself, and make sure your case is forwarded quickly from one stage to another. If you are going to petition the Tax Court, stop at whatever stage you've reached just short of the ninety days and file your petition. Tell the IRS when you file.

A revised audit report decreasing the tax can be issued during the ninety-day period as a result of new information you present or reconsideration of what you originally submitted. An audit report cannot be written increasing the tax. This requires "reopening" and is only done if fraud or a gross error is involved. If there are some issues you agree to, ask for a partial report and sign it, agreeing to just those issues. This will not prevent you from going to Tax Court on the other issues, and it will stop the interest from running on the portion of the deficiency you are in agreement with.

What if you never receive the statutory notice, or ninety-day letter? My advice is to make sure you do. If the letter is mailed to your last known address and for some reason returned by the Postal Service, no further effort will be made to contact you. (The same holds true, of course, if it is not returned but not delivered to you for some reason.) At the end of ninety days, the tax will be assessed by default. If you know your case has been closed out of the audit group unagreed and you do not receive the statutory notice within a month or two (there is no specific time within which the notice must be issued), call your auditor and ask her to find out if the case is in

Notices yet and whether the letter has been mailed. By the same token, tell your auditor if you move before you receive the letter and ask her to forward your new address to Notices.

We have been talking about cases that have statutory deficiencies. If you disagree with an audit report that shows no statutory deficiency or a statutory overassessment, you will not be issued a statutory notice of *deficiency,* and you have no appeal to the Tax Court (for example, if the audit report is for a refund you believe is too small). The same is true for any additional tax due because of a decrease in your prepayment credits (e.g., withholding or earned-income credit). The only way you can protest adjustments that result in a statutory overassessment or a decrease in prepayment credits is to pay any tax due and file a claim (Form 1040X).

APPEAL WITHIN IRS

Your case is closed unagreed and sent forward for issuance of a statutory notice if you disagree (or agree but remain silent for too long). You must inform your auditor if you want to exercise your administrative-appeal rights instead, and you must do so within thirty days after the audit report is written.

The administrative-appeals process consists of an "informal" level of appeal and a "formal" level. Neither level is open to you until the audit is complete. If an audit report has been issued to you because you have failed or refused to provide required information, you do not yet have the right to appeal. Only after all the issues have been fully developed and an audit report written, based upon all the facts you can possibly provide, will you be granted an appeal. (This is the ideal; practice sometimes varies, but it is nothing you can count on.)

At the informal level, you meet with the auditor's manager or a senior auditor. Either has full authority to change the audit report upon reconsideration of the issues and the documents you provided. This change can be an increase in the tax as well as a decrease, and taxpayers are sometimes sorry they didn't agree with the original audit report. Be sure of the solidity of your position before you come in.

You can obtain an informal conference by telling the auditor at the end of the interview that you disagree or by calling or writing during the thirty-day period. An appointment will then be arranged for you. The manager will not usually hold an informal conference with you "on the spot," unless you have become unmanageable and the auditor feels the need for reinforcement.

FORMAL APPEAL

If you do not want an informal conference or if you are dissatisfied with the results of your informal conference, you may request a hearing with the Appellate Division. This is the path the Pittances have elected. When you get to Appellate, you have reached the end of the line within IRS. If you cannot resolve your case at that level, your only recourse becomes the courts.

The Appellate Division will refuse to hear your case, however, if your protest is based on moral, religious, political, constitutional, conscientious, or other similar arguments. If you are out to kick up a little dust in these areas, you will have to do it in court. Obviously, the IRS has no authority to make rulings regarding any law, human or divine, other than the Internal Revenue Code. Unless your argument pertains strictly to tax law, you will have to seek another forum.

To request an appellate hearing, simply tell the auditor or group manager that you want to make a formal appeal. You do not have to put your request in writing, although you certainly may do so if the spirit moves you.

There is one exception: If your audit was conducted by a revenue agent (not an office auditor) and the proposed deficiency is greater than ten thousand dollars, you must file a written protest in order to appeal. The written protest should state:

1. Your desire to appeal;
2. Your name and address;
3. The date and symbols on the letter sent with your audit report;
4. The tax period(s) involved;
5. A list of the audit adjustments you disagree with;
6. The facts supporting your position, followed by a statement "under penalties of perjury" that to the best of your knowledge and belief the facts are true; and
7. The law or other authority you are relying on.

For deficiencies between $2,500 and $10,000, a written protest is optional. However, you must briefly state in writing which issues you dispute.

When your oral (or written) request is received, your case will be sent to the Appellate Division, which may not be where you were audited. For this reason, you may want to ask where your appellate hearing will be held and whether you have a choice of offices. When your file is received in Appellate, it will be assigned to a conferee, and an appointment letter will be sent to you. If the appointment date is not convenient for you, call the conferee and arrange a better time.

THE PITTANCES MEET THE CONFEREE

Let's join Noel and Annie Pittance as they prepare for their hearing. Although an appellate hearing is a "formal conference," it isn't really all that formal. In fact, it's similar to the audit interview the Pittances have already been through.

First, Noel and Annie must decide whether to hire someone to represent them. They've been told, however, that the representative must be an attorney, C.P.A., or enrolled agent, and in the end, Noel decides he doesn't want to incur the extra expense. He believes he can do some research and present his own case as long as Annie is there for moral support.

When they requested a conference, Noel and Annie told the auditor they disagreed with her adjustments on three issues: the theft loss, noncash contributions, and entertainment expense. They also felt the negligence penalty was unfair and insulting. At the conference, these will be the only four issues for which the Pittances will be allowed to present evidence. The appellate conferee will not listen to evidence on agreed or uncontested issues or on issues not raised before.

In arguing for allowance of the theft loss, noncash contributions, and entertainment expense, the Pittances will be permitted to give oral testimony or to call witnesses to testify on their behalf. They may also present the same documentary evidence that was shown to the original auditor. They may not introduce any new evidence. If Noel should suddenly discover receipts to prove additional entertainment expenses, for example, the case would be sent back to the auditor to determine whether the audit results should be changed. Appellate conferees do not audit.

On the day of the hearing, Noel and Annie sit nervously outside the conferee's office in the Federal Building downtown. They have brought along Mrs. Schaeffer, their neighbor, as a witness to their casualty loss, and Noel has found a point of law he hopes will allow him his entertainment expense. He has also compiled some figures to back up the fair market value of their noncash donations.

While they wait, the conferee reviews the Pittances' case file one more time. He runs an eye over the audit report, paying careful attention to the written explanations of adjustments. During the conference, the conferee will be bound to the legal basis for any audit adjustment contained in the explanation sent to the Pittances with their audit report. If you refer to Chapter XI and the sample audit report, you will see that next to every adjustment to the Pittances' return are one or more explanations on Form 886-A, which accompanies the audit report. At the audit level, these explanations may be changed at any time to take into account new information submitted or to correct errors or imprecise wording. This was true at the informal-conference stage as well.

The conferee, however, can rely only on the written explanations. Although the Pittances don't know it, this is an important limitation on the conferee's powers. Why is this a limitation? Quite bluntly, these explanations are often incomplete or, more rarely, inaccurate. Let me illustrate: You are an insurance salesman claiming education expense to study banjo repair. This expense is not deductible, because it qualifies you for a new trade or business. However, because you were unable to locate any receipts, the explanation for disallowing the expense reads, "It has not been verified that the expense was incurred." This is an incomplete explanation, because it doesn't mention the other, solid, legal basis for not permitting you the expense (it qualifies you for a new trade or business). If you were suddenly able to unearth receipts to verify the expense, the conferee would have to allow you the deduction, even though it is clearly not deductible. He is bound to the auditor's explanation, for better or for worse.

Obviously, this limitation could work to the Pittances' advantage if the explanations sent them were deficient. Unfortunately for the

Pittances, the auditor has not been so gracious, and the conferee breathes a sigh of relief. He doesn't mind compromising in order to settle the case, but he hates to have to give the case away outright because someone else made a mistake.

When the conference begins, Mrs. Schaeffer testifies that she had seen all the items the Pittances reported stolen before the burglary and has seen none of them since. She states that, from her own observation, the articles were worth at least as much as the Pittances claimed. The conferee wants to know if she is qualified in any way as an appraiser, and Mrs. Schaeffer replies, "No, but I have a good idea what household items are worth."

Noel then hands over the police report and the four receipts he showed his auditor. The conferee examines them and realizes that Noel has nothing new to present and therefore has not met the burden of proof. The police report and purchase receipts are no better evidence of the amount of the loss at the conference level than they were when originally presented to the auditor. Nor has the conferee been swayed by Mrs. Schaeffer. Her testimony carries no legal weight. She does not have the experience or training to overrule the auditor's judgment.

Furthermore, because of the adjusted gross income limitation, the conferee would have to decrease the auditor's adjustment by more than six hundred dollars to allow Noel and Annie just one dollar of deduction. This he is unwilling to do.

"All right," says Noel, "but there's no such limitation on contributions." He pulls out a sheet of paper in Annie's handwriting. She has visited a thrift shop and listed the sales prices of various articles of clothing and furniture similar to the items they gave away. Noel claims they substantiate the fair market value deducted on the return.

The conferee examines the list. It is not signed or dated by an employee of the thrift shop. But even if the figures are truthful, there is no evidence the donated items were of the same age, quality, or condition as the articles on the list. At this point in time, such evidence is unobtainable. If the Pittances were facing a second auditor, the adjustment would have to stand.

That is not true in Appellate. A conferee has broader authority to settle a case than the auditor. The conferee has two conflicting goals: (1) He wants you to pay the correct tax and (2) he wants to keep you from going to court. He is like a defensive tackle on a football team. He wants to hold you to short yardage (the maximum amount of tax you owe), but he'll give up a lot of ground if it's the only way he can keep you out of the end zone (court).

In plain terms, the conferee is willing to deal. And unlike the auditor, he has the power to do so. Settlement authority allows the conferee to consider and accept settlement offers made by taxpayers when the proposed tax deficiency is less than twenty-five hundred dollars. The conferee may settle the disputed issues in the taxpayer's favor, even though it is contrary to the Service's official position. That means the conferee can allow the Pittances the full amount of the loss they claimed without any legal basis at all.

If all this sounds too good to be true, then you won't be surprised to learn that there are some conditions attached. Settlement authority is used only when the outcome if the case goes to court is in doubt. This can happen, for instance, where the law laid down by the courts conflicts with the Service's announced position. Another example may be where it seems likely the court will believe the taxpayer's admissible oral testimony even though he does not have perfect documentation.

A settlement may take the form of mutual concessions, both sides giving a little until a reasonable compromise is reached. This type of settlement occurs when both the IRS and the taxpayer have strong positions, so that neither side is willing to concede the issue in full. The conferee will weigh the relative strength of the government's case against that of the taxpayer to decide how much of a concession to make.

In other cases, if the conferee does not believe he would recommend trial, the issue may be conceded in full. If no other method of settlement is appropriate, a proposal of settlement based on a percentage or stipulated amount of tax may be considered. Regardless of the type of settlement, it is always based on the merits of the case. The IRS will not settle simply to avoid the cost and inconvenience of a trial.

The conferee believes the Service's chances of winning the Pittances' case in court are good, but he would still like to reach an agreement short of court. For that reason, he is willing to be convinced that Noel and Annie are entitled to more than they got from the auditor. All Noel has to do is persuade the conferee that this is so.

When the problem is lack of proof, the conferee is usually more receptive to oral testimony than the auditor. He is the last line of defense within the IRS, and he has to be more flexible if he wants to keep a large percentage of Noels and Annies out of court. With this in mind, the conferee questions the Pittances about the age and condition of the donated articles, listening for any plausible oral testimony he can accept as justification for lessening the tax.

Noel summons all of the sales techniques he has been taught in seminars and makes a well-reasoned, persuasive argument for allowing a larger deduction. The conferee listens carefully and decides he is satisfied. He knows that although the auditor's judgment would stand up in court, it was to a certain degree arbitrary. If the Pittances had been assigned to another auditor, with a different outlook or experience, they might have been allowed a greater or lesser amount. Basing his decision on Noel's oral testimony, the conferee says he believes an additional allowance of three hundred dollars is fair.

Noel is disappointed. He had hoped the conferee would give him at least half of the amount disallowed after reviewing the list.

"Five hundred dollars," he says tentatively, unsure whether he is permitted to bargain or whether the conferee's decision is final.

The conferee does not take offense. He expects the taxpayer to try his hand at horse trading. He runs down the auditor's list in the work papers again. In most instances, the auditor's adjustments are reasonably in line with the conferee's own view of their fair market value. He does not believe he can support an additional allowance of five hundred dollars without using settlement authority. He is unwilling to do this, though, because he feels the Service's position is sound. But Noel has evidenced a desire to deal instead of going to court, and the conferee wants to appear reasonable.

"Four hundred dollars," he counters. "That's as high as I can go."

Noel and Annie confer briefly and decide to wait until the other issues are resolved before making up their minds about their contribution.

The next issue is the entertainment expense of five hundred dollars for which Noel had no receipts and that the auditor disallowed in full. Noel says the auditor was wrong not to allow him anything at all just because he could not show exactly how much he spent. The letter from his employer proved that he must have spent something. He has done research, and the *Cohan* rule applies: a reasonable amount should be allowed based on his oral testimony.

The conferee asks if Noel can come up with any documentation at all. Noel says, "No, I didn't keep any." He insists that the *Cohan* rule is the only evidence he needs.

The conferee knows that the *Cohan*-case rule has been superseded by the record-keeping requirements of section 274, and that unlike the gray and subjective nature of determining fair market value, these requirements are black-and-white. Either Noel has substantially complied with the law by maintaining adequate records or he has not and is consequently not entitled to the deduction.

After explaining why the *Cohan* rule no longer applies, the conferee tells Noel that the auditor's adjustment will have to stand. Noel, emboldened by his mild success on the contribution issue, offers to settle for two hundred dollars. The conferee refuses. Why? Because with Noel's complete lack of records, the Service has an airtight case for disallowing the expense. The government is assured of winning the issue in court. Therefore, the conferee has no reason to make any concessions or to accept a proposal of settlement.

The last issue is the negligence penalty. Annie says being penalized makes her feel like a criminal. Failing to report the money she earned as a private-duty nurse was an honest mistake. Hasn't the conferee ever made a mistake before? She feels the auditor was petty and unjust.

The conferee believes that the negligence penalty was justified in this case. Whether or not the omission was intentional, the Pittances should have exercised more care to ensure they reported all of their income. However, he personally feels that because the amount of the penalty (5 percent of the statutory deficiency) is so low, it is little more than a slap on the wrist anyway, and in that regard, it has already served its purpose. Assertion of the penalty is discretionary, and if it is the sole obstacle to resolving the case, the conferee is not averse to giving it away, even though in his opinion it is deserved.

Sounding Noel and Annie out, the conferee asks if they will agree to his findings on the other two issues if the negligence penalty is removed. After a whispered discussion, the Pittances agree. The conferee eliminates the penalty but reinforces its effect by warning them that if an omission of this kind occurs again, the penalty will not be mitigated and the recurrence may even be looked on as fraud. The Pittances promise to be more careful in the future.

The conferee concludes the hearing by giving the Pittances a

Form 870, Waiver of Restrictions on Assessment, to sign. This form shows the revised amount of tax due as a result of the conference. Allowing an additional $400 for contributions and removing the negligence penalty, the Pittances now owe $2,224.50, a decrease of $174.23 in tax. Once they sign the waiver, the tax will be assessed.

If the Pittances and the conferee had been unable to come to an agreement, a statutory notice of deficiency would have been issued, and they would have had ninety days to petition the Tax Court or pay the tax and file a claim.

Unless the law is clearly arrayed against you or you have a serious deficiency of proof, you will probably come out of an appellate hearing owing less tax than when you went in, if only by a few dollars. The factors to weigh in deciding whether an appeal is worthwhile are the time, the cost, and the merits of your case versus the expected decrease in tax. From my experience, the taxpayer benefits from an appeal in the overwhelming majority of cases.

XIII. COURTS OF LAST RESORT

When all your appeals within Internal Revenue fail, you are faced with the decision to either throw in the towel or continue your fight in court. If this is the end of the line for you, wait for the bill, pay the tax, and go back to living normally again. If, however, you utter those deathless words of John Paul Jones, "I have not yet begun to fight," start drawing up a battle plan. You are at still another crossroads, and there are two ways you can go: to Tax Court or to district court. Where you end up depends on whether you pay the tax.

With a statutory notice in your hand and a resolve to do battle, you can either refuse to pay the tax and petition the Tax Court or pay the tax and file a claim, which starts you on the road to district court. How you feel about paying up may be decided by how large the tax deficiency is, how solvent you are, or which court you believe will be most advantageous to you.

Let's assume you have decided not to pay and therefore are going to Tax Court. What is the Tax Court, and how do you go about getting there? The United States Tax Court is a specialized court that hears only tax cases. To bring your case to Tax Court, you must have a statutory notice, or 90-day letter. The Tax Court operates to the advantage of the small, low-income taxpayer especially. The court comes to you; you do not have to go to it. Its justices are like the circuit-court judges of yesteryear: they travel from city to city for your convenience and to save you high travel costs. Furthermore, you do not need a lawyer (although you may have one). You may represent yourself if you cannot afford or do not want legal counsel.

There are two types of Tax Court procedures, one of them designed for cases in which the disputed tax is ten thousand dollars or less. This small-tax-case procedure is simpler, the rules of evidence are more relaxed, and the trial is more informal than when larger cases are involved. The other-than-small-tax-case procedures are complex enough to make a lawyer advisable although not required. A lawyer is far less necessary when the small-tax case procedures are used. If you choose legal counsel, he does not need a power of attorney, as he would have during the audit. He must, however, be admitted to practice before the U.S. Tax Court.

If you want to use the small-tax procedure, but the tax at issue is more than $10,000, you can concede part of the deficiency to come within the limit.

PETITIONING THE TAX COURT

You get to the Tax Court by filing a petition. This petition must be filed with the court within *90 days* after the mailing date of the statutory notice (or 150 days for taxpayers outside the United States). Ninety days means ninety days—not three months. The day the notice was mailed is not counted, but the day of filing the petition is. As long as the petition is postmarked on or before the last day, it will be considered to be filed on time. If the last day for filing falls on a weekend or a legal holiday in the District of Columbia, the time is extended to the court's next business day. Your best protection is to mail your petition by certified mail and request a receipt.

Note: Your petition must be *postmarked* to be timely filed. Do not use a private courier service or an electronic transmission to send your petition.

A sample preprinted petition for a small-tax case (Form 2) is shown here. A petition for other than a small-tax case is also shown. If you want to use the small-tax procedure, you must *elect* to do so, or the other procedure will apply. This request is made when you file your petition and is included on the small-tax-case form. Form 2, the small-tax-case petition, may be obtained in preprinted form by writing the Clerk of the Tax Court. You may type either petition yourself, using the samples as models. Do not leave out any item shown on the sample. A typewritten petition must be typed on plain, white paper, 8½ × 11 inches and weighing not less than 16 pounds to the ream.

The petition must list all the issues that are in dispute and the facts

UNITED STATES TAX COURT

(FIRST) (MIDDLE) (LAST)

(PLEASE TYPE OR PRINT) Petitioner(s)

V.

COMMISSIONER OF INTERNAL REVENUE
Respondent

Docket No.

PETITION

1. Petitioner(s) disagree(s) with the tax deficiency(ies) for the year(s) ____________ as set forth in the NOTICE OF DEFICIENCY dated ____________, A COPY OF WHICH IS ATTACHED. The notice was issued by the Office of the Internal Revenue Service at

____
(CITY AND STATE)

2. Petitioner(s) taxpayer identification (e.g. social security) number(s) is (are)

____

3. Petitioner(s) dispute(s) the following:

Year	Amount of Deficiency Disputed	Addition to Tax (Penalty) if any, Disputed	Amount of Overpayment Claimed

4. Set forth those adjustments, i.e. changes, in the NOTICE OF DEFICIENCY with which you disagree and why you disagree.

____

Petitioner(s) request(s) that this case be conducted under the "small tax case" procedures authorized by Congress to provide the taxpayer(s) with an informal, prompt, and inexpensive hearing at a reasonably convenient location. Consistent with these objectives, a decision in a "small tax case" is final and cannot be appealed to higher Courts (the Courts of Appeals and the Supreme Court) by the Internal Revenue Service or the Petitioner(s). *

SIGNATURE OF PETITIONER — DATE — PRESENT ADDRESS—STREET, CITY, STATE, ZIP CODE—TELEPHONE NO.

SIGNATURE OF PETITIONER (SPOUSE) — DATE — PRESENT ADDRESS—STREET, CITY, STATE, ZIP CODE—TELEPHONE NO.

SIGNATURE AND ADDRESS OF COUNSEL, IF RETAINED BY PETITIONER(S) — DATE

*If you do not want to make this request, you should place an "X" in the following box. ☐

T.C. Form 2 (Rev. Sept. 1982)

upon which your argument is based. Make sure that you cover both issues and facts completely. The portion of any deficiency attributable to a partnership item cannot be considered as part of your personal tax case. It must be decided in a separate partnership proceeding.

You must also attach a copy of the statutory notice of deficiency, plus any statement that accompanied the notice or prior notices referred to in the notice. On Form 4 or a separate sheet of paper, request the city in which you want your hearing.

An original and four copies of the petition must be filed; for small-tax cases, an original and only two copies are needed. There is a sixty dollar filing fee, which may be paid by cash, check, or money order made out to "Clerk, United States Tax Court." If you are unable to pay the fee and the amount of tax at issue is small, you may request a fee waiver. Mail your petition with the filing fee to Clerk, United States Tax Court, 400 Second St. N.W., Washington, D.C. 20217.

When your petition is received by the Tax Court, a copy of it is served on the Commissioner of Internal Revenue, who then has sixty days to file an "answer" or forty-five days to make a motion on the petition. If this is not a small-tax case, the Commissioner's answer must fully set forth the IRS defense. It must also specifically admit or deny each material allegation in your petition or state that the Commissioner lacks the information or knowledge to form a belief as to the truth of any allegation. Every ground on which the IRS relies and has the burden of proof must be stated. Any allegation the Commissioner does not expressly admit or deny will be considered to be admitted.

Now it's your turn again. If the Commissioner's answer alleges material facts (ones that tend to establish any of the issues raised in the Commissioner's favor), you have forty-five days after service of the answer to file a "reply" or thirty days for motions on the answer. When you reply, you have to admit or deny every affirmative allegation in the Commissioner's answer or the allegation will be deemed admitted by you. If you have elected the small-tax-case procedure, however, a reply does not have to be filed unless the court or the Commissioner requires it.

If all this is beginning to sound terribly legal, that is a trait most court trials have in common. The small-tax-case procedure is com-

PETITION (Other Than In Small Tax Case)

UNITED STATES TAX COURT

____
Petitioner(s)

v.

COMMISSIONER OF INTERNAL REVENUE,
Respondent Docket No.

PETITION

The petitioner hereby petitions for a redetermination of the deficiency set forth by the Commissioner of Internal Revenue in his notice of deficiency [Service symbols] dated __________, 19____, and as the basis for his case alleges as follows:

1. The petitioner is an individual with legal residence now at ____.
(Street) (City) (State) (Zip Code)
Petitioner's social security number is ___________. The return for the period here involved was filed with the Office of the Internal Revenue Service at _________________________________.
(City) (State)

2. The notice of deficiency (a copy of which, including so much of the statement and schedules accompanying the notice as is material, is attached and marked Exhibit A) was mailed to the petitioner on ______________, 19____, and was issued by the Office of the Internal Revenue Service at ____________________.
(City and State)

3. The deficiencies as determined by the Commissioner are in income taxes for the calendar (or fiscal) year 19____, in the amount of $__________, of which $__________, is in dispute.

4. The determination of tax set forth in the said notice of deficiency is based upon the following errors: [Here set forth specifically in lettered subparagraphs the assignments of error in a concise manner and avoid pleading facts which properly belong in the succeeding paragraph.]

5. The facts upon which the petitioner relies, as the basis of his case, are as follows: [Here set forth allegations of fact, but not the evidence, sufficient to inform the Court and the Commissioner of the positions taken and the bases therefor, in orderly and logical sequence, with subparagraphs lettered, so as to enable the Commissioner to admit or deny each allegation.]

WHEREFORE, petitioner prays that [here set forth the relief desired].

(Signed)__________________________
(Petitioner or Counsel)

____
(Post Office Address)

Dated: ______________, 19____

____
(Telephone Number)

paratively simple, however, and you shouldn't be intimidated. If you are appearing without legal counsel, a court is usually tolerant and the judges helpful. Thousands of your fellow citizens have gone before you and survived. So can you.

There are other procedures for amended or supplemental pleadings, motions, discovery, depositions, admissions, and stipulations, which I am not going to cover here. If you want details about these procedures, locate a government bookstore or write the Superintendent of Documents, U.S. Government Printing Office, Washington, D.C. 20402, for a copy of *Rules of Practice and Procedure United States Tax Court.* You may also be able to get answers to specific questions from the IRS Appellate Division or Regional Counsel.

Your case will be docketed after the petition is filed. This means the court will set a date and a city for the hearing. There is a good chance that your case will be settled out of court, however. Because of the heavy (and increasing) caseload in the Tax Court, every effort is made to resolve cases before trial. It is often possible to obtain a favorable settlement if you are willing to give and take a little.

To facilitate settlement at an earlier stage and decrease the number of cases actually tried by the Tax Court, the IRS Appellate Division has been given sole authority to dispose of a docketed case that it had not previously considered. This means that even though you somehow bypassed Appellate on your way to Tax Court, you wind up there before your hearing. The Appellate Division has four months to negotiate a settlement with you. A settlement conference will be arranged within forty-five days after Appellate receives your case. If a settlement is reached, the settlement documents will be filed with the Tax Court, a decision will be entered, and the tax agreed upon will be assessed.

At the end of the four-month period or if Appellate decides the case cannot be settled, it will be sent to IRS Regional Counsel. Now Counsel will have authority to dispose of your case and will arrange another conference within forty-five days to obtain any additional evidence or facts. After your case has been fully developed by Counsel and the chances of winning it in court have been appraised, a settlement may be offered to you by Counsel. Appellate will be consulted before this settlement offer is made, but Counsel makes the final decision. Only if all settlement negotiations fail will you finally come to trial.

UNITED STATES TAX COURT

.... Petitioner(s)	)
	)
v.	) Docket No.
	)
COMMISSIONER OF INTERNAL REVENUE, Respondent	)

DESIGNATION OF PLACE OF TRIAL

Petitioner(s) hereby designate(s) ....
City and State
as the place of trial of this case.

....
Signature of Petitioner or Counsel

Dated: ...., 19....

FORM 4
Rev: 1/84

☆ U S GPO 1988 - 207 - 787/79275

PRESENTING YOUR CASE

When the hearing begins, you must present sufficient evidence to prove your case. The Tax Court will be trying your case *de novo,* or anew. It will consider all of the evidence you present at the hearing and not merely review the evidence you gave the IRS. Because it is reviewing your entire liability for the year in issue, the court's finding may be for more tax than the IRS claims you owe.

It is up to you to prove that the statutory notice is incorrect. The burden of proof is yours in court, just as it was in the audit. You must produce evidence that does more than merely establish your case; it must *overcome* the government's case. The burden of proof is on the IRS only if fraud is alleged.

If this is not a small-tax case, you or your counsel will make an opening statement and formally present your evidence. The government then presents its case. At the end of the hearing, the court may ask you to make an oral argument and to file written citations of the authorities you have relied on. You then have seventy-five days after the conclusion of the hearing to file a tax brief. In small-tax cases, oral arguments and briefs are not generally required.

After the hearing, the court writes a "Report," stating its findings of fact and opinion. This is not the court's decision. The decision is usually entered immediately after the Report is published if the court finds the notice of deficiency is correct. If it finds that the deficiency should be revised, either up or down, the decision will be entered after you and the IRS agree on the new tax due in light of the court's opinion. If you cannot agree, the court itself will determine how much you owe.

The court's decision is an order that finds the amount of tax due, finds there is no deficiency, or dismisses the case for any reason. The date of the decision determines the time for filing an appeal. It also controls the period when the statute of limitations on assessment and collection is suspended pending the Tax-Court proceeding.

Seeing a case through the Tax Court takes an average of fourteen months from the date of filing to the date of closing. During the 1987 fiscal year, the court closed 45,366 cases, but still ended the year with a backlog of 87,816 cases. For this reason, you should not expect a speedy disposition of your case.

DECISION AND APPEAL

The Tax Court decision is final if you have chosen the small-tax-case procedure. There is no appeal. You will have to abide by the decision and pay any additional tax the court determines you owe.

If the small-tax-case procedures were not used and you are not pleased with the Tax Court's decision, you have ninety days after the decision is entered to appeal. At this point, it is advisable to hire an attorney, even though you represented yourself in Tax Court. Appeal is to the U.S. Court of Appeals for the circuit in which you legally reside. The notice of appeal may be filed by mail addressed to the Clerk of the Tax Court. The postmark is deemed the date of delivery. The notice of appeal must state the party or parties who are appealing, the judgment appealed from, and the name of the court to which the appeal is taken. (If you intend to pursue the appeal without benefit of legal counsel, obtain a copy of the *Federal Rules of Appellate Procedure* from the U.S. Government Printing Office [see address on page 205].)

Your appeal does not postpone the assessment and collection of the tax deficiency determined by the Tax Court. To avoid assessment, you must post a bond on or before you file your notice of appeal. This bond may be up to double the amount of the deficiency.

If you are unsuccessful in the Court of Appeals, your last hope is the U.S. Supreme Court. The Supreme Court naturally is pretty choosy about the cases it hears, and you are not guaranteed a review by that august body.

To give you an idea of your chances on appeal, during the fiscal year 1987, 395 Tax Court cases were closed on appeal. The dispositions were as follows: three hundred thirty-five cases affirmed, *twelve* cases *modified,* and *forty-six* cases *reversed* on one or more issues. The Tax Court's decisions were unchanged in 85.3 percent of the cases. In fewer than 12 percent were the decisions competely reversed.

STAKING YOUR CLAIM IN DISTRICT COURT

Tax Court is only one alternative. If you choose to pay the deficiency, your avenue is to the U.S. District Court (or Court of

Claims) via the filing of a claim. At any stage of the audit process, you may pay the tax and file a claim for refund of the overpayment. A Form 1040X is used to make your claim. The claim must be filed within three years of the due date of the return (or date it was filed, whichever is later) or within two years after the tax is paid if the two-year period ends after the three-year period.

Let me distinguish a (formal) claim from an audit protest or reconsideration (informal claim). Any time a taxpayer protests his audit results at the time he receives his bill, without paying the tax due, he is lodging an audit protest, or informal claim. At the grace of the IRS, he is often given still another chance to prove he does not owe the tax that has now been assessed and billed. The IRS is not obligated to reconsider the deficiency, and if the decision is made to let the tax stand, the taxpayer has no right to appeal. He must first pay the tax and file a formal claim.

Your claim is mailed to the IRS service center where you filed your tax return for that year. Fully state all the facts and your legal arguments on the Form 1040X. You will be limited to these facts and arguments in the district court. A written declaration that your statement of the facts and grounds is made under penalties of perjury must accompany the claim.

When your claim is received at the service center, it will be forwarded to the local district office where you were originally audited. Now you will begin the audit process all over again. Your chances for success at the audit level depend on how far along in the audit process you got the last time before paying the deficiency and filing the claim. If for some reason, such as absence from the country, you never really presented any evidence, your claim will probably be allowed to the extent you can verify it. If, however, you had a full audit and went to a district conference or appellate hearing, don't expect the auditor to suddenly reverse such a hard-fought Service position.

If the auditor hands you a notice of claim disallowance (in part or in full), you are entitled to a district conference, followed by a hearing with the Appellate Division. Again, if you have been this way before, you can be fairly certain your claim will not be recognized. You are merely biding your time until you can go to court.

You may bring a suit to recover taxes in either the Court of Claims at Washington, D.C., or in the U.S. District Court where you reside. Unless you live in the Washington area, you will probably want to sue in district court and not the Court of Claims. You can obtain information about procedures for filing suit in either court by contacting the Clerk of your local district court, or the Clerk of the Court of Claims, 717 Madison Place N.W., Washington, D.C. 20005. However, you probably should have an attorney for this appeal. Unlike the Tax Court, there are no informal court procedures for small taxpayers in either of these federal courts. You have a right to a trial by jury, which is not true in Tax Court.

You must wait six months from the date your claim was filed before suing to recover, unless the IRS makes a decision before then.

You cannot file suit more than two years after receiving the notice disallowing part or all of your claim.

Your opponent in district court or the Court of Claims will not be the IRS but, rather, the U.S. Department of Justice. Its Tax Division litigates civil tax cases that are appealed to these two courts. (The IRS's Regional Counsel litigates in Tax Court.) As with cases brought to Tax Court, an attempt is usually made to settle out of court and avoid expensive litigation. The Tax Division has the authority to compromise the tax, after obtaining the recommendation of the IRS.

If your case does eventually come to court and the judgment is not in your favor, you will have to decide whether you want to appeal further. Appeal from the district court is to the U.S. Court of Appeals, just as it is from the Tax Court. From the Court of Appeals, you may appeal to the U.S. Supreme Court, but, again, the Supreme Court may refuse to hear your case. If you have chosen the Court of Claims, your appeal is direct to the Supreme Court.

All this can become expensive. Under certain circumstances, you may be able to recover attorney's fees from the government. You must show that you have "substantially prevailed" in any federal court, including the Tax Court and Claims Court, that the IRS was unreasonable, and that you exhausted all administrative remedies. Your recovery is limited to $75 an hour, unless the court determines a higher rate is justified.

When court is your last resort, which court are you going to choose? The Tax Court is simpler, less costly, and more convenient.

You can save the high legal costs normally attendant upon going to court, whether you elect the small-tax-case procedure or the regular procedure. Procedures are less formal. Court is held at or near a city where you reside. Furthermore, you may suspend payment of the deficiency until the Tax Court enters its decision.

Why, then, would you ever want to pursue the lengthier, costlier, more complex appeals offered by the U.S. District Court or the Court of Claims? Perhaps cost is no object, and you already possess a battery of expensive legal talent. A better reason is the stand one court has taken on issues similar to yours. A study of tax-law decisions by the three courts may reveal that one court has taken a position favorable to the argument you are advancing, while the other two have not. These courts are not necessarily in agreement over the interpretation of the tax law. It is possible to choose a legal forum that is weighted in your favor.

Note that your best odds are overwhelmingly in Tax Court, where, in 1987, 62 percent of taxpayers were full or partial winners. In District Court or Claims Court, only 19 percent could claim any sort of victory.

These considerations should all play a part in your strategy if your last roll of the dice is before a judge, whether with a jury or without.

XIV. PAYING YOUR DUES

Whether you decide to accept the auditor's findings or fight tooth and nail to the Supreme Court or accept your fate somewhere in between, you will come at last to the final reckoning. Time to pay up and move on—to better luck and records next year.

Once you've made your decision to pay (or it has been made for you), you will probably wait for the additional tax to be assessed and billed to you before settling your account. You don't *have* to wait, however. You may pay the auditor at the time you agree to and sign the audit report. Or, at any stage of the appeals process, you may sign a waiver of restrictions on assessment (Form 870) and pay the IRS employee who is handling your case at that point. If you don't want to pay at the time you agree, allow at least six to eight weeks for your file to be processed and the bill to be sent to you from your service center.

Your bill will show the balance of tax due plus interest and, in some cases, penalties. The amount of tax due should match the balance-due figure on your final audit report. If the tax is less than the amount you signed for, an error was corrected in your favor.

ERR NOW, PAY LATER—INTEREST

Interest is computed on the additional tax you owe, because in theory you have had the use of the government's money since the due date of your return. That is the date you would have paid the additional tax determined in the audit if you had filed a correct return. The rate of interest has been bobbing up and down for the past several years. The various rates and the dates they were in effect are shown in the table. The interest runs from the due date of your return until the date the IRS receives the signed (agreed) audit report or waiver of restrictions. If you filed your return late after applying for an automatic extension to file, the interest still runs from the original due date of the return.

INTEREST AND CERTAIN PENALTY RATES

The interest rate on underpayment of taxes and the penalty for underpayment of estimated tax are as follows.

Period	Interest Rate and Estimated Tax Penalty Rate
April 1, 1988, through June 30, 1988	10 percent a year
January 1, 1988, through March 31, 1988	11 percent a year
October 1, 1987, through December 31, 1987	10 percent a year
July 1, 1986, through September 30, 1987	9 percent a year
January 1, 1986, through June 30, 1986	10 percent a year
July 1, 1985, through December 31, 1985	11 percent a year
January 1, 1985, through June 30, 1985	13 percent a year
July 1, 1983, through December 31, 1984	11 percent a year
January 1, 1983, through June 30, 1983	16 percent a year

The rate of interest for deficiencies of more than $1,000 due to tax shelters or sham or fraudulent transactions is 120 percent of the regular rate, rounded to the nearest tenth of a percent. For example, if the normal interest rate is 11 percent, the interest rate for tax shelter deficiencies will be 13.2 percent.

This higher-interest rule applies if underpayment in excess of

$1,000 is due to (1) deductions based on the overvaluation of property by 150 percent or more; (2) losses or investment credit disallowed under the at-risk rules; (3) tax straddles; (4) deductions on activities not engaged in for profit; (5) sham or fraudulent transactions; and (6) additional income or disallowed deductions or credits due to the use of accounting methods that materially distort income.

What if the audit results in an overpayment? Interest will be paid on your refund. But the rate will be one percent *lower* than the interest on an underpayment.

Your auditor or the person handling your appeal will compute the interest for you if you want to pay "on the spot." Because the interest is compounding daily and the rates fluctuate so wildly, you probably should not attempt the calculation yourself unless you have access to a computer and a truckload of aspirin.

PENALTIES

In addition to interest, your bill or audit report will also show any penalties you may have incurred. There are three types of penalties that can result from an audit: (1) delinquency, (2) negligence, and (3) civil fraud. The assertion of the negligence and civil-fraud penalties is largely at the discretion of the auditor and will be discussed in the next chapter.

The delinquency penalty is asserted on the additional tax resulting from the audit if you filed your tax return late without applying for an automatic extension of time to file (Form 2688). The penalty is 5 percent of the additional tax for every month (or fraction thereof) that the return was late-filed, up to a maximum of 25 percent.

Only that part of your additional tax which is delinquent is subject to the penalty. If all or part of your total tax was prepaid through withholding or estimated-tax payments, that amount is not delinquent. It is only when your total tax exceeds your withholding or estimated tax that you are penalized on the excess. Your auditor will reduce the penalty by any amounts already assessed by the service center at the time you filed.

The delinquency (or failure-to-file) penalty is also imposed by your auditor on the tax due on any return you were required to file but did not. These are usually payroll-tax returns, Forms 940, 941, and 942. Your auditor will file the return(s) for you and indicate the amount of the penalty on the return(s) or report forms.

The delinquency penalty will not be imposed if you can convince your auditor you had "reasonable cause" for not filing a required return timely. A reasonable cause is one that would prompt an ordinary, intelligent person to act in the same manner you did. An example might be reliance on the advice of competent tax counsel. I have also known auditors to decide there was reasonable cause if they believed that, because of his educational or cultural background, the taxpayer was truly ignorant of the tax law.

No interest is computed on penalties if they are paid within ten days of the date of notice and demand. If you let payment slide by, the resulting interest will run from the date of notice and demand to the date you finally pay the penalty.

The delinquency, negligence, and civil-fraud penalties arise from the audit. There is another penalty you can incur for failure to pay the audit deficiency. This penalty is ½ percent for each month or less that the deficiency remains unpaid, up to a maximum of 25 percent. If you cannot show reasonable cause for failing to pay within ten days of the date of notice and demand, this penalty will keep upping the ante until you pay.

PAYING UP

Now that you're ready to settle your account, what forms of payment are acceptable? If you don't want to wait for the bill but would rather pay your auditor, a check or money order payable to the Internal Revenue Service is best. Your auditor may not accept cash. The payment you make is immediately forwarded to the Collection Division, which is responsible for the collection of tax. The audit group is not involved in the collection process and accepts checks or money orders only at the time of audit as a convenience to taxpayers and also because of an IRS motto: "A check in the hand is worth two uncollected."

If you don't make payment at the time you sign your audit report, wait for your bill. Once the auditor receives your signed agreement, your case is mailed back to the service center. Any payment arriving after your case has left the audit group cannot be associated with your file and will wander through the IRS like the flying Dutchman while you receive bills demanding payment.

When you wait to be billed, you may pay by either check, cash, or money order. Send your payment to the address shown on the bill (your service center) and *not* to the audit group. Your social security number should be written on your check or money order or in some way affixed with cash payment. This will ensure that your payment is credited to your account and not to another "John Smith." Make checks or money orders payable to the Internal Revenue Service; do not leave the PAYEE line blank. Do not endorse over your salary check or any other check made out to you.

During the filing season, it is sometimes possible to have the refund on your current year's return applied to your audit deficiency. In fact, if you don't make payment, this will be done for you. You must not rely on this exact timing, however. Write the service center or call your local collection office if you want to explore this possibility.

If, through some misfortune, your check for payment bounces, an additional penalty of 1 percent of the check is imposed, unless the check was tendered in good faith and with reasonable cause to believe it would be paid. If the check is for less than five hundred dollars, the penalty is the lesser of five dollars or the amount of the check.

FAILURE TO PAY

By law, you are required to pay your tax bill within ten days of the notice and demand. We have already discussed the monetary penalty that attaches if you fail to meet this deadline. However, even more serious consequences can ensue. If the tax is unpaid after the ten-day period has elapsed, a statutory lien attaches to your property and rights to property.

The best advice I can give you is to pay promptly. There is leeway in the system to let payment slide, but the longer you wait the higher the interest and penalties, so there is no real financial advantage to inviting a siege. If you cannot pay, either because you are financially unable or for some other reason that will cause delay, call or visit your local IRS collection office as soon as possible. Do not ignore the bill. Your tax problems will not wither away from neglect. They are like weeds: if you don't take immediate steps to control them, they will soon be completely out of hand.

If you cannot immediately pay in full, communicate with your local collection office as soon as you receive your first notice. Several payment options are open to you, but you must ask for them. However, if you have the money or can borrow enough to pay in full, you should do so. Because of the IRS's drastic enforcement power and the lack of compunction with which it is used, you are better off owing money to a bank or finance company than the IRS.

If you think you can borrow, call or write your local collection office asking for an extension of time to fully pay the tax. The IRS will give you a short-term extension of up to sixty days. A revenue representative will fill out Form 433-D, Installment Agreement. You will need to supply: (1) the name and address of your employer (and your spouse's employer if it is a joint return); (2) the amount of your take-home pay and the dates you are paid; (3) names and addresses of your bank accounts (you are not required to supply the account numbers); (4) a description and license number of each motor vehicle you own; and (5) the location, description, equity, and mortgage holder of all real estate you own.

You may also be granted an automatic installment agreement of up to twelve months. You must make your request before the third week after you receive your fourth notice, and the total tax deficiency must be less than the IRS secret tolerance amount. Again, your request can be made in person or by mail.

No agreement will be granted if you are delinquent in filing a return or if you already have an installment agreement outstanding. You must sign Form 433-D or Form 2159, Payment Deduction Agreement, and pay in equal installments.

If you are unable to pay in sixty days or you do not qualify for automatic installment payments, special arrangements can still be made. However, you must visit the collection office and submit to an interview.

The collection representative will determine whether you are as poor as you think you are or whether you have the resources to pay in full. You should take any records with you that will be useful in supporting your report of your financial condition, such as loan payment books, mortgage or rent books, unpaid bills, and information about your income, assets, and personal living expenses. From the information you furnish, the representative will complete Form 433-A, Collection Information Statement for Individuals. Once you have supplied this information, the representative will consider the statement and your records to determine how you can best pay the amount due. Try to remember that the government is sentimental only about collecting the tax. If you have assets that can be sold, mortgaged, or used as security for loans, you are expected to sell or encumber them in order to pay. If you have to go into debt, that is one of the harsh consequences of spending your refund check before it is approved by audit. The representative may also decide you are able to pay in full; if you neglect or refuse to pay, enforced collection action will then be taken (see below).

Often, if it appears that asking you to make immediate payment will result in undue hardship, a payment agreement may be reached that allows you to make payments in installment form. The amount of each monthly payment will be based on your maximum ability to pay and is conditioned upon your paying all future taxes timely. Sometimes a payroll deduction is arranged, in which your employer withholds a set amount from your salary. Another method is named the Advance Dated Remittance Program. Under this plan, you give the IRS postdated checks for each month of the installments. The IRS processes one check each month, and your responsibility is to make sure there is enough money in the bank to cover it. If you are given a part-payment agreement, you must, of course, make each payment on time, or collection action will be taken. You must also keep the IRS informed of any windfalls or increased income that could be used to pay the tax. Under a part-payment agreement, interest continues to accrue on the unpaid balance at the rate of ½ percent per month (up to a maximum of 25 percent).

In cases of extreme hardship, collection action may be delayed. This does not mean we wipe the slate clean. You are still obligated to pay when your financial conditions improve. A federal tax lien is filed on all currently uncollectible cases of $1,000 or more.

The Collection policy in your district may vary somewhat from the guidelines outlined above. Negotiated agreements to pay in monthly installments over a lengthy period of time are entirely discretionary with the IRS and are subject to the approval of the representative's supervisor and other reviewers.

THE COLLECTOR ON YOUR DOORSTEP

You are given four warning notices if you fail to pay or make arrangements to pay within the specified ten days. These notices are sent from your service center. After the fourth, and final, notice, which is pretty stern stuff and warns you of a levy, your account is sent to your district collection office as a Taxpayer Delinquent Account (TDA). The collection-office group will then contact you in a last-ditch attempt to get your attention. If this fails, a revenue officer is assigned to your account and unpleasant things begin to happen.

Now the enforced-collection action begins, with a notice of levy. A "levy" is a taking of property to satisfy a tax liability. There are two types of levy: levy on property that is being held for you by third parties, such as your employer or your bank, and levy on property in your possession. You are given the opportunity to respond to the notice of levy and to pay the tax or make arrangements to pay.

Failure to respond usually first results in a levy on your salary or your bank account. Your paycheck may be garnished at the time a notice of levy is served on your employer. This levy remains in effect until the tax deficiency is paid in full. The levy attaches to all of your wages after subtracting a minimum exemption amount. You are allowed to keep $75 per week for yourself and $25 per week for your spouse and each of your dependents. For example, if you have a wife and three children, you can keep $175 of your wages ($75 for yourself, $25 for your wife, and $75 for your children). The IRS will take the balance.

Although wages and bank accounts are the most popular properties to levy against, other property such as accounts receivable, promissory notes, and securities are also likely targets. However, some property is exempt from levy, including (1) clothing (except furs and jewelry) and school books; (2) food, fuel, furniture, and personal effects up to $1,500 in value; (3) books and tools used in your profession, up to $1,000 in value; (4) unemployment benefits; (5) income needed to pay court-ordered child-support payments; (6) certain annuity and pension payments; (7) workmen's compensation; and

Form 433-D. Installment Agreement. (cont'd)

Form **433-D** (Rev. July 1987)

Department of the Treasury – Internal Revenue Service

Installment Agreement

Name and address of taxpayer*(s)*	Social security or employer identification number	Agreement locator number
	Kinds of taxes *(Form numbers)*	
	Tax periods	Agreement review date
	Amount of tax owed	

The undersigned agrees that the Federal taxes shown above, plus any interest and penalties provided by law, will be paid as follows: $________ to be paid on ________ and $________ to be paid on the ________ of each ________ thereafter until the liability is paid in full, and also agrees that the above tax installments will be increased as follows:

Date of increase					
Amount of increase	$				
New installment amount	$				

Conditions:

- This agreement is based on your current financial circumstances and is subject to revision or cancellation if subsequent financial information required by IRS reflects a change in your ability to pay.
- If this agreement is still in effect after 36 months, your financial circumstances will be reevaluated. The agreement may be changed or canceled at that time.
- All Federal taxes that become due during the term of this agreement will be paid on time.
- All Federal tax returns that become due during the term of this agreement will be filed on time.
- Any Federal or State refunds that might otherwise be due will be applied to this liability until it is satisfied.
- Permission to make installment payments may be withdrawn and the entire tax liability may be collected by levy on income or by seizure of property if the conditions of this agreement are not met or if it is determined that collection of these taxes is endangered.
- This agreement may require managerial approval. If it is not approved, you will be so notified.

Additional conditions:			Originator's name and IDRS assignment number:
Your signature	Title *(if corporate officer or partner)*	Date	For assistance call:
Spouse's signature *(if joint income tax return)*		Date	or write:
Agreement examined and approved by *(signature)*		Date	

Note: When making an installment payment, please be sure to:

1. Write your social security or employer identification number on each payment.
2. Make each payment in an amount at least equal to that specified in this agreement. For example, do not double one payment and skip the next without contacting us.
3. Enclose with each payment a copy of the reminder notice (if you received one), in the envelope provided.
4. Mail your payment on time to the proper IRS office, even if you did not receive a reminder notice.
5. Contact us immediately if you cannot meet the terms of this agreement.

Part 2 – Taxpayer's Copy

Form **433-D** (Rev. 7-87)

(8) undelivered mail. These are specifically exempt by law. However, as a matter of policy and good public relations, the IRS rarely levies on social security benefits, Medicare or welfare payments, the cash loan value of insurance policies, death benefits, or pension plan proceeds, including IRA and Keogh accounts.

Only the written notice of levy sent to your last known address is required before levy action is taken. No court order or approval is needed. Levy may be made if no response is forthcoming within ten days. Note, however, that if the IRS believes the tax is in jeopardy (e.g., you bought a ticket to Buenos Aires), levy may be made without waiting ten days.

A brief word here about who is responsible for paying the tax. If a joint return was filed, both husband and wife are responsible for the tax. The IRS may come after either one of you and leave you two to fight it out between yourselves later. An assessment against a child related to income he earns has the effect of an assessment against the parent, and collection action may be taken against both parent and child.

Certain "innocent spouses" may be relieved of joint liability. You will not be held liable for an audit deficiency in excess of $500 if: (1) the underpayment was due to the omission of income by your spouse or disallowance of deductions or credits claimed by your spouse; (2) you did not know or had no reason to know there was an understatement of tax liability; and (3) under the facts and circumstances, it would be inequitable to hold you liable.

This rule does not apply unless the tax deficiency exceeds ten percent of the innocent spouse's adjusted gross income of $20,000 or less (twenty-five percent of an adjusted gross income over $20,000).

Besides the innocent spouse rule, you are not liable for a joint return if it was signed as a result of fraud, trickery, or duress.

If the levy against your more liquid assets, such as your salary or bank account, fails to satisfy the deficiency and you still refuse or neglect to pay or make arrangements to pay, levy will next be made on other property you own, property that must be sold to convert it to cash. Levy on this type of property is called a "seizure."

Any property, including your home, may be seized and sold to settle your tax liability. Unlike a levy on your cash assets, a court writ is required before seizure. Before deciding to seize property, the IRS considers what the net sales proceeds are likely to be and whether the seizure and sale will create an undue hardship on you and your family. Seizure of the family home is done only as a last resort, but be certain: it will be seized if deemed necessary.

A levy or seizure may be released if you deliver a cash bond to the IRS, sign a payroll deduction agreement, agree to an acceptable installment arrangement, or pay the property's forced-sale value to the IRS.

After property is seized, it is put up for sale. You have the right to remain in your seized home until the day it is sold. At least a ten-day notice of the proposed sale must be given to you and the public (unless the property is perishable). This notice should be issued as soon as practicable after the necessary arrangements for sale have been made. The revenue officer will set a minimum bid—the lowest price at which the property will be sold. If no one offers that amount, the property is deemed purchased by the United States.

You have the right to object to the minimum bid price if you think it is too low. You also have the right to request that your property's true forced-sale value be determined by an IRS valuation engineer or a private appraiser. However, the costs of obtaining a private appraisal will be charged to you.

The sale must take place within ten to forty days after public notice is given.

Whatever proceeds are derived from the sale are first applied to the expenses of levy and sale, then to the tax bill. If the sale proceeds are less than the tax bill, further collection action will be taken to satisfy the portion still unpaid. When the sale proceeds exceed the tax bill, the excess money will be credited or refunded to you, unless someone to whom you owe money submits a superior claim.

You have a right to redeem your property prior to sale by paying the tax due plus the expenses of seizure. Real estate may be redeemed within 180 days after the sale if you pay the purchaser the amount he paid for the property plus interest at the rate of 20 percent per annum.

In some cases, collection is impossible—not just now, but forever. You might meet this criterion, for example, if you are elderly and ill, with no savings and living on a small pension.

If there is doubt that the tax you owe can ever be collected, you may be able to settle for a lesser amount by making an offer in compromise. If you owe $1,000 but the most you believe you can afford to pay is $200, you can ask the IRS to wipe the slate clean by accepting that amount. If the IRS also believes the full amount will never be paid, they may accept. Collection on your debt will be not merely suspended. Your debt will be considered paid in full.

Your offer must be sincere, not frivolous. It must reflect your maximum ability to pay and must be accompanied by a completed Form 433, Statement of Financial Condition. The offer itself is made on Form 656, Offer in Compromise. Never suggest an offer to an IRS employee without specifying that you want to compromise your tax liability. The word "offer" could be construed as a bribe if your intent is not clear.

An offer in compromise can also be made when there is doubt as to liability—a *bona fide* dispute about a question of fact or law. This might occur if you were audited without your knowledge and agree you owe some tax, but not as much as you were assessed.

Although the IRS must consider all offers in compromise, they are only grudgingly and rarely accepted.

Earlier I said that a statutory lien attaches to your property and rights in property if you fail to make payment within the specified ten days after you receive your bill. This has no real effect on you, however, unless the IRS decides to file a Notice of Federal Tax Lien. This is a notice to your creditors that the lien exists against your property, including property acquired after the lien is filed. Once a Notice of Federal Tax Lien is filed, it becomes a matter of public record and can have an adverse effect upon your business or other financial interests. It may affect your credit rating.

The Notice of Federal Tax Lien is filed at the place prescribed by the state where the property is situated. If your state prescribes more than one place or none for filing, the notice is filed with the Clerk of the U.S. District Court for the district in which your property is situated.

When the tax due (plus interest and penalties) has been satisfied, the notice is released. All state fees for filing and releasing the notice must be paid by you.

The best way to avoid the harshnesses of the collection process is to work with Collection. What the Collection representative or revenue officer is looking for is some assurance that the tax will be paid as soon as you can manage payment without hardship. He is not out to bring you to ruin. If you're not making money, neither is your government. Cooperate, act in good faith, and keep the collector away from your door.

XV. I CAN GET IT FOR YOU WHOLESALE

Some taxpayers, despite the occupations listed on their returns, are secretly gravediggers. Unfortunately, the graves they are digging are their own. While most taxpayers philosophically accept the records they have and valiantly make the best of it, a few are busy making the worst of it. They are so wrapped up in shoveling that hole, they don't see the resulting heap threatening to bury them.

As if an audit weren't trouble enough, a few taxpayers insist on heightening their peril. Pehaps they like to live dangerously. Whatever the reason, these taxpayers risk penalties, fines, and imprisonment just to avoid paying tax. I don't expect you to be among their number, of course, but it's possible to court trouble without even being aware of it, unless you're familiar with the laws and the IRS interpretation of them. I'm talking about the laws relating to bribes, threats, assaults, negligence, fraud, and the ever-popular tax evasion. In some of these cases, you're going to think the IRS is overreacting; in others, it's the taxpayer who is.

GRATUITIES

An IRS auditor may not accept any gratuity from a taxpayer whose return she is examining or over which she has influence. A gratuity includes a gift, favor, entertainment, loan, discount, or any other thing of monetary value. And this is true even within a reasonable time after the audit is completed.

It is the auditor's responsibility to politely refuse a proffered gratuity, but you can do yourself a favor by not offering in the first place. No matter how well intentioned, your generosity can be easily misconstrued. Turning you down can be awkward for the auditor, embarrassing to you, and at worst, make the auditor suspicious of your return and anxious to prove she has not been influenced by you. The most tangible way to prove that is to have you leave the audit owing more tax. Remember that an auditor has discretion to accept your oral testimony when your records don't suffice, and in many cases (unless your records are now letter perfect) this can be the difference between owing tax and not owing tax. You don't want to put a strain on your fragile relationship with the auditor by unwittingly becoming too friendly.

Where does the IRS draw the line between a harmless gratuity and a bribe? The difference lies in your intent, not in the size of the offer. A true gift has no strings attached; you do not expect anything in return. A bribe is the consideration for a smaller tax bill. It is tendered with the intent of receiving a gift in exchange: the auditor's agreement to look the other way. If this is what you hope to achieve, even a cup of coffee can be a bribe.

The outright offer of a sum of money to lessen or wipe out a tax deficiency is easy to call. This is your classic bribe, and it is a stupid and risky way to beat the government out of what is, after all, only money. It makes even less sense when you consider that you have to spend money to do it. The odds on finding an auditor or a revenue agent who wants to play this form of Russian roulette with you are slim indeed, and if you guess wrong it's hard to get the auditor to believe it was just a joke. It is especially difficult in office audit, where the tax deficiencies rarely run into the thousands, to find an employee who is willing to share the risk for a short-term reward.

The subtle bribe attempt, the offer than can be taken for innocent friendliness, is harder to detect and harder to prove. And it is in this area that you can become suspect without meaning to. A good example is the line that heads this chapter: "I can get it for you wholesale." I have been offered discounts on portable televisions, even clothes. Usually these are spontaneous expressions of good will. Often they are whipped out by salesmen who probably say them in their sleep and for whom discounts are just good business. The problem with intent here is that it is not readily apparent. The auditor does not know what you are thinking, only what you said. Your words are her only clue to whether you are as innocent as you appear. Offering an item at cost or for a discount has serious implications and should always be avoided.

If an auditor or agent is conducting the audit at your place of business, an action open to unfavorable interpretation is to leave cash out in the open, especially in such a manner as to make the auditor aware it is available. Don't leave a cash-register drawer open near the auditor and leave the room, for instance. Not only can this be construed as an indirect offer of a bribe, but it makes the auditor extremely wary that you may later accuse her of theft.

Another example can be illustrated by a taxpayer who startled and disconcerted a friend of mine by pulling an enormous, gift-wrapped package out of his shopping bag and setting it squarely in front of her. He was Korean, with a big smile and little English, and my friend decided he was used to a different form of government. As large as the package was, she tried to ignore it, but he kept edging it closer and closer, smiling and nodding, until the audit became a tug-of-war, she pushing it away and he shoving it back.

Other gratuities, more awkward than incriminating, include tickets to sporting events, plays, or concerts, or free passes to an amusement park or miniature-golf course the taxpayer manages or owns. I have had actors invite me to little theaters they were appearing in, with tickets to be left at the box office. One gospel singer brought in an album her choir had recorded, as a Christmas gift. Which brings us to Christmas cards: Don't send one to your auditor. We really hate sending back Christmas cards, because of the spirit of the season, but we feel guilty keeping them.

Probably the most uncomfortable position an auditor is placed in is when the taxpayer offers to buy or give her a cup of coffee or a soft drink or when the audit takes place at the taxpayer's or representative's place of business and lunchtime rolls around. The *IRS Handbook of Employee Responsibilities and Conduct* permits an auditor to accept a "nonalcoholic" drink "where circumstances would make it uncomfortable to refuse. . . . " On the whole, it is frowned upon, however, and in my district, auditors and agents must buy their own coffee, thank you. Overreacting? Maybe; maybe not. Personally I prefer a government agency that won't even accept a cup of coffee from the citizenry to some of the others, who have their hands out.

Don't offer to buy the auditor lunch, either, even if she's a woman and it wounds your male pride to have her pick up her own check. As a woman, this is one of the stickiest situations I face: fighting for the check. Let the auditor do her job without taking it personally. I have seen several good working relationships go sour over lunch. Also along the business line, your auditor or agent should not accept validated parking—at least in my district, where the stated policy is to find a pay parking lot where possible, rather than park free in the taxpayer's lot. We simply cannot accept any favors, no matter how trivial, from you.

How does the auditor decide whether a bribe has been offered if no words are spoken? She must evaluate your intent from your actions, and although the size of the gift is not controlling, it can bear a relationship to your true intentions. The smaller the gift the less likely it is a bribe. The size of a bribe is usually in proportion to the taxpayer's expected gain. A fifty-cent cup of coffee is not going to buy even a ten-dollar tax reduction. Using the same reasoning, a discount on a dress sounds more innocuous than a discount on a television set. The television set is borderline, and I am unsure to this day whether a bribe was intended. In addition to the amount, the timing is important. Becoming suddenly generous when the audit report is handed to you is not going to create a favorable impression. Two tickets to the Rams game arriving in the mail after the taxpayer has already signed an agreement seems to lack any intent: the case is closed and the auditor is no longer in a bargaining position with the taxpayer. The tickets must not be accepted, but they certainly cause no alarm. The auditor also considers the taxpayer's cultural and educational background. The Korean with his silver-wrapped package had no knowledge of our laws or customs. Many immigrants come from countries where bribing tax officials is traditional, even expected. (Unmistakeable oral bribe attempts by immigrants have been prosecuted, however.)

Where the nature of the offer is ambiguous, the auditor will usually give you the benefit of the doubt. Bribery is a serious charge and not an accusation we throw around lightly. The auditor may pretend not to have heard you or may laugh it off as a joke. Only if by your persistence you convince her that a bribe offer is being made will she take steps to nail you. If you bring or send a gift of nominal value to your auditor, she will hand or mail it back to you without repercussions, stating she is not permitted to accept the item.

If an auditor suspects you of attempted bribery, she will report the incident to the IRS Inspection Division. Suspicion is all that is required, so it is possible for you to be investigated even though your intention was honest. That is why the best policy is to avoid offering *anything* to your auditor. The auditor will say nothing to you about her suspicions. She will not even tell her manager. The possible bribe is reported directly to Inspection.

The Inspection Division is an independent arm of the IRS, independent so that it cannot be wrongfully influenced or controlled by IRS, because one of its primary functions is to investigate misconduct by IRS employees. In this role, Inspection is like an internal police force; it investigates prospective employees and uses a network of inside informers to uncover integrity violations by employees. But Inspection also steps in to investigate violations of the law by taxpayers when those violations involve IRS employees. A taxpayer who attempts to bribe an auditor poses a threat to that employee's integrity, and it does not matter that he refused the bribe and his integrity remains unimpaired.

Inspection decides whether the auditor's suspicion that a bribe was intended has merit and whether an investigation is warranted. If a sound case is eventually developed, prosecution will be recommended. Inspection does only the fact-finding; the Justice Department prosecutes. An attempted bribe is a federal offense, punishable by imprisonment up to fifteen years and/or a fine up to three times the amount of the bribe.

THREATS

Inspection also becomes involved whenever an employee is physically endangered by a threat or assault. Depending on the degree of violence, these can be serious crimes, and if you have a bad temper I advise you to leave it at home. The combination of one auditor, one taxpayer, and one audit report can be highly inflammable, and otherwise calm, rational persons can suddenly find themselves ranting and raving. In that condition, it is easy to say or do something you may later regret.

Because her safety is at stake, an auditor is not going to wait around to see whether you really mean it if your tone of voice or actions become threatening. No benefit of the doubt here. If there is an escape route available, she'll leave you alone to do your explaining, red-faced, to Inspection.

How can you avoid having to try to prove you're not a violent criminal? Don't let your emotions get the worst of you. Remember, it's only money and you have half a dozen levels of appeal. Don't shoot the first person who doesn't let you have your own way. Think before you speak: Can your words be taken two ways? The same is true for action.

You may have no intention of hitting the auditor when you shake your fist at her, but it's unlikely she's going to take it for a new form of greeting, either. Especially if you are yelling at the same time. Suddenly rising to your feet and standing menacingly over the auditor may also be taken as a threat of imminent assault. One man who had to account to Inspection belligerently told the auditor, "I'll pay, but you're going to pay too!" It may well have been merely blurted out with the taxpayer having no idea what he intended to do, but a threat was definitely implied, however ambiguous. He was sufficiently shaken by a visit from Inspection that no action was taken against him. This is the type of rash remark it is easy to blunder into if you are angry, and it is a good example of why you should consider the implications of what you say or do.

Here are a few more tales of taxpayers who gave us a start, all quite unwittingly. A mod young man in tight-fitting Levi's whipped out a switchblade—and began cleaning his fingernails. A highway patrolman who must have zipped in between crimes showed up fully armed, revolver bristling at his side. A golf-course manager deducting the cost of feeding his guard dogs brought them in to give me an idea of how much they ate: two German shepherds trained to attack anyone who said a harsh word like "tax" to their master, as big as horses and no doubt possessed of voracious appetites; I believed every word he said and sent the dogs out to wait in the car.

One auditor asked his taxpayer, a shabby, down-and-out man in his fifties, for identification. The man dutifully handed over an ID card from the veterans hospital. In one corner of the card was printed a small letter code. Any other auditor would have nodded and given it back. But this auditor had worked at a VA hospital, and he almost panicked when he saw that code, an innocuous-looking letter of the alphabet meaning "homicidal psychopath." The audit was unusually quick, with not a word about owing tax, the audit report to be mailed from a discreetly safe distance. As soon as his outpatient left, the auditor called the hospital to demand why he had been allowed to come to the audit. "Oh," the woman said brightly, "we didn't think it would do him any harm." If she had ever seen how normally "sane" taxpayers react in audits, her optimism would have been as shaken as the auditor.

Inspectors are on twenty-four-hour call to ride to the aid of threatened employees. Auditors have telephone numbers at which an inspector can be reached day or night. The threat or assault does not have to be made during business hours on government property. Even heavy breathing on the telephone late at night by a taxpayer trying to frighten an auditor may be construed as a threat.

I don't want to leave you with the impression that we live behind barricades, nervously looking over our shoulders and jumping whenever the telephone rings. Most of us have unlisted telephone numbers, but that is usually the extent of our paranoia. In my experience, only one taxpayer actually told an auditor he was going to kill her. A couple of years ago, a citizen drove his car through the window of an audit group, but it was probably just an accident. And of course there are always the bomb scares for diversion. It really doesn't bother us at all.

NEGLIGENCE

Your return can get you into another kind of trouble—with a little help from you, of course. This trouble is strictly monetary, but paying over good money to the government is what you are trying to avoid. And when it comes to the negligence and fraud penalties, it's just as easy to steer clear of them as it is to incur them.

The penalty for negligence, or intentional disregard, of tax rules and regulations in the preparation of your tax return is 5 percent of the additional tax, or statutory deficiency, you owe as the result of the audit, plus 50 percent of the interest due on the underpayment. If your return was delinquent (not timely filed), the penalty is 5 percent of the total tax due on the return, not just the additional tax uncovered in audit.

The negligence penalty amounts to a slap on the wrist for being naughty. There is no intent to defraud here—rather, irresponsible and reckless behavior similar to driving faster than the speed limit. When the negligence is gross, the line between fraud and negligence blurs, however. Intent to defraud can be implied from the taxpayer's actions: the higher the speed the less it looks as though you just forgot to check your speedometer.

The assertion of the negligence penalty is in the discretion of the auditor, and as one of mine said to me, "It's not an exact science, is it?" As is true in other areas, the auditor will often give you the benefit of the doubt, preferring to believe that you made an honest mistake or that you really incurred the expense but are a poor record keeper or that the issue involves an area of the law most taxpayers have trouble applying.

Your signature on your tax return is an affirmation that to the best of your knowledge it is true and correct. The phrase "to the best of my knowledge and belief" does not excuse you from negligence by crying, "But I didn't know the law." You are expected to make a good-faith effort to learn the law that applies to you. Failure to do so is negligence. But auditors realize that some areas of the law are tricky, vague, or not often used by individual taxpayers, for instance installment sales, recapture of depreciation, and deferring the gain on the sale of a residence. Ignorance of the law and errors are common when more complex issues are involved, and negligence in those cases would probably only be considered if the taxpayer was sophisticated in tax matters.

The average taxpayer is expected to know such basics as exemptions, itemized deductions, and business expenses. Taking a deduction for expenses that are clearly not deductible, such as your children's school uniforms or repairs on your pleasure boat, is inviting that slap on the wrist. The same is true if the expense is deductible but not by you, for example automobile expense where your employer reimburses you completely.

Exaggerating your expenses may also be negligence. If your auditor finds you consistently rounding off to the nearest fifty or one hundred, expect to be penalized. If the amount on your return bears no relation to what you actually spent or if you didn't spend anything at all, you may have let yourself in for fraud.

Failure to report all of your income can be either negligence or fraud. Which penalty the auditor decides to apply is governed by the reason you give for the understatement and the amount involved, among other factors. Omitting income almost always results in one penalty or the other, however, and is considered a serious offense.

The fact that you relied on a tax preparer to fill out your return correctly will not absolve you from responsibility for negligence. You are charged with inspecting your return before it is mailed in, to make sure it is accurate. One computer-printed return with gross income of $15,000 showed an interest expense of $34,000. The auditor discovered that, through a data entry error, the true amount, $340.00, had been entered, without the decimal point, as $34000. Even the most casual inspection by the taxpayer would have prevented this error. Because of his evident neglect, a penalty was asserted.

Negligence is prevented before the audit by exercising reasonable care. Educate yourself in the law, and you need never know the indignity of being penalized.

FRAUD

When a taxpayer sets out to evade the tax, he goes beyond negligence and crosses the borderline into crime. Tax evasion is a criminal act for which prosecution is a real possibility, and the resulting fraud on the tax return can lead to a stiff civil penalty. If evidence of fraud is uncovered during the audit, a taxpayer can be in for a rocky ride that may lead to fines and imprisonment.

As an honest taxpayer, this dire prospect is nothing for you to worry about. You cannot commit fraud accidentally. Fraud is willful. It is a deliberate intent to evade tax. The taxpayer knows that the figures on his tax return are false and that his tax liability is understated as a result. His purpose is dishonest, and he has resorted to lies, deceit, concealment, or misrepresentation of the facts to achieve it.

Tax evasion and fraud must be proved, and this is one area in which the IRS has the burden of proof. In order to find a taxpayer guilty of criminal tax evasion, the government must prove he is guilty "beyond a reasonable doubt." If the evidence will not sustain this burden of proof, then the taxpayer will escape prosecution. The civil-fraud penalty will be considered instead. The civil-fraud penalty is 75 percent of the underpayment of tax due to the fraud, plus 50 percent of the interest due. This is a much steeper penalty than the 5 percent for negligence and can add up to a substantial amount if the fraud was great. To prove civil fraud, the evidence must be "clear and convincing." There may be some doubt, but the evidence must be sufficient to convince a reasonable person that the understatement was due to fraud.

Unless the taxpayer confesses, intent to evade tax or defraud is usually proved by circumstantial evidence. As I've discussed before, intent is a state of mind, and to determine what is in a person's mind, we look to his actions. Can we infer from his acts of concealment, false explanations, or false documents, among others, that he deliberately intended to evade taxed and succeeded?

What are some of the indications of fraud your auditor is looking for? Where the taxpayer has failed to report all of his taxable income, evidence of fraud includes:

1. Omissions of specific items of income where similar items are included, for example, not reporting fifteen hundred dollars interest income from Bank A but reporting fifty dollars interest income from Bank B. By reporting the fifty dollars, the taxpayer has shown he knows interest income is taxable, so omitting the larger amount appears deliberate.
2. Omission of an entire source of income, for example, failure to report tip income. Another possible mark of fraud when tips are not reported is leaving "occupation" blank on the return. This can be interpreted as an attempt to conceal the fact that you earn tips (although it is usually easy to spot from the W-2), and concealment is an indication of intent to defraud.
3. Personal expenditures in excess of known sources of income, that is, you are spending more money than your return shows you earn. What usually alerts an auditor is a low or even negative taxable income.
4. Total bank deposits in excess of the amount of income shown on your return. Bank deposits are routinely totaled whenever the taxpayer is self-employed; they may also be added up for persons with W-2 wages if the auditor suspects unreported income. This is usually accomplished by asking the taxpayer to bring in his monthly bank statements for the year in question. If he refuses to cooperate, the auditor will subpoena these records from the taxpayer's bank.
5. Concealment of bank accounts, brokerage accounts, or other property. A favorite hiding place for taxable goodies has long been the safety-deposit box. But be forewarned: a bank does not provide

sanctuary. Just as the IRS can subpoena your bank records, it can also pry its way into your "safe" treasure chest with a court order. Before you rise up in arms against this invasion of privacy, however, please note that I have brought this subject up only in connection with fraud. In the handling of a routine office audit, such a procedure is unheard of. So, unless you are involved in criminal activity or stashing unreported cash income, don't lose any sleep worrying about this.

6. Failure to deposit receipts, especially cash, into a business bank account, as is normal business practice. This goes hand in hand with keeping loose controls on business receipts.

7. False explanations of your sources of income, for example, stating you borrowed five thousand dollars when in fact you won five thousand dollars on a TV game show.

When the fraud involves fictitious or improper deductions, it usually takes one of the following forms:

1. Substantial overstatement of deductions, for example, deducting six thousand dollars as travel expenses when the amount was actually one thousand dollars.

2. Deduction of large amounts of personal expenses as business or itemized expenses, for instance, personal rent deducted as business rent.

3. Burying obviously unallowable items in an unrelated account or mislabeling an expense. Examples would be including political contributions under "Advertising" or labeling your TV set "Machinery."

4. Claiming completely fictitious deductions, such as a casualty loss when no loss occurred.

5. Claiming exemptions for nonexistent, deceased, or self-supporting persons (or for dogs, cats, iguanas, etc.).

A taxpayer's records or lack of them can also be an indication of fraud. If a taxpayer has been audited before and told what records he needs, his subsequent failure to keep adequate records could indicate his intent to make reconstruction of his income and expenses deliberately difficult. Keeping two sets of records or a set of records that do not agree with the tax return are other evidences of fraud.

The most common evidence of fraud an auditor encounters is false or altered documents. These are usually crude and often comically obvious. The fraud is actually less irritating to the auditor than an obvious insult to her intelligence. Some examples are shown below:

18th day of Jan **19**86

ITEMS	AMOUNT	
Breakfast		
Lunch		
Dinner		
Hotel		
□Plane □Train		
To		
To		
To		
Baggage		
Bus and Taxi		
Postage		
Telephone, Telegrams	2	00
Tips		
Entertainment		
Auto Allowance		
Auto Rental		
Gas and Oil		
Lubrication and Washing		
Repairs, Parts, etc.		
Parking and Storage	3	50
Tolls		
Miles @ ¢		
Total Expense for today	5	50

19th day of Jan **19**87

ITEMS	AMOUNT	
Breakfast		
Lunch Howard	23	90
Dinner Davidson		
Hotel Riverside		
□Plane □Train		
To		
To		
To		
Baggage		
Bus and Taxi		
Postage		
Telephone, Telegrams	1	90
Tips	4	00
Entertainment		
Auto Allowance		
Auto Rental		
Gas and Oil		
Lubrication and Washing		
Repairs, Parts, etc.		
Parking and Storage	2	00
Tolls		
Miles @ ¢		
Total Expense for today	31	80

Diary prepared by a dishonest, but absentminded, taxpayer. It was presented as a timely kept record, though actually made up after the fact; the taxpayer had difficulty remembering which year was being faked.

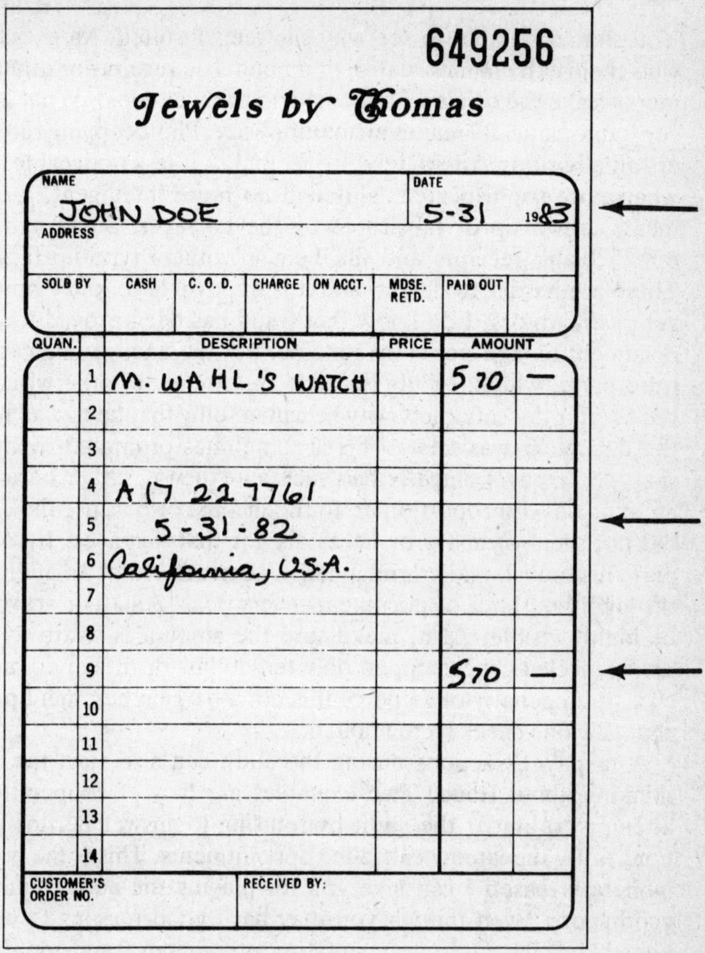

649256

Jewels by Thomas

NAME	DATE
JOHN DOE	5-31 1983
ADDRESS	

SOLD BY	CASH	C. O. D.	CHARGE	ON ACCT.	MDSE. RETD.	PAID OUT

QUAN.		DESCRIPTION	PRICE	AMOUNT	
	1	M. WAHL'S WATCH		570	—
	2				
	3				
	4	A 17 227761			
	5	5-31-82			
	6	California, USA.			
	7				
	8				
	9			570	—
	10				
	11				
	12				
	13				
	14				

CUSTOMER'S ORDER NO.	RECEIVED BY:

This jewelry receipt was altered twice. But an experienced eye would soon notice the discrepancy between the two dates and the heavy penmanship that transformed $10 or $70 into $570.

You should be able to see why she feels insulted. Most taxpayers who change the names, dates, or amounts on receipts or other documents leave the originals at home and bring us copies. That is why a copy automatically makes an auditor wary. Photocopying rarely covers an alteration completely; it just makes it less noticeable. Somewhat more sophisticated, although no more intelligent, are documents drawn up or fabricated by the taxpayer. Some manage to obtain blank receipts and fill them in; others type up facsimiles. These are harder to detect, and it is impossible to know how many get past auditors. I do know that fraud has been proved where the document looked perfectly genuine, but the auditor had called the third party, who allegedly issued it and found out otherwise. Often the auditor doesn't know why he called, only that he had a "feeling" the document was false. This is sometimes prompted by disbelief that the taxpayer actually had such an expense, either because the amount was disproportionate to the income or because the expense did not seem ordinary or necessary for that taxpayer. If you must play this foolish and criminal game, remember that an auditor sifts through thousands of documents every year. Amateur artwork can be highly visible. Also, make sure the amount is worth it. I have seen canceled checks upped only ten dollars or fifteen dollars. The civil-fraud penalty of 75 percent is not a bargain basement price for changing one check by ten dollars.

A taxpayer's actions during the audit can also start the auditor thinking about fraud. Two examples are lack of cooperation and attempts to hinder the audit by refusing to answer pertinent questions or by repeatedly canceling appointments. This is the best nonmonetary reason I can give you for playing the audit game like a good sport. Even though you may have good reasons to be tight-lipped, hostile, and procrastinating other than fraud, don't invite suspicion on yourself. It will cause needless delay and unpleasantness, and eventually you may have to talk a blue steak to get yourself out of the pickle your auditor has imagined you into. Lying to your auditor is even more foolhardy, no matter how legitimate your excuse. Information you give an auditor is confidential; don't be so bashful that you cast doubt on your entire credibility.

What action does an auditor take when she suspects fraud? What she *won't* do is let on she suspects anything. The taxpayer will be the last to know. She will continue the audit just long enough to gather

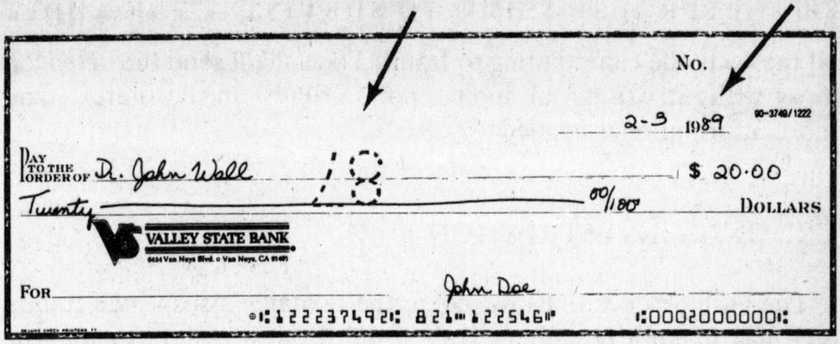

No.

2-9 1989 90-3749/1222

PAY TO THE ORDER OF Dr. John Wall $ 20.00

Twenty 00/100 DOLLARS

VALLEY STATE BANK
6454 Van Nuys Blvd. ○ Van Nuys, CA 91401

FOR John Doe

⑆122237492⑆ 821⑈122546⑈ ⑆0002000000⑆

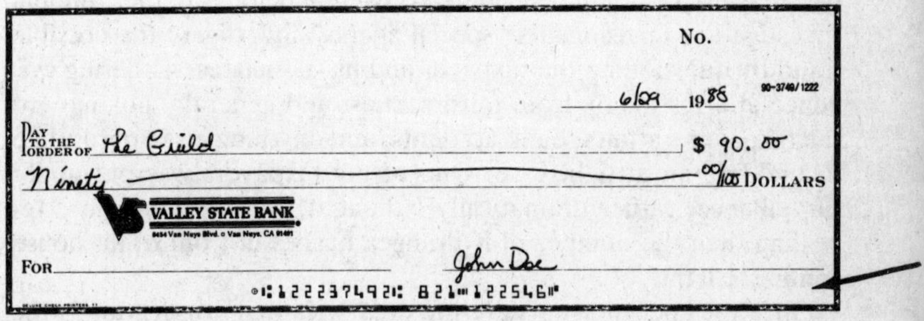

No.

6/29 1988 90-3749/1222

PAY TO THE ORDER OF the Guild $ 90.00

Ninety 00/100 DOLLARS

VALLEY STATE BANK
6454 Van Nuys Blvd. ○ Van Nuys, CA 91401

FOR John Doe

⑆122237492⑆ 821⑈122546⑈

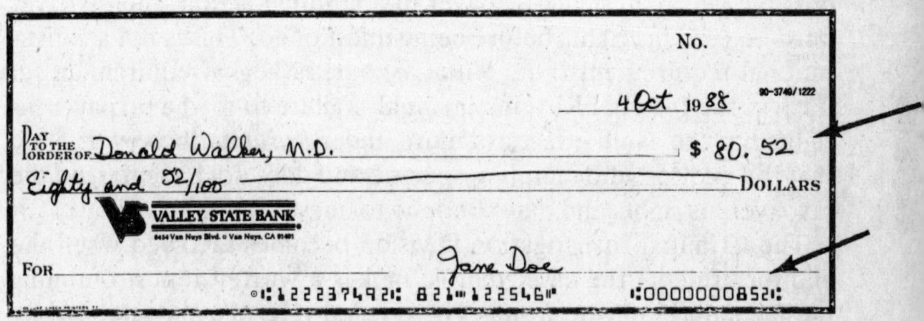

No.

4 Oct 1988 90-3749/1222

PAY TO THE ORDER OF Donald Walker, M.D. $ 80.52

Eighty and 52/100 DOLLARS

VALLEY STATE BANK
6454 Van Nuys Blvd. ○ Van Nuys, CA 91401

FOR Jane Doe

⑆122237492⑆ 821⑈122546⑈ ⑆0000000852⑆

Three examples of fraudulent checks. The point of interest in the first check is not just the change of date, which is fairly obvious from the odd-looking "9" in "89." The confirmation comes from the holes punched into the check by the bank, which read "87" upside down. The second check was never cashed. How can you tell? There is no magnetic number in the lower right-hand corner. On the third check, the amount has been changed from $8.52 to $80.52. The magnetic number in the lower right-hand corner states the original amount.

all the facts she can pointing to fraud. Then she'll send the taxpayer away without writing an audit report, usually on the pretext that more information is needed.

CRIMINAL INVESTIGATION

The auditor does not investigate the taxpayer's suspected fraud. She may make a few phone calls to third parties who can confirm her suspicions, but the real job of developing a fraud case beyond that reasonable doubt needed for conviction belongs to the Criminal Investigation Division. Its "special agents" investigate the possible fraud by questioning the taxpayer and his associates, gathering evidence and testimony from third parties, and generally poking into the taxpayer's affairs, bank accounts, and anything else appropriate to building an airtight case. One of my taxpayers was put under surveillance, rather dramatically I thought, with nothing more revealing than the number of hydrangea bushes in front of his house coming to light.

Once the special agents are involved, criminal prosecution is the likely result. Because the special agents are gathering evidence for possible use against the taxpayer in a criminal action, the taxpayer must be read his rights before being questioned. This is not a constitutional requirement (i.e., *Miranda*) but, rather, a requirement set forth in the Internal Revenue manual. Failure to read a taxpayer his rights has the same effect as failure under *Miranda,* however. Note that the auditor who merely suspects fraud does not have to read the taxpayer his rights and may continue to question him.

The Criminal Investigation Division becomes involved when the auditor "refers" the case, that is, makes a written report outlining the facts that indicate fraud. These fraud referrals are screened by Criminal Investigation for their prosecution potential. If the special agent who does the screening believes that the case is weak and that it cannot be proved beyond a reasonable doubt, the referral will be rejected and sent back to the audit group for assertion of the civil-fraud penalty instead of prosecution. The civil-fraud penalty cannot be asserted unless the case has first been referred to Criminal Investigation.

If a fraud referral is accepted, it is given a score and placed in a case pool. How high a score a case gets depends on how good its prosecution potential is. Some of the factors considered include the amount of tax involved; the availability of witnesses or evidence to prove the case; the cost of prosecution compared to the expected results; the age, state of health, or educational background of the taxpayer; the taxpayer's occupation; and how prominent the taxpayer is in the community. A criminal prosecution is used for publicity. Besides wanting an airtight case to ensure a conviction, the IRS also wants that conviction to get media coverage and put a little fear into the rest of us. A well-known or influential taxpayer can serve that purpose. Sometimes the IRS is trying to improve compliance in a particular occupation or ethnic community and will recommend prosecution even though the taxpayer is not known outside his profession or community.

The higher the score the more likely a case will be investigated. If a case is not picked out of the pool by a special agent within ninety days, it will be returned to the auditor, and the civil-fraud penalty will be asserted. Even after a case is selected for investigation, it can be sent back for the penalty if the investigation fails to turn up sufficient evidence for trial. When the special agent has completed his investigation and recommended prosecution, Criminal Investigation's job is over. The actual prosecution is approved and carried out by the U. S. Department of Justice.

If you are guilty of tax evasion or fraud and you believe it has been detected, hire an attorney and keep your mouth shut. Better still, pay your taxes like the rest of us and sleep easier during an audit.

XVI. TAXPAYER CONFIDENTIAL

When you file your tax returns, what guarantee do you have that the personal information they reveal won't be broadcast to the public at large? What prevents the IRS from becoming a back-fence gossip, regaling your neighbors with tales told from your tax return?

Because of the threat to privacy inherent in computerized government, laws have been enacted in recent years governing the maintenance of government files and public access to them. These laws protect your privacy by preventing government agencies from keeping secret files and from making information about you public. As a taxpayer, the legal provisions respecting privacy of major importance to you are section 6103 of the Internal Revenue Code (as amended by the Tax Reform Act of 1976), the Freedom of Information Act, and the Privacy Act of 1974. We will discuss each of the provisions separately.

PRIVACY AND THE INTERNAL REVENUE CODE

What keeps your auditor silent about you and your tax return? Internal Revenue Code section 6103 mandates that all returns and return information are confidential. This is the general rule, and as usual, there are some exceptions providing for limited disclosures that are in the public interest. We'll deal with some of these exceptions later. Because of Code section 6103, your auditor may not disclose your return or return information without incurring severe penalties.

A protected "return" includes any tax or information return, along with their supporting schedules or attachments, which are filed by you or on your behalf. Examples of returns are Forms 1040,

941, 1120S, W-2, and 1099. "Return information" is any information taken from a return, such as your address or social security number, audit reports, special agents' (Criminal Investigation) reports, Appellate Division statements, and computerized data about your tax account. The information that you were or are being audited is also confidential, as is any information you or your representative submits during an audit. Data in a form that cannot be associated with or identify you in particular are not return information.

How do these rules forbidding unauthorized disclosures affect you in an audit? Because of section 6103, your auditor will not discuss your return or the audit with anyone but you. If you want a representative to act on your behalf, you must give him a written authorization, or power of attorney (see Chapter VI). Without a power of attorney, your representative can present the requested documents, but the auditor will examine them in silence. She may not discuss her findings with him or say anything that would give him any information about your return. Instead, the auditor will have to communicate with you personally to resolve the audit.

Even spouses who filed separate returns and close relatives fall under this prohibition. Neither the appointment clerks nor the auditors will discuss your case with anyone who does not have a valid power of attorney on file. If a taxpayer is deceased, the case may be discussed with the executor, administrator, or trustee of the estate; however, a Form 56, Notice of Fiduciary Relationship, and letters testamentary naming the executor, etc., must first be submitted. A guardian or trustee of the estate of an incompetent may receive return information upon written request.

A representative, friend, or relative does not need a power of attorney to accompany you to the audit, either to act as an advisor or to be a witness. As long as you are present, the auditor may discuss your return in front of the unauthorized person who came with you. The disclosure is being made to you and not to the other person. Nor is a power of attorney needed for someone to make or change an appointment for you or your representative.

Although an auditor may not reveal return information, or the fact that you are being audited, to an unauthorized person, she may contact third parties for information about you needed to conduct the audit. For instance, if you have a doctor bill showing the total amount of charges for the year but no canceled checks as proof of payment, the auditor may call the doctor's office to confirm your oral testimony that you did indeed pay. She will not tell the doctor that you are being audited, although he may come to that conclusion by himself. Rather, she will say, "I need to know the total amount of charges paid by Mr. X in 198-." It is necessary to identify you to get this information, but the reason the auditor called is left unspoken.

Similarly, where a divorced parent is claiming a child as an exemption, it is permissible common practice for the auditor to contact the other parent to inquire whether the exemption is being claimed by both. The letter tells the other parent that an audit is being conducted, but it names only the children claimed as exemptions, not the person under audit. The letter reads, "We are reviewing *another person's* income-tax return. . . ." Again, the parent may deduce who is being audited, but this is not expressly stated in the letter. An auditor may also tell a noncustodial parent the amount of support provided to a child by the custodial parent.

The IRS may send inquiries to the Postal Service or to your W-2 employer in an effort to locate you for an audit. These inquiries do not mention that you have been chosen for an audit; they ask only for your current address of record. If you do not respond or refuse delivery of our letters at your home address and we know you are still working for your W-2 employer, we may mail our correspondence to you at your employer's address. When we do this, we stamp the envelope TO BE OPENED BY ADDRESSEE ONLY to save you from prying eyes.

As mentioned above, the IRS may make limited disclosures of returns and return information that are in the public interest. Section 6103 of the Internal Revenue Code lists the persons or agencies to which such disclosures may be made and for what purposes. Some of the permissible disclosures are to committees of Congress, to the President, to officers and employees of the Department of the Treasury for tax-administration purposes, and to attorneys of the Department of Justice involved in court proceedings involving tax administration. Returns or return information may also be disclosed for statistical use to the Bureau of the Census, the Bureau of Economic Analysis, the Federal Trade Commission's Bureau of Economics, and the Department of the Treasury.

Federal employees investigating nontax criminal violations or preparing for an administrative or judical proceeding related to a nontax crime have limited access to returns or return information, but only by order of a U.S. District Court. If an auditor or other IRS employee discovers or is given evidence of a possible crime unrelated to income tax in the course of his duties, this evidence may be disclosed to the proper federal, state, or local law-enforcement authority. An IRS employee who witnesses a crime en route to or during an audit may disclose the facts of the crime to the police, but otherwise may say only that he was on official business, without disclosing what that business was or the taxpayer's identity.

State tax officials may also receive returns or return information. The IRS has negotiated agreements with forty-eight states and the District of Columbia to release audit results to the states' taxing authorities. A copy of the final audit report is automatically provided to a state tax employee in each of these states. This saves the state an audit—the taxpayer's state-income-tax return is adjusted in accordance with the IRS audit findings and he is billed. The state does not have to do an independent audit of its own.

Other agencies to which otherwise confidential information may be disclosed for specified, limited purposes are the Social Security Administration; the Railroad Retirement Board; the Department of Education; the Department of Health and Human Services; federal, state, and local child-support-enforcement agencies; and the General Accounting Office. In addition, the IRS may disclose letter rulings and technical-advice memoranda (after deleting the taxpayer's identity), accepted offers-in-compromise, and the amount of outstanding liens.

Any person or agency to whom the IRS discloses returns or return information must safeguard that information and keep it confidential. Only persons whose duties require them to have the information may be given access to it, and it must be stored in a secure area. Records must be kept of any disclosures. The IRS polices these agencies. If an agency does not establish safeguards and ensure confidentiality, the IRS may refuse to disclose return information to it until the lack of security is remedied.

The IRS is charged with protecting your privacy, but how good a job does it do? Let's say that the Service is trying. It is limited not by desire but by lack of funds. Ardent security requires capital; little by little, as the money trickles down from the fount of Congress, safeguards such as high-security file cabinets and paper shredders are being installed. A Security Branch has been created and is responsible for ensuring that all returns are properly protected.

The following are some of the steps your audit group takes to guard your privacy:

1. All files, correspondence, and other documents containing the names or other identification of taxpayers are placed in locked cabinets overnight.
2. The identity of anyone requesting confidential information over the telephone is verified by asking the caller to give us pertinent information from the return that would be known only to the taxpayer. For example, you may be asked to tell us your social security number, the names of your children, your employer, etc. If the clerk or auditor is unsure that she is speaking to the taxpayer, the requested information will be mailed to the address on the return.
3. A valid power of attorney or written authorization must be in the taxpayer's file before confidential information will be disclosed to his representative.
4. Documents that identify taxpayers under audit are disposed of by shredding, rather than being thrown away.
5. Non-IRS employees are not permitted in areas where they have no business.
6. Confidential matters are not discussed by auditors or clerks in public places or in the audit office if other taxpayers are within hearing distance.
7. Employees must justify their need for returns and return information before obtaining them.
8. Audits are conducted in enclosed booths that are meant to be soundproof. In practice, these booths are usually inadequate to prevent other taxpayers in surrounding booths from hearing your audit. Most auditors, including myself, believe this is a violation of your privacy. Lack of money to provide offices with more privacy seems to be the villain. To date, however, there has been no public outcry, so change is unlikely. It could just be the pleasures of eavesdropping outweigh the limited invasion of privacy.

What are the penalties for unauthorized disclosures? Under Internal Revenue Code section 7213, the unauthorized disclosure of tax-return information by IRS employees or anyone else is a felony punishable by a fine not to exceed five thousand dollars or not more than five years in prison, or both. For this criminal penalty to apply, the disclosure must be intentional and made with the knowledge that it was not authorized by law. Criminal prosecution is brought by the Department of Justice.

AUDITING THE IRS—THE FREEDOM OF INFORMATION ACT

The Freedom of Information Act (FOIA) provides for public access to certain nonexempt government records. In some cases this is accomplished by publishing the records, by setting up reading rooms open to the public, or by supplying records upon specific request from the taxpayer.

As a taxpayer, you have a right to inspect or request copies of IRS policy statements and legal interpretations, internal manuals, training materials, statistical reports (except TCMP and those which identify taxpayers), digests, and nonexempt portions of investigative files. You do *not* have access to other taxpayers' tax returns or return information (because of Code section 6103, discussed above), interagency or intra-agency memos stating legal opinions, case-selection criteria, trade secrets and other commercial or financial information that is confidential, the Law Enforcement Manual (used by the Criminal Investigation Division), or the identity of informants. Nor can you examine portions of your own investigatory file compiled for law-enforcement purposes, which would interfere with enforcement proceedings against you or reveal protected investigative techniques and procedures or confidential sources. (Such a file would only exist if you were being investigated for possible criminal prosecution, for example, in a fraud or bribery case.)

Of what value is the Freedom of Information Act to you in an audit? If you are a fairly average taxpayer undergoing audit for routine issues (e.g., exemptions, itemized deductions, rental expenses, business expenses), access to the available government records will be of no real benefit. The questions of law and fact are usually simple, and there are no "secret" audit techniques being used. For most issues, the IRS position can be found in the Internal Revenue Code or Regulations or selected court cases or Revenue Rulings. Your auditor will show you any of these if they form the basis for her determination. All you have to do is ask during the interview to see the statement of law upon which she is relying. Poring over the Internal Revenue manual may give you an insight into the audit process and procedure, but this book tells you all you really need to know. If some point needs clarifying, ask your auditor.

In most cases, then, asking to inspect the IRS records available to you will be educational but will probably not save you any money. If you delay the audit to request certain records and wade through them, it will even cost you money, because there are fees for searching and making copies. Delay can also mean more interest expense if, after all, you owe additional tax.

Access to policy statements and legal interpretations may be of value to you if one or more of the issues on your return are highly technical, unique, or singled out by the IRS for individual treatment (e.g., commuting to and from a temporary jobsite), usually because of indecision or controversy regarding the correct interpretation of the law. Portions of the Internal Revenue manual may also be helpful if you are the subject of an audit technique you do not thoroughly understand, for instance, one of the indirect methods of determining your correct income (see Chapter X). Normally, however, the auditor will explain the procedure she is using if you ask.

If you wish to exercise your rights under the Freedom of Information Act and the records you desire have not been published or you do not have access to a public reading room (situated in each regional office and the National Office, in Washington, D.C.), you may make a specific request for the records. This request must be in writing and signed by you. It must state that the request is being made "pursuant to the Freedom of Information Act, 5 U.S.C. 552." The records you seek must be "reasonably described"; ask your auditor for help if you are unsure how to describe the records you want. If you are asking for disclosure of your own tax records, identify yourself as the taxpayer whose records you are requesting, either by having your request notarized or by enclosing a photocopy of your driver's license. State also whether you want to inspect the records or have copies made without first inspecting them. You must either state that you agree to pay the fees for search and duplication or set a ceiling on the amount you are willing to pay. You may also request a reduction or waiver of fees, giving the justification for your request (e.g., indigency). Lastly, include your address.

Mail or hand deliver your request to the IRS official responsible for control of the records you want. Ask your auditor which official your request should be addressed to if you do not know. If your auditor is unable to help you, send your request to the office of the director of the IRS district in which you reside or to:

Chief, Disclosure Staff
Internal Revenue Service
Freedom of Information Request
c/o Ben Franklin Station
P.O. Box 388
Washington, D. C. 20044

When your request is received, the responsible official will determine whether the request can be granted. This determination must be made and notification mailed to you within ten working days after receipt of your request. If the request is granted, copies of the records, along with a statement of fees, will then be promptly mailed to you. If you asked to inspect the records, you will be notified when and where the inspection can take place.

If your request is denied, you will be told the grounds for not granting it, the name and title of the official responsible for the denial, where the records are, and your appeal rights. Where the records cannot be located and a determination made within the ten-day limit, you will be notified and advised that this constitutes a denial unless you agree to a voluntary extension of time not to exceed ten days. You may appeal if you do not want to extend the time.

Administrative appeal is to the Commissioner and may be filed at any time within thirty-five days of the date of notification. The letter of appeal must be in writing and signed by you and must reasonably describe the records requested and the date of the request. Enclose a copy of the denial and your original request. Include any arguments in support of your request. Mail your appeal to:

Freedom of Information Appeal
Commissioner of Internal Revenue
c/o Ben Franklin Station
P. O. Box 929
Washington, D.C. 20044

The Commissioner or his delegate must make a determination to affirm the denial (in whole or in part) or to grant the request within twenty working days after receipt of your appeal, unless an extension of time is agreed to. (The total of all extensions of time must not exceed ten days.) If your appeal is denied, you may bring an action directly against the IRS in the U.S. District Court in the district in which you reside or where your business or records are. The burden of proof in court is upon the IRS to justify its actions in not making the requested records available. The government may be assessed court costs and your attorney fees if the court decides in your favor.

What is the cost of requesting records? The fee charged for search services is ten dollars per hour of personnel time spent to locate or retrieve the records. Fees for computer searches and printouts is the actual cost. Transportation or shipping costs of moving records from one location to another or of transporting an employee to the record site for a search may also be incurred. The fee for duplication is fifteen cents for each photocopy and the actual cost of photographs, films, or other materials. Copies of returns cost $4.25 and a transcript of tax information is $2.25. Payment should be made by check or money order payable to the Internal Revenue Service.

OBTAINING ACCESS TO YOUR FILES

The Privacy Act of 1974 was passed to safeguard individual privacy from misuse of federal records and to provide individuals with access to their own records. This Act applies to all government agencies, not just the IRS. To a large extent, the provisions of the Privacy Act designed to protect an individual's privacy are duplicated by section 6103 of the Internal Revenue Code, discussed at the beginning of this chapter.

To briefly highlight some of the provisions of the Act, the law requires each government agency to:

1. Annually identify its record-keeping system.
2. Keep detailed accounting of all disclosures of records other than disclosures under the Freedom of Information Act.
3. Limit record keeping to only what is necessary, relevant, and lawful.
4. Inform individuals who are asked to provide information, of the authority for the request, the purpose for collecting the information, the uses to which it will be put, and the legal consequences of not complying.
5. Assure the accuracy, relevance, timeliness, and completeness of records to prevent harm to an individual.
6. Maintain no record relating to First Amendment rights (freedom of speech, religion, assembly).
7. Establish safeguards to assure the security and confidentiality of records.
8. Notify an individual when a record relating to him is disclosed under compulsory legal process that has become a matter of public record.
9. Collect information directly from the individual, if possible, when collecting it from a third party may adversely affect the individual.
10. Permit an individual to examine, correct, or amend records pertaining to him.

The last provision, granting you access to your records and the opportunity to correct them, is the only one that is likely to prove important to you in an audit. Occasions may arise over the long course of an audit when you may want copies of your return, the auditor's work papers, conference or appellate statements, correspondence between you and the IRS, or the status of your tax account. You have a right to any of this confidential tax-return information, as does your authorized representative, unless criminal proceedings have been started against you.

When and under what circumstances would you want to see the documents in your audit case file? Ordinarily there is precious little to see that you don't already know about. The notes your auditor makes list only what documents you have presented and the facts as you related them. They also include the auditor's conclusions of law, but these are given to you in writing along with the audit report. You may want to know how the auditor arrived at certain figures, but usually this can be accomplished by asking her to explain her computations.

Your file contains your tax return, and if you have lost your copy or were never given one by your tax preparer, you will probably need to request a copy before your appointment date for reference in getting your records together. Simply call the appointment clerk and ask her to mail you a copy. Similarly, you may have given the auditor a letter or statement to verify a deduction or credit without keeping a copy for yourself. If you find you need a copy, ask your auditor for one.

Perhaps the auditor has solicited information from a third party about you and has relied upon this information to your detriment. You may want to see this unfavorable information to make sure it is accurate and to contest it if you believe it is not. Or you may believe that the auditor has misunderstood the facts and recorded them incorrectly in her notes. An inspection of her work papers can confirm or deny this.

An auditor should not make personal or derogatory comments about a taxpayer in her work papers. If you believe that the auditor has included prejudicial statements about you in the file that indicate you may not have been judged fairly, copies of such statements can work to your tremendous advantage. If an auditor does make the mistake of recording her personal feelings about a taxpayer, the IRS will probably not uphold her findings or defend them in court. A prejudicial comment might be, "Taxpayer is a cheat," because it expresses an opinion not supported by fact. Quoting a taxpayer would not be prejudicial, however, e.g., "Taxpayer says she is a 'hooker.' " Nor has an auditor overstepped the bounds if she records the facts: "Taxpayer used abusive language and otherwise behaved in a hostile manner."

Copies of the auditor's work papers and conference and appellate statements should probably be requested if you have exhausted the administrative appeals process and are taking your case to court. If, conversely, the IRS is bringing you to court for a criminal violation of the tax law, a request to examine or be provided with copies of your investigative file may be denied if disclosure would interfere with the proceedings against you or reveal nonroutine investigative techniques or confidential sources.

The same procedure applies for requesting to inspect or receive copies of your audit file as for any other Freedom of Information Act request. However, in the audit situation, it is generally possible to make your request informally to the auditor or conferee without going through the prescribed procedure. If the records requested are not voluminous, they will probably be copied on the spot with no fee charged.

XVII. LETTING OFF STEAM

(A Collection of Letters from Taxpayers)

Dear District Director:

For years, without question, I have stood idly by while hundreds of dollars have been taken out of my earned pay. Without knowledge of your organization, I followed the masses, with the assumption that this was the way it was done. Now that I have started a business of my own, I am curious to know just who are you (IRS) and why is it you are called a service organization that provides me (a small businessman) no service? But you want to be paid in full! For what?

I paid sixty dollars ($60.00) for the past two years for a tax accountant to decipher your rules for taxes and file with you my business. Not once have I received any paper work from you about your "Internal Money Service." Now you mail me a letter requesting to see all paper work on my recently started business. Keeping in mind you have not, at this time, explained who you are and what you are here for. I would like to know more about you.

Your unannounced service organization is requesting a lot of my time and money. I have no money (as my tax return shows) and very little time to spend researching for a service that I get no service from. If you are a service to me, then mail me what you offer before you request to be paid. If you offer me no service, then what part do I play in your organization?

I am not appealing your examiner's findings nor am I agreeing with them. I would like to know who the hell are you (IRS)? Why do you want to see my paper work? Why am I to send to you my business history?

I would like to talk with you about <u>you</u> before I talk about me and my little business.

Seriously,

Dear Commissioner,

I love you, love you, love you! I knew it yesterday when I received your latest letter wherein you stated that I'd been selected for an audit. It's like an engagement, isn't it?

True, we have only been penpals since sometime in March but I can't deny my heart.

The snows were still piled high in the roadways. The peaks were white all the way down their jagged slopes when I first went to place my dowry at your feet.

After a number of your letters I still was not about to be swayed by your reconsiderations. Like any woman I was only interested in how much you could give me.

You were adamant, relentless and still you pursued me and now you have won. I don't care one iota what you can give me. You see I am in love with you. I'm yours. Take me.

My days are magic and full of hope. I await the mailman with the 11 o'clock post; – my nights are only a little lonely because I know someone really cares – that's the glory of true love – my dearest.

I must run now, dear one, but keep your letters coming. Let's hope your father – what's his name – Audit Division – approves of our plans.

Love and Kisses

Note: This letter was originally published in The American Way of Taxation, Internal Revenue 1862-1963, edited by Lillian Doris, Prentice-Hall, 1963.

Dear Sirs:

Please forgive me but I certainly do not owe the money which was indicated by the two papers Mrs. ____________ had me sign.

I am of foreign birth and in our country government officials are not questioned for if any one does a great deal of trouble ensues. So therefore I signed the papers without any explanation. However I was informed by an officer of the Internal Revenue Service that in [the] USA you may question a government official if you believe yourself to be unjustly treated.

I did not make a mistake as the lady in question formulated an amount from somewhere, but certainly not from my books.

Perhaps the treatment I'll receive will be like other countries but the gentleman officer reassures me that in spite of beliefs and appearances the U.S. government always tries to rectify.

I place myself at your mercy. Kindly let me know and please help me.

Thank you.

Attention: Mr. ____________

I do not agree with your re-vised report, but! In order to get IRS off my back I am enclosing a check for the amt. of $68.00. I must voice my opinion. Number 1, as I explained and tried to show you the death certificate, all I can go by are the statements (my husband) told the tax preparer as to how many miles to work (but you asked me to estimate) Number 2, since I did not go to work with him how do I know he took the same route every day or that he did not pick up a fellow rider, or bring one or any some days, and Number 3, although he was my joint tax filer how can you audit a dead man? (and how do you expect me to remember every detail of 1976?) But then no one can play God; retribution comes to all.

I do not agree that I should pay cash for a remote control Zenith color console, a Gibson washer and dryer and furnish you with contracts. I paid (sales) tax, but you disallowed it. I have already talked to one of your tax auditors, and his mumbo-jumbo explanation seems to be that you come to whatever finding you wish.

So this is my reply.

A Taxpayer

RE: Dishonesty, stupidity and incompetence of IRS Personnel

TO: The President of the U.S.A.
Congressman ___________
Senator ___________
Commissioner of Int. Rev. -
Sec. of the Treasury

This morning I reported to the Los Angeles IRS office for an appellate hearing on an audit wherein the auditor displayed typical stupidity and dishonesty in an attempt to steal $146.00 from me, claiming fence repair on my rental property must be capitalized.

Today, I suffered the humility of another stupid audit by an equally stupid, dishonest, and incompetent civil service welfare recipient whose lack of knowledge and incapability of performing her duties, clearly established why she is in civil service and with IRS; she couldn't, I believe, hold a job 15 minutes in industry where a wee bit of ability would be required. I have been denied my right to an appellate hearing on this thieving injustice.

I have a couple of pieces of paper - obviously merely misleading propaganda - that the auditor gave me explaining my appeal rights. I am wondering why you, whom we entrust with the administration of our once great, proud and respected government, fail to oversee this criminal organization, why you fail to correct the abuse by this master of intimidation, this extravagantly financed and legalized mafia - condoned and financed by the United States Congress.

I want an appellate hearing per the Internal Revenue Code by someone who has enough self respect to hold a fair hearing and enough intelligence to know the difference between capital expenditures and repairs and who doesn't the moment he/she gets an unknowing taxpayer by herself, intimidate that taxpayer and further harass her.

Sincerely,

Dear Sir

I wrote you a few days ago about the letter you wrote me Since thin I have Ben to the [income tax] man that fix thim out anyway I got no receipts of all Bills. I think that is just like Digging Up the Dead in the mean time this have happen four times in a Row. I am not trying [to] get out of paying my bills I do not like to pay any one [I] dont owe

I think things is mest up some whear I am no longer working and my ex wife is disable to work, also I have to take care [of] her out of what little I get. But anyway I am willing to do what is write.

If you still say I owe you I wish to pay, if I can, and God Will.

I have my tax fix because I dont know how but I found out when a mistake is mad I is the one who pays

I am sending $50.00 and hope to get a answer soon I still disagree with you finding

Yours truly

Dear Mrs. ____________

We really appreciate your great help - by spending your time and efforts to make it possible. We will remember it forever. Thanks again.

____________ & Family

INDEX